Selah

Pause and Consider

Daily Devotional

Lois M. Tupyi

Selah: Pause & Consider © 2009, Lois M. Tupyi.

ISBN: 978-0-615-32230-8

Cover photography © 2009, Mark Winchester.

www.selahdevotional.org

Acknowledgements

Words are inadequate to express my profound gratitude to all who helped make the book a reality. The editors donated hundreds of hours word-smithing my thoughts into something readable. The beautiful photographs were all donated from friends and family not wanting personal recognition, but so important in completing the daily thought.

My thanks to Pacific Press Publishing Association; Josh who was patient with all my questions and Mark who did an amazing job helping an amateur look professional through the design of the book.

To my immediate family who extended grace and understanding as I spent countless hours hidden away in the office writing; thank you for giving me the freedom to work.

The finished product is a direct result of those who believed and prayed each step of the way. For that I am eternally grateful to all of you.

Editors
    Gwyneth Bledsoe
    Terrance and Gayellen Smith

Contributing photographers
    Norma Berens
    Gwyneth Bledsoe
    Becki Boyd
    Renee Howe
    Suzy Ketterling
    Gloria Mozingo
    Jill Oosterman
    Connie Rowe
    Rebecca Stoller
    Lois Tupyi

Preface

My personal passion is to see others become all God has planned for them and for each of us to live life to the fullest in Him. Hence, I felt led to write a daily devotional that includes a daily thought supported by Scripture verse(s), an image or picture and a hymn stanza, which makes this devotional unique from others I have read.

Each day's devotion includes an analogy from everyday life and I often share personal stories of my own journey that I hope you can relate to. Though I include a daily Scripture verse, I recommend you read the complete chapter containing the selected Scripture because I find it helps me to understand the Scripture better when read in context.

I suggest you begin your devotional time with a short prayer asking the Lord to open the eyes of your heart. Read the devotion and Scripture pausing to reflect on your life. Continue by reading the suggested Bible chapter listening for God to highlight a specific passage. Look over the hymn and let the lyrics move you to worship. Conclude with prayer allowing the Holy Spirit to speak to your soul. A suggested application has been included to further incorporate the thought in your day whenever appropriate or possible.

I pray that as you use this daily devotional your personal walk with God will become more intimate and rich. May all glory and honor go to God; our Lord, Savior and friend. And may you be abundantly blessed with the peace of the Holy Spirit throughout each day.

For years I had a desire to write a devotional book, but was hesitant, and unsure where to start. I questioned whether what was on my heart was put there by God. I started praying daily for discernment, believing He would provide direction and wisdom, if it was within His will. It was on a whim that I sent an e-mail to a publishing house asking if they ever published books for unpublished authors. I was surprised to see the door start to open with possibilities, and the rest is history. My prayer is that God will use my thoughts to encourage others in their life journeys. Perhaps it will also encourage them not to be afraid to do something that doesn't make earthly sense and seems utterly impossible. When it is the Lord's will, He opens all the doors and provides everything needed to make it happen. We need to

have the faith to believe and be willing to take the first step. God has always chosen unlikely people to do His work. Is God calling you to attempt the impossible in something?

"Now to Him who is able to do immeasurably more than all we ask or imagine, according to His power that is at work within us, to Him be glory in the church and in Christ Jesus throughout all generations, for ever and ever! Amen."
Ephesians 3:20-21

"Praise the Lord, praise the Lord, let the earth hear His voice!
Praise the Lord, praise the Lord, let the people rejoice!
Oh, come to the Father, through Jesus the Son,
And give Him the glory, great things He hath done."

Commit to praying daily about something God has put on your heart but you've been afraid to do.

> *"I love to tell the story,*
> *'Twill be my theme in glory,*
> *To tell the old, old story*
> *Of Jesus and His love."*

Most of us have made a New Year's resolution. I don't like to call them resolutions but I find myself thinking about what I hope to achieve in the coming year. Often thoughts include things I want to do or change. Attending a regular exercise program, losing a few extra pounds, not watching TV, devoting more time to God, spending more time with the family, playing the piano more—these are some of my more common ones. So why is it I often cannot commit to these positive changes? It seems the things I hope to accomplish at the first of the year get pushed aside as life takes over. Having an accountability partner helps keep me on task. But the partner has to be committed to helping me or my goals still get lost in the shuffle. Change is difficult even when the results are positive. Perhaps our resolution each year should be to focus on becoming all that God desires and ask Him what that means. Maybe we need to make Him our accountability partner and ask for His help when we are weak or tempted to quit. When my motivation is to please God I find myself more focused and committed than when I'm just doing it for myself. Did you make a New Year's resolution this year?

"No, in all these things we are more than conquerors through Him who loved us."
Romans 8:37

Ask God to help you discern if you need to make a change in your life.

*"Rescue the perishing, care for the dying,
Snatch them in pity from sin and the grave;
Weep o'er the erring one, lift up the fallen,
Tell them of Jesus, the mighty to save."*

Spiders build webs to trap their prey. The spun silk is sticky, and unsuspecting houseflies and other insects fly into it and become trapped. A spider web appears fragile and of no danger to anyone. But the intricate pattern along with the strength of the silk fiber makes the web much stronger than one would think at first glance. I have found it challenging to wash off spider webs hidden in the eves of my house. Satan sets snares for us hoping we will be trapped. He uses many ploys that are attractive and unassuming, but deadly to the unwary. If we are not careful we become ensnared before we know we've walked into danger. The only safe way to live our lives is to constantly keep our eyes upon God and ask Him to direct our steps, protecting us from those who want to harm us. If we get so busy buzzing around like a fly and haven't taken time to pray for God's direction we could find ourselves in a sticky mess crying out for Him to rescue us. Do you pray every day for the Lord to protect and guide you?

*"But my eyes are fixed on you,
O Sovereign Lord;
in You I take refuge—
do not give me over to death.
Keep me from the snares
they have laid for me,
from the traps set by evildoers.
Let the wicked fall into their own nets,
while I pass by in safety."*
Psalm 141:8—10

Memorize today's scripture and pray for God's protective covering.

> *"Let us ever love each other, with a heart that's warm and true.*
> *Ever doing to our brother, as to us we'd have him do.*
> *Kind and loving to each other, gentle words to all we meet;*
> *Thus we follow Christ our Savior, proving all His service sweet."*

There's an old disco song that says "What's love got to do with it?" According to the Bible it has everything to do with it. 1 Corinthians Chapter 13 is often called the love chapter and aptly so. I can have the greatest gifts, the strongest faith and give abundantly to those around me, but if I lack love none of it matters. The complete book of 1 John is about loving each other. In Chapter 4 we are challenged that if we don't love our brother then we cannot love God. These words from the Bible convict me and show me how far I have to go. My ability to love falls short of total patience and kindness. I can get angry and be self-seeking in my relationships. My love has failed at times especially when I have been wronged by another. I find myself irritated by some people and have difficulty loving those who are mean, obnoxious and belligerent. Yet God has commanded me to love all of mankind not just the loveable or those who love me. This is impossible in my own strength and means I must spend time with Him calling on Him to fill

me with His love. I need His eyes and His heart to see the potential in others as He does. What's love got to do with it? It's the barometer of where my relationship is with God. How does your love life stack-up to the Bible's definition?

> *"Dear friends, let us love one another, for love comes from God.*
> *Everyone who loves has been born of God and knows God.*
> *Whoever does not love does not know God, because God is love."*
> *1 John 4:7 & 8*

Read the attributes of love in 1 Corinthians Chapter 13
and see how you're doing.

*I*n the past when I went on a vacation I would be so focused on getting there that I wouldn't enjoy any part of the trip until I arrived. I didn't want to stop and take a break, much less take a side trip and see something along the way. Needless to say I wasn't the most enjoyable traveling companion. But my husband keeps gently reminding me that life is the journey and we need to enjoy every minute. He has helped me relax and be less goal orientated. Years ago I used to come home from work frustrated because no matter how hard I worked I never could get to the bottom of the in-box. But I have learned through the years that I will never have an empty in-box. There is always another thing to do and I need to enjoy each task thanking God for the energy and ability to work. We don't know if we have tomorrow, we only have today so we need to make the most of it. When I'm focused on where I'm going I lose sight of the beauty and joy of the moment. I don't want to arrive at my final destination and realize I missed living. Are you able to enjoy each day or are you looking ahead and missing out on life?

"Then I realized that it is good and proper for a man to eat and drink,
and to find satisfaction in his toilsome labor under the sun during the few days of life
God has given him—for this is his lot. Moreover, when God gives
any man wealth and possessions, and enables him to enjoy them
to accept his lot and be happy in his work—this is a gift of God."
Ecclesiastes 5:18 & 19

"Sweeter as the years go by,
Sweeter as the years go by,
Richer, fuller, deeper, Jesus' love is sweeter,
Sweeter as the years go by."

Go for a day trip and stop often along the way to see the sights.

"For we will all stand before God's judgment seat. It is written: 'As surely as I live,' says the Lord, 'Every knee will bow before me; every tongue will confess to God.' So then, each of us will give an account of himself to God."

Romans 14:10–12

"What can wash away my sin?
Nothing but the blood of Jesus;
What can make me whole again?
Nothing but the blood of Jesus."

My grandson, playing hide and seek with a plastic bucket, reminded me that toddlers experience a stage in their development when they think because they cannot see us, we cannot see them. It's cute when little ones do it, but when we do the same thing with God it's not nearly as cute. We rationalize that because we can't physically see God He isn't seeing us, especially when we make choices we prefer He didn't witness. The reality is that He sees it all, just as I saw my grandson wiggle with delight under the bucket. We pretend we can get away with things, but we can't. We will have to stand before the judgment seat of God and give an account of what we've done in our life. I don't know about you, but I don't want God to remind me of all the times I had a bucket on my head and thought I was getting away with something. Is there something in your life you're pretending is hidden from God?

Ask God to reveal any hidden sin and seek forgiveness and healing from it.

What are you afraid of? I'm afraid of snakes and heights. I work at not letting either of them control me and have killed rattlesnakes to protect my children, but I'm still afraid of them. Two of my grandchildren came to spend the weekend with me. We were having a great time until they noticed our two dogs, and they became afraid. It wasn't just fear, it was a crawling up the leg, shaking fear, even though the dogs were in the kennel and couldn't hurt them. I finally took the kids inside but they could see the dogs through the window and cried for us to take them away. Though they were inside and the dogs were outside in a kennel they couldn't overcome their fear. Their unfounded fear of the dogs ruined their play time and interfered in the fun weekend I had planned. All our efforts to show them the dogs were friendly and would not harm them failed. Sometimes we let our fears consume us and we are unable to move past them. At times like these we need to remember that God has promised to always be with us and we have nothing to be afraid of. Some fears are real and should caution us to be careful. But many things we fear are imagined and if left uncontrolled can take the joy out of our life. What are you afraid of and does it interfere with your ability to enjoy life?

*"'Because he loves me,'
says the Lord,
'I will rescue him;
I will protect him for he
acknowledges my name.
He will call upon me,
and I will answer him;
I will be with him in trouble,
I will deliver him and
honor him.'"
Psalm 91:14 & 15*

*"And it holds, my anchor holds:
Blow your wildest, then, O gale,
On my bark so small and frail;
By His grace I shall not fail,
For my anchor holds, my anchor holds."*

Work at overcoming something you fear.

*E*ating every day is important to the health of our bodies. In fact we are told that we need to eat three meals a day to keep our body running at the best metabolic rate to burn calories and have energy. Except for times when we purposely choose not to eat, most of us don't neglect ourselves when it comes to eating. Usually at the first sign of hunger, we're in the kitchen seeing what we can scour up to eat, satisfying our appetite with food. The Bible tells us we should hunger and thirst after righteousness and we will be filled. In order to grow our faith we need to keep it fed on a regular basis

through the reading of the Bible and prayer time. If we develop a habit of doing this, we will notice when we skip it, much the same as when we skip a meal. It will become something we desire and we will experience hunger pangs for God. There was a time in my life when I did not understand what it felt like to hunger and thirst after God, but I have learned to recognize the urge to feed my faith with some God time. Eating regular meals keeps us healthy, and spending daily time with God will keep our faith vibrant and strong. Do you hunger and thirst after righteousness and are you quick to satisfy it?

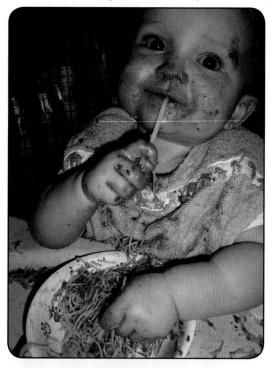

"Blessed are those who hunger and thirst for righteousness,
for they will be filled."
Matthew 5:6

"My soul is satisfied,
My soul is satisfied;
I am complete in Jesus' love,
And my soul is satisfied."

Try to notice and respond to that pang of desire to spend time with God.

A friend of mine in his eighties recently lost his wife. He shared with me that he was having an estate sale and selling most of their things. His house had already sold and he was downsizing significantly, simplifying his life. His wife had many beautiful collections, some of them valuable, and they had been a source of joy to her. But her collections held little attraction to her widowed husband. His memories of the many wonderful years together, the life they had built, the family they had raised and the churches they had served were what he placed value in now. We often collect things at different times in our life. These collections take our money, time and space but they never can return love or affection to us. They are just things to which memories are attached. What's stored within our heart is of far greater value than anything money can buy. These lasting treasures come from within us, not from things around us. Let us spend our days collecting beautiful memories and precious moments with those we love. We will never need to sell the investment of time and love we put into our relationships, no matter how much we downsize. Is your life cluttered with things?

"Sell your possessions and give to the poor. Provide purses for yourselves that will not wear out, a treasure in heaven that will not be exhausted, where no thief comes near and no moth destroys. For where your treasure is, there your heart will be also."
Luke 12:33 & 34

"Than to be the king of a vast domain,
Or be held in sin's dread sway;
I'd rather have Jesus than anything
This world affords today."

De-clutter your life by getting rid of some of your things.

January 10
Read Psalm 66

he Rocky Mountains are known for winter skiing and sledding, and many people move there to be closer to winter sports. I'm really not a fan of outside winter activities, especially if I have to personally participate in them. I find they usually involve the cold, ice, and speed. Often I find myself slipping, falling, and freezing, instead of enjoying the activity. There are times in my life when I feel like I'm on an icy mountain, speeding out of control down a course I'm unfamiliar with, and thinking the only way I'm going to stop is to fall and endure the pain. When my grandchildren feel this way, they call out to their daddy to catch them, which he always does. We can do the same thing to God. Sometimes I just need to take off my skis, or get off the sled, and go inside for a nice warm cup of hot chocolate with Jesus. I don't think God wants us to live our lives out of control, stopping only when we crash into something. Does it feel like your life is speeding down an icy slope, out of control, and is it time for a hot chocolate break with a special friend?

"Praise our God, O peoples, let the sound of His praise be heard;
He has preserved our lives and kept our feet from slipping."
Psalm 66:8 & 9

"Lord, lift me up and let me stand,
By faith, on Heaven's tableland,
A higher plane than I have found;
Lord, plant my feet on higher ground"

Make your favorite beverage, curl up and talk with Jesus about what's on your heart.

When we were framing our new house we held a signing party. Over eighty people came and wrote Scriptures all over the framed walls. By the end of the day, there was hardly a bare board in the house. Many Scriptures had been chosen to fit the rooms. My bedroom wall contained the Scripture from Ephesians 4:26 that says "do not let the sun go down while you are still angry." More than once I have thought of those words hidden beneath the wallboard when I've been upset about something. We've lived in our home for many years now and there is something powerful about knowing that when I'm there I am covered with God's Word. It's like a protective blanket pulled around me and sheltering me from any storm I may come up against. There is power, comfort, assurance, promise and hope in God's Word. Find a way to wrap yourself in His Word and see if it doesn't make a difference in your day. Do you have any Bible verses displayed in your home?

"Take to heart all the words I have solemnly declared to you this day, so that you may command your children to obey carefully all the words of this law. They are not just idle words for you— they are your life."
Deuteronomy 32:46 & 47

"Tell me the story of Jesus,
Write on my heart every word;
Tell me the story most precious,
Sweetest that ever was heard."

Tape a favorite Scripture on your bathroom mirror and start your day out right.

January 12
Read Acts chapter 15

I was a guest speaker at a community event and shared about the ministry of Love INC with the crowd. Afterwards I was approached by a man who felt I had turned my back on a former client, abandoning him and his children during their time of need. He was very vocal about his disappointment in the ministry and his words cut deeply. We had invested months trying to help this family caught in destructive lifestyles, but there was only so much we could do and eventually they left the program due to an unwillingness to change. I found myself deeply discouraged by this encounter and went to work the next day burdened and hurt. My staff specifically prayed for God to encourage me. As I opened the mail later that day there was a letter addressed to me from someone I did not know. It contained words written to encourage me about the ministry and the profound way it was touching so many lives. Tears flowed as I thanked God for these very personal words penned several days ago by a stranger. God had written me a love note knowing I would need to hear words of acceptance and love on that exact day. I don't know how God orchestrates the timing in these things—it amazes me. But I do know that He cares intimately about each one of us—so much so that He even sends love letters in the mail to lift us up. Have you ever received encouragement from someone exactly when you needed it most?

"The people read it and were glad for its encouraging message."
Acts 15:31

"Love lifted me!
Love lifted me!
When nothing else could help,
Love lifted me!"

Write someone an encouraging note today.

What do you see when it starts to snow—slick roads and cold weather or beautiful flakes and earthly refreshment? Do you hunker down, afraid to venture out, or do you grab your winter garb and run out to enjoy it? Snowstorms bring all of these things and our response dictates whether we will enjoy or dread them. Challenges in life are like snowstorms. We can see all the difficulties and discomfort they'll bring and hunker down in fear. Or we can face them head on as an opportunity for God to teach us something new. Every difficulty has unforeseen blessings that will not be realized until we pass through them. Each time we retreat we miss something God has planned for us. Nothing comes to us except through His hand and with His permission. Nothing can live in constant sunlight. There must be times of rain and snow to nourish the earth and promote growth. The next time you find yourself in a storm look upward in awe and know that God has a blessing for you—you just have to look for it. When difficulties arise what do you see—an obstacle or an opportunity?

"Blessed is the man you discipline, O Lord, the man you teach from your law."
Psalm 94:12

"Praise Him! Praise Him!
Tell of His excellent greatness;
Praise Him! Praise Him!
Ever in joyful song!"

Enjoy a cold day with a hot beverage and warm memories.

A blessing from God encourages us and glorifies Him. The Bible is filled with blessing after blessing bestowed by God upon His people. One of my favorite blessings in the Bible is found in 2 Corinthians. It speaks of the triune God and gives me great comfort and encouragement. First it reminds us that Jesus extended grace to us by dying on the cross for our sins so that we might live with Him in eternity. Then it speaks of God's great love for us—undeserved love that surpasses all understanding. He woos us to Him, beckoning us to come and live with Him forever. And finally we are reminded that while on earth we have the sweet, sweet fellowship of the Holy Spirit—Emanuel, God with us. He is our present-day companion to encourage, guide, discipline and instruct us while on earth. Only a triune God could meet all our needs. Grace, love, and fellowship are blessings we should offer to each other. Do you recognize God's blessings upon your life?

*"May the grace of the Lord Jesus Christ, and the love of God,
and the fellowship of the Holy Spirit be with you all."*
2 Corinthians 13:14

*"To Thee, great One in Three,
Eternal praises be, hence, evermore;
Thy sov'reign majesty may we in glory see,
And to eternity love and adore!"*

Give a blessing of peace and joy to someone you meet today.

Where I live in southwestern Idaho, an inversion during the winter is quite common. The stagnant cold weather becomes trapped close to the ground as the warmer air sits above it like a cap. A dense frost-like fog covers everything in its path and ice crystals create a fairy landscape. It's not uncommon for the inversion to turn into weeks of icy fog. The reality of the bitter cold strikes out like a slap in the face, and as the days go by my mood can slip into a cold and lethargic state. Then one day a gusty wind blows the inversion out, and the winter sun shimmers on the ice-laden fantasy, warming up the earth and lifting my spirit. I need God's warmth found in His love and the Holy Spirit's refreshing breeze to melt my heart and rejuvenate my spirit. Have you ever had a frosty mood that needed thawing out with some "Son" time?

"May God Himself, the God of peace, sanctify you through and through. May your whole spirit, soul and body be kept blameless at the coming of our Lord Jesus Christ. The one who calls you is faithful and He will do it."
1 Thessalonians 5:23 & 24

"Send the light, the blessed Gospel light;
Let it shine from shore to shore!
Send the light, the blessed Gospel light;
Let it shine forevermore!"

Play some worship music, grab a good book,
and let the "Son" shine into your soul.

January 16
Read Ephesians chapter 4

Many of us have heard the saying, "you can't judge a book by its cover." Writing this book has made me more aware of how important the cover will be. People will be drawn to pick it up or pass it by based on how it looks on the outside. We often do the same thing with people. We tend to categorize them by how they look and speak before we get to know them. Often we are wrong. I was made keenly aware of this through a volunteer who served with Love INC. The first time I met him he came to my house with his wife. He struggled to walk with a walker and carried an oxygen tank. The short trip from his car to my entryway tired him so I was surprised when he said he wanted to become a budget mentor. My first impression was that this was not a good fit for a man of his health, age, and physical restrictions. I immediately tried to think of ways to discourage him but could find none so enrolled him in the next training. Much to my surprise he and his wife became one of our most powerful and effective mentors. They were wise, loving and possessed a wealth of knowledge. The clients who were blessed to be matched with them loved them dearly. I had the honor of speaking at his memorial service and shared how he had changed my perspective. I no longer judge a person by their cover. I seek to get inside and see what rich treasures wait to be discovered. Are you quick to form an opinion of someone based on how they look or speak?

"From Him the whole body, joined and held together by every supporting ligament, grows and builds itself up in love, as each part does its work."
Ephesians Chapter 4:16

Make a decision not to judge people before you get to know them.

> *"At the cross, at the cross where I first saw the light,*
> *And the burden of my heart rolled away,*
> *It was there by faith I received my sight,*
> *And now I am happy all the day!"*

To get on a commercial airplane you need a ticket. It does not matter who you know, your social status, if you're a good, moral person or have done a multitude of good deeds throughout your life. While some of these are good things without a ticket you will not be allowed on the plane. Even if you throw a tantrum, threaten the attendant or try to pay off the airline personnel, without a purchased ticket the plane will leave without you. Many people believe they can get to Heaven through a variety of ways. They think if they are a decent person who models good morals it will get them to Heaven; or if they do a lot of good works and serve others it will earn them a place. Some may think that if they are successful and affluent they will be allowed in because of their status or position. But the Bible is very clear that no matter who we are or how we live our lives, if we have not accepted Jesus as our Lord and Savior we will not receive eternal life. We have to recognize that salvation is not earned nor are we born into it. It's a gift of grace from God, given freely to all who accept, and it's the ticket to Heaven. Do you have your ticket to board the eternity plane or are you still trying to get on some other way?

"For it is by grace you have been saved, through faith—and this not from yourselves,
it is the gift of God—not by works, so that no one can boast."
Ephesians 2:8 & 9

Recall when you accepted Jesus as your Lord and Savior
and make it a day of celebration.

> "I love my Lord,
> He loveth me;
> The life of a Christian suits me,
> I'm happy, redeemed, and free."

I enjoy the reality show "The Biggest Loser" and am amazed by the contestants' transformation as they commit to changing their life-style and becoming healthy. One of my favorite episodes is late in the season when they compete in a challenge with all the weight they have lost strapped to them. Many of them can hardly lift the pounds they have shed and it reminds them how far they have come. Sin weighs us down, is difficult to carry and affects everything else in our life, much like being overweight. God has told us that once we sincerely confess and seek forgiveness for our sins, He casts them away as far as the east is from the west. He lifts the burden from our souls and gives us new life. But many of us struggle to let go of our failures and put them back in our minds continuing to feel the weight and burden even though God has cast them away. It's similar to the contestants strapping their lost pounds on and trying to move. They don't really have the weight anymore but it feels like it. Strapping confessed sin to ourselves burdens us unnecessarily—we don't have to carry it anymore. God has lifted it and cast it aside. He wants us to have the freedom that comes from living in Him. Is there some burden you continue to carry around even though you've given it to the Lord?

"For as high as the heavens are above the earth, so great is His love for those who fear Him; as far as the east is from the west, so far has He removed our transgressions from us."
Psalm 103:11 & 12

Praise God for His forgiveness and cast off the burden.

"If the whole body were an eye, where would the sense of hearing be?
If the whole body were an ear, where would the sense of smell be?
But in fact God has arranged the parts in the body,
every one of them, just as He wanted them to be."
1 Corinthians 12:17 & 18

"All things bright and beautiful,
All creatures great and small,
All things wise and wonderful:
The Lord God made them all."

Discrimination of any sort causes division. Whether it's the color of skin, cultural or educational background, financial status—when we make judgments based on our differences we cause segregation not unity. God created us all uniquely different. He obviously loves diversity. But there are also many common characteristics inherent in each of us. The need to be loved and accepted is desired by everyone. None of us likes to be made fun of and we all have emotions, good and bad. We laugh, cry, feel fear, anxiety, stress, anger—our trigger points are different but the emotions are the same. We all feel physical and emotional pain although our tolerance levels are different. We are much more alike than we are different. I've worked with thousands of clients from a wide range of ethnic, cultural, financial and educational backgrounds. While each one had personal characteristics they had much in common. God sees us as His creation, a blend of uniqueness and similarities. He didn't have pet projects when He created us making one color or culture better than another. He created diversity because He knew the body needs many parts, not just one or two. It's exciting to know I'm unique. But it's also good to know that if I'm a good toe I don't have to try and be an elbow too, because God made someone else to be that part. It's time we overcame our differences and started celebrating them. Diversity is a good thing—God said so. Do you feel you're judgmental of others because they're not like you?

Get to know someone who is distinctly different from you.

January 20
Read 1 Corinthians chapter 10

Winter can be such a beautiful, pristine season but underneath the beauty grave danger can lurk. A thin layer of ice may form over a flowing river. If the ice has been covered with freshly-fallen snow, it is almost impossible to know that you are literally walking on thin ice until you hear the cracking sound under your feet. I've heard stories of people who have fallen through the ice and been swept under it or down river by the swiftly-flowing current. Sin can deceive us in the same way if we're not careful. We can be awestruck by the outward beauty and find ourselves wandering onto thin ice. Often, we realize too late that we do not have firm footing under our feet and find ourselves swept away before we can retreat. The Bible warns us to be wise and avoid all temptation. Satan knows our weaknesses and he will entice us by disguising the danger until he has us on thin ice with a roaring, raging river beneath. It's at those times we need to cry out to God to set our feet back on solid ground. Have you ever found yourself on "thin ice" and cried out to God to rescue you?

"No temptation has seized you except what is common to man. And God is faithful; He will not let you be tempted beyond what you can bear. But when you are tempted, He will also provide a way out so that you can stand up under it."
1 Corinthians 10:13

"Fear not, I am with thee, oh, be not dismayed,
For I am thy God, and will still give thee aid;
I'll strengthen thee, help thee, and cause thee to stand,
Upheld by My gracious, omnipotent hand."

Evaluate your life to see if you're walking on any thin ice and if so make a fast retreat.

"For God did not give us a spirit of timidity,
but a spirit of power, of love and of self-discipline."
2 Timothy 1:7

"Would you do service for Jesus your King?
There's pow'r in the blood, pow'r in the blood;
Would you live daily His praises to sing?
There's wonderful pow'r in the blood."

My four-year old granddaughter is learning to read. Because she has a desire to read she spends time reading aloud to herself and to others. If she never opened a book and always chose to play she would not become a good reader. I would like to lose some weight but am I willing to put forth the effort and sacrifice to achieve this goal? I don't want to give up the foods I really enjoy. I don't want to only eat at meal times and never after 6:00 pm. I don't want to commit to an exercise program at least three times a week. I won't reach this goal until I decide I want to make the necessary

sacrifices. Most of us have things we want in life but often make choices that contradict those desires. Many people say they want to be involved in regular Christian work but they won't invest the time it takes to grow in their personal relationship with God. They don't want to read the Bible and spend daily time in prayer. They don't want to give up their extra-curricular activities. They want to be used by Him but they won't put forth the effort to become useable for Him. Achieving any goal requires a sacrifice on our part. It must become a priority so we'll make choices that make it happen. Do your actions support what you say you want to do or do you talk one way and live another?

Identify a goal you've yet to meet and put steps in place to make it happen.

*"He leadeth me, O blessed thought!
O words with heav'nly comfort fraught!
Whate'er I do, where'er I be
Still 'tis God's hand that leadeth me."*

Why is it often a struggle to find God's will for our life? I sometimes feel discerning His will is like finding a needle in a haystack—nearly impossible. Yet that is not what His Word says. The Bible repeatedly tells us that if we seek Him we will find Him. A face-to-face conversation or an e-mail sent directly to me would make knowing His will much easier. But I think His first priority is for me to know Him and out of that I will find His will. After I received the call on my heart, I waited six years to be placed in ministry. Daily I prayed, and sometimes even cried in the struggle, searching for what He wanted me to do. Once during a very emotional time I distinctly felt in my spirit the verse from Jeremiah 29:11, where He talks of having plans for me, plans to prosper and not harm me. I clung to that promise but did not know where it was found in the Bible. Then one day I saw a plaque in a bookstore with the verse. I bought the plaque, ran home and looked up the Scripture. It was then I found the rest of the story in verse 13. God would be found when I sought Him with all my heart. It was the key that unlocked the door. When I quit seeking His will and started seeking Him I was placed in ministry. Do you struggle knowing God's will for your life?

*"You will seek me
and find me
when you seek me
with all your heart."*
Jeremiah 29:13

Think of a time God made His will known to you.

odern vehicles are designed with many built-in safety features and warnings. They have seat belts, air bags and child restraint car seats for our children; alarms to let us know when the road is slick, the tires are low or a door isn't closed. The dash is filled with gauges and gadgets telling us everything going on under the hood. Safety is of the utmost concern. Whenever one of the warning lights go on I'm quick to take my car into a mechanic and fix whatever is wrong. If I ignore the warning light I might end

up stranded one day with a broken-down car and no one around to help. Our bodies have built-in warning systems also. When we feel anxious, grumpy, moody or out of sorts it's saying something's wrong. Depression, discouragement and worry are all signs that something's out of kilter internally and we need to get it fixed. God has given us this warning system to alert us that our soul needs attention. We need to go to God, the master mechanic, and find out what's wrong. If we'll just park ourselves in His garage and let Him look us over He'll find the cause of our problem and get us back up and running in no time. We can't afford to run ourselves into the ground or we could end up beside the road, broken down and of no use to anyone. Are you paying attention to your eternal warning system?

"Why are you downcast, O my soul? Why so disturbed within me?
Put your hope in God, for I will yet praise Him, my Savior and my God."
Psalm 42:5

"Search me, O God, and know my heart today,
Try me, O Savior, know my thoughts, I pray;
See if there be some wicked way in me;
Cleanse me from every sin, and set me free."

Check under your spiritual hood and see if you need a tune-up.

> "Oh, to grace how great a debtor daily I'm constrained to be!
> Let Thy goodness, like a fetter, bind my feeble heart to Thee.
> Prone to wander, Lord, I feel it, long I cried to be made pure;
> Here's my heart, O take and seal it, work in me Thy double cure."

When you look at a river from an airplane you can see it winding back and forth across the landscape. It meanders its way, taking the path of least resistance across the land. Many of us live in the same manner. We take the path of least resistance going with the flow of those around us. Pretty soon we're entrenched in a lifestyle that is contrary to our beliefs and we wonder how we got there. We can't afford to wander aimlessly downstream oblivious to the course we are on. We have to make a conscious choice to pick our way carefully. Sometimes we find the way blocked and have to move something to keep going in the right direction. Sometimes we find ourselves needing to go uphill and have to dig deep to find the strength. Other times we find ourselves at an impasse and have to turn around until we find a different route. But if we don't control the flow of our life it won't be long before we find our random meandering has taken us far away from where we want to be. It's a lot harder to redirect water in a new direction than to purposely control the direction to begin with. Stop and take a look at your life. Have you been wandering aimlessly without purpose or direction? It might be time to take control and make sure you end up where you want to be.

"We must pay
more careful
attention, therefore,
to what we have heard,
so that we do not
drift away."
Hebrews 2:1

List your long—and short-term goals for your life.

*"Praise the Lord. Praise God in His sanctuary; praise Him in His mighty heavens.
Praise Him for His acts of power; praise Him for His surpassing greatness...Let every-
thing that has breath praise the Lord. Praise the Lord."*
Psalm 150:1,2 & 6

*"Church of the Living God, The pillar of the truth,
Thou dost enclose within thy walls, the aged and the youth;
Here in thy light of love, the saints with gladness meet;
Here every tribe and kindred come in fellowship so sweet."*

A pastor friend related a touching story to me. He shared how one
of his young granddaughters had come to church with him and his
wife, something she rarely got to do. After the service he asked
her what her favorite part had been, and without hesitation she said, "That's
easy Grandpa. It was after the sermon when I got to run down the aisle and
hug you. That was my favorite part." As the pastor shared this with me he
said it had caused him to contemplate why people come to church. Perhaps
it's because they feel obligated, or
they like the speaker, or the music,
or to see their friends. Wouldn't it
be great if they came to church
because they loved God, desired an
intimate and personal relationship
with Him and found nothing more
rewarding than meeting Him there?
We should come to church because
we know God is there waiting for
us—we're part of His family. God
meets us any time and anywhere, but
there is something special about
going to His house to spend close,
personal time with Him. Why do
you go to church, or even more
important, if you're not going have
you asked yourself why not?

Invite a friend to go with you to church.

> *"Be an overcomer, only cowards yield*
> *When the foe they meet on the battlefield;*
> *We are blood-bought princes of the royal host,*
> *And must falter not, nor desert our post."*

When we visited the island of Saipan, we toured the abandoned bunkers left by the Japanese from World War II. These bunkers were dug into the landscape and mountains and were invisible to the untrained eye. Many American soldiers were killed by the Japanese hiding in them. Satan works in the same way. Ephesians 6:12 says, "For we do not wrestle against flesh and blood, but against principalities, against powers, against the rulers of the darkness of this age, against spiritual hosts of wickedness in the heavenly places." We cannot see our greatest foe and he knows our every weakness, attacking us where we are vulnerable. But the battle has already been won by Christ on the cross. We have not been asked to conquer new ground but to stand firmly in Christ's victory and hold our ground. Put on the full armor of God every day and live without fear. Christ has conquered death and we have victory through our Lord and Savior. We may not be able to see our enemy but knowing Christ won the battle we can stand firm and claim the victory. Do you stand your ground or retreat in fear when the enemy attacks you?

"For the eyes of the Lord range throughout the earth
to strengthen those whose hearts are fully committed to Him."
2 Chronicles 16:9

Recite the Scripture about the armor of God we are told to wear.

*"Jesus, my Lord, my life, my all,
In Thee I trust, in Thee I hide;
I know Thou wilt not let me fall
If I stay by Thy side."*

After Elijah prophesized to Ahab, the Lord told him to hide in the ravine of Kerith. God promised He would supply water from the brook and send ravens to feed him. So Elijah did as he was told and God provided. But after some time the brook dried up because there was no rain in the land. As I contemplate this Scripture, I try to imagine the emotions Elijah must have felt as day by day the water diminished. It looked like God's provision was running dry. Would I have stayed there until it dried up completely or would I have panicked and left to find other provision before I was up a creek, so to speak? God was not delinquent in caring for Elijah. He sent another resource the day it dried up. But I'm not sure I would have been around by that time. I probably would have taken off in desperation, sure God had forgotten and changed His plan without informing me. Because of my lack of faith I would have missed the next blessing. How often do we feel led by God to do something and the minute it starts to look like He's left the scene, we take over and make our own plans to bail us out? Just how much do we really trust God—enough to sit still when our brook runs dry? There's a lot to learn from this simple story and I'm not sure I would pass the test. Would you?

*"So he did what the Lord had told him. He went to the ravine of Kerith,
east of the Jordan, and stayed there. The ravens brought him bread and meat
in the morning and bread and meat in the evening, and he drank from the brook."*
1 Kings 17:5 & 6

Think of different times God has met your need.

> *"Let your light so shine that the world may see*
> *How to come to Christ who will set them free;*
> *Let its rays gleam bright when the darkness falls,*
> *Till each sinful soul for the Savior calls."*

I am always amazed at how much light just one little candle can give off. The glow is soft and inviting, creating an atmosphere of warmth. When the power goes off, it's a real blessing to have a candle nearby to help cut through the darkness. When Christ comes to live inside of us, our soul takes on an inner glow like the candlelight. It cuts through the darkness in the world and brings comfort to those around us. Have you ever been part of a church service where each person held a small candle and the light was passed down the row, lighting one after another until all the candles were lit? Our lives can illuminate a dark world in the same way. We need to pass the light of Jesus to those who are in the dark or suffering. Everyone has the potential to shine, but life can hurt at times and the inner glow can become dim or go out. Sometimes bad choices leave them wandering in the dark, lost and cold. Our one light can shine God's love deep into their lives and spread warmth, one person at a time. If we are willing to help light the world with Christ's love, even after we die, the soft glow reflected in their lives will continue to penetrate the darkness, as they pass it on to the next person they meet. Have you passed the light of Jesus onto someone in your life?

> *"In the same way, let your light shine before men, that they may see*
> *your good deeds and praise your Father in heaven."*
> Matthew 5:16

Turn out the lights and sit in the soft glow of candlelight.

> "Take my life and let it be
> Consecrated, Lord, to Thee;
> Take my hands and let them move
> At the impulse of Thy love."

Now that it is just my husband and I at home a gallon of milk lasts a long time. In fact there are times it goes sour before we can use it all and it has to be discarded. The gifts and talents that God has given us are to be shared and used in Kingdom work. They are not to be stored and hidden inside us. Unused talents are worthless, like a sour jug of milk. God has said He will discard those who do not use their talents. When I was young and newly married we moved to a new community and began attending a local community church. At a Bible study I confessed I had always been one of the worship musicians at other churches I attended. I had not told anyone at this church I could play the piano or sing even though we had been attending there for several months. I'll never forget the older woman who heard my confession and came up after the study. Shaking a bony finger at me she said, "How dare you!" Confused, I asked her, "How dare I what?" She replied, "How dare you hide your talent and not use it for the Lord." Her words startled and convicted me and within the month I was at the piano using the gifts and talents God had given me. Are you hiding a God-given talent and not using it in Kingdom work?

"Take the talent from him and give it to the one who has the ten talents. For everyone who has will be given more, and he will have an abundance. Whoever does not have, even what he has will be taken from him. And throw that worthless servant outside, into the darkness, where there will be weeping and gnashing of teeth."
Matthew 25:28–30

Find a way to use your God-given talents in His service.

January 30
Read Philippians chapter 2

*O*ur present-day culture is focused on self more than others. If it feels good, do it, and if it doesn't, don't put up with it. We're told our personal happiness and comfort should be our number one priority. But in a Christian's life this present-day philosophy is far from right. We are told to put others first and ourselves second, to be a servant rather than the one served. Dying to self does not come easily. In fact, I believe we are incapable of this except through the strength of our Lord, Jesus Christ. We can play out the actions of putting others first—turning the other cheek when we've been wronged; holding back a retort when we are falsely accused; offering a helping hand to someone when we're so far behind with our own work we can't see how we'll manage. If we do all of these things, but harbor resentment, anger or feelings of being used, we have not honored God with our actions. It's not just what we do, but how we do it and the attitude of our heart when we do it, that matters. God doesn't want us to put on a false front to others when in our soul we are fighting a battle of self-indulgence. Dying to self is a daily action that requires His strength to accomplish—or it's a losing battle. Do you serve others with a pure heart?

*"Do nothing out of selfish ambition
or vain conceit, but in humility
consider others better than yourselves.
Each of you should look
not only to your own interests,
but also to the interests of others."*
Philippians 2:3 & 4

*"I've one little heart to give to Jesus,
One little soul for Him to save,
One little life for His dear service,
One little self that He must have."*

Do a secret act of service to help someone.

> *"I'm a child of the King,*
> *A child of the King:*
> *With Jesus my Savior,*
> *I'm a child of the King."*

Do you believe in miracles? I do. One of the greatest miracles God has given me was restoring sight for my second son. At birth he was pronounced perfectly healthy and we celebrated as we took him home to join his older brother. But it wasn't long before we began to suspect that something was wrong. He was not responding visually to the world around him. We took him to the doctor and our worst fears were confirmed, he was blind. They had been unable to detect a problem at birth because his eyes had formed, but the part of his brain that would tell his eyes to see had not developed. From the age of five months on we worked with his eyes doing exercises, patching one then the other, glasses, surgery—everything we were told. The doctors said there was a slight chance we could bring limited vision into one eye at a time, but not to get our hopes up. We were working on borrowed time having only until he was four years old to teach his brain to see. Believing God could heal his eyes we never gave up hope that one day he might have good vision. That was over thirty-one years ago and, though he has some vision restrictions, he sees better than was ever thought medically possible. We learned a lot through those years of dealing with his disability. Who would have known that God would use my son's personal journey to help equip him for the blessed birth

of his deaf daughter twenty-eight years later. Our God is a God of miracles and He works all things for His good and His glory. Can you recall a miracle God has done in your life?

> *"When he had gone indoors, the blind men*
> *came to him, and He asked them,*
> *'Do you believe that I am able to do this?'*
> *'Yes, Lord,' they replied. Then He touched*
> *their eyes and said, 'According to your*
> *faith will it be done to you,'*
> *and their sight was restored."*
> *Matthew 10:28 & 29*

Recount a miracle from your life to encourage someone else.

February 1

"Sing them over again to me, wonderful words of life,
Let me more of their beauty see, wonderful words of life;
Words of life and beauty, teach me faith and duty
Beautiful words, wonderful words, wonderful words of life;
Beautiful words, wonderful words, wonderful words of life."

I taught piano lessons for several years and found you could teach anyone who wanted to learn how to play notes. The challenge was in helping them turn the notes into music. Some of my students were able to understand the difference and make beautiful music. Other students never seemed to grasp the concept, and while they may have learned to play difficult compositions, they lacked emotion and feeling. The difference was whether they were playing with their head or from their heart. If they played with their head they played notes never hearing how it sounded. If they played from their heart they listened to the sound they were making and the music would swell from the keyboard resonating from somewhere deep within. We can live our lives in the same way. We can methodically live life without feeling or thought. Or we can choose to live passionately from the depth of our soul using all of our senses to embrace each day, and live life to the "full" as Christ has promised. How are you living your life? Are you just playing notes or are you making beautiful music?

"Serve the Lord with gladness; come before Him with joyful songs."
Psalm 100:2

Pick one of your senses and focus on it throughout your day,
thanking God each time you use it.

To me reputation is what other people believe about you, not necessarily reflecting who you are, while character is the person you are behind closed doors when no one is looking. We can build a reputation based on our behavior in public, but that doesn't mean people know our true character. One of the things I strive for is to be the same person at home, alone, in the car, at work or out in public. I have to admit this can be challenging. Road rage is becoming more common as people have less patience for those around them. While I wouldn't say I have road rage, sometimes I get irritated when I'm behind the wheel and the driver in front of me seems to be crawling along. I have been tempted to give them the look—something my kids could tell you about— when I finally get a chance to pass them. More convicting than the embarrassment I would feel if I knew the other driver, is

the realization that my heart is not right and needs correcting. I have a ways to go in developing consistent character in all areas of my life. Do your reputation and character match, or do you have some work to do when you're alone too?

"In everything set them an example by doing what is good. In your teaching show integrity, seriousness and soundness of speech that cannot be condemned, so that those who oppose you may be ashamed because they have nothing bad to say about us."
Titus 2:7 & 8

"I have decided to follow Jesus;
I have decided to follow Jesus;
I have decided to follow Jesus;
No turning back, no turning back."

Imagine Jesus is riding in the passenger seat of your car
and see if you drive differently.

February 3
Read Romans chapter 5

*H*ave you ever felt insignificant and wondered what difference your life makes in the bigger scheme of things? Satan wants to convince us that our actions don't matter, that we're just one person so we can do what we want. But through history we have seen how the actions of a single individual have impacted and even changed our world. Think of Mother Theresa or Billy Graham whose lives impacted thousands for Christ. Think of Adolf Hitler or Bin Laden who destroyed and devastated lives on a massive scale. Then there are Adam and Eve who through one single decision changed the course of history. And Christ who came to earth to restore the lost. How we live does matter. What I do and believe will shape the future generations of my family. Let us not be deceived—we have the ability to make an impact on the world for good or bad. Let us live as if it makes a difference because it does. Doing our best one day at a time through Christ's strength and for His glory is all He asks. Do you believe how you live can make a difference in the world?

"For just as through the disobedience of the one man the many were made sinners, so also through the obedience of the one man the many will be made righteous."
Romans 5:19

"O Jesus, Lord and Savior, I give myself to Thee,
For Thou, in Thy atonement, didst give Thyself for me;
I own no other Master, my heart shall be Thy throne;
My life I give, henceforth to live, O Christ, for Thee alone."

Reflect on a past decision that changed the direction of your life.

> "We gather together to ask the Lord's blessing;
> He chastens and hastens His will to make known;
> The wicked oppressing now cease from distressing;
> Sing praises to His Name; He forgets not His own."

As my marriage started to crumble my husband moved out and my three teenage children and I struggled to deal with our emotions. I had watched other couples go through divorce and knew that families in crisis often fell apart. I felt I had failed my marriage but I didn't want to fail my children. I knew we were going to need something to draw us together when everything seemed to be coming apart. I prayed to God for help and He gave me an idea. I was reading a book at the time that listed positive points and I thought why not add Scripture to these points and together as a family memorize a different one each week. I presented the idea to the kids and they bought into it. Each week one of us would present a new thought and Scripture. Through the week we would recite it and all the previous ones, working up to twenty-two in all. Even the early 6:00 time-frame didn't seem to phase the kids as we gathered to focus on God's Word and prayer before we started our day. God walked us through that difficult time and my children still talk about the difference it made in their ability to cope. We all have times when we have to make a choice—will I let my circumstances make me bitter, or will I allow God to use them to make me better. Through prayer and God's Word it is possible to walk through a difficult time and be better because of it. Have you ever thought of memorizing Scripture and praying with your children before their day begins?

> "And we know that in all things God works for the good of those who love Him, who have been called according to His purpose."
> Romans 8:28

Commit to memorizing a different Scripture each week.

> *"Peace, peace, wonderful peace!*
> *Flowing so deep in my soul;*
> *Peace, peace, sweet peace,*
> *How it maketh the sad heart whole."*

I have been on a life-long quest for peace and have often found it elusive and fleeting. My husband is a man of peace and it is one of his more endearing qualities. After I married him, I was determined to find the source of his deep, inner tranquility but the more I tried to understand it the further away I felt. One night God gave me a dream that helped me in my quest. In my dream I was sitting beside a beautiful pond and I wanted to know what made it so special. I dove into the waters searching for its source of beauty only to find the water muddied by my efforts. The more desperate I became the dirtier the waters grew. Finally in desperation I crawled to the side crying over my inability to understand the secret. As I lay exhausted the waters stilled and became peaceful and beautiful again. I carefully peered over the edge and realized I could see the depths of the pond if I rested and observed rather than forcing my way inside. I realized peace was not something I could chase after or dig up. It is something I would learn as I paused and rested in the Lord. When we quiet ourselves before God He will, in time, settle the answer in our soul and we'll find the peace that transcends all understanding (Philippians 4:7). Are you a peace-filled person or is peace elusive to you?

"I will keep thee in perfect peace whose mind is stayed on thee."
Isaiah 26:3

List things that disrupt your peace and ask God how to find peace in them.

> *"Here for all your talent you may surely find a need,*
> *Here reflect the bright and Morning Star;*
> *Even from your humble hand the Bread of Life may feed,*
> *Brighten the corner where you are."*

There are many varieties of flowers, and each is beautiful in its own way. Some have large vibrant blossoms, others have tiny delicate shapes. Some are exquisite in their colors and others have subdued, gentle coloring. I don't compare one flower with another, I enjoy each one for what it has to offer. God made all of creation, and while we embrace the uniqueness of His world, we sometimes struggle to embrace our own uniqueness. My sisters-in-law are both very knowledgeable in certain areas and sometimes I feel uneducated and inferior when I'm around them because I'm not gifted that way. Satan is delighted when we compare ourselves to others. It's a great tactic of his to tear us down and control us. When we start comparing ourselves to someone else, a whole range of emotions can set in including jealousy, dissatisfaction, envy, discouragement, criticism, slander, and even anger or malice. All these are listed as sins in the Bible. God has gifted us uniquely and we have developed our gifts at different levels. Instead of

looking at someone else and wishing for their gifts, we need to explore who God created us to be and excel in our gifts. Prayerfully discern your uniqueness and use it to glorify Him. Do you know what gifts God has blessed you with and are you using them to His glory?

"Each one should test his own actions. Then he can take pride in himself, without comparing himself to somebody else, for each one should carry his own load."
Galatians 6:4 & 5

Thank God for the unique creation you are.

> "*Amazing grace! How sweet the sound*
> *That saved a wretch like me!*
> *I once was lost, but now am found;*
> *Was blind, but now I see.*"

One of my granddaughters was born severely hearing-impaired. At the age of one she underwent surgery and had Cochlear implants put into each side of her head. At first she could not understand what sound was and it took several weeks before she started to comprehend that she was hearing the world around her. It was a joy to see her adjust and begin to say words a few months after the surgery. At night and when she swims the hearing devices must be removed. As we take off her "ears" she enters the deaf world and we must find other ways to communicate with her. We can be spiritually deaf too. Even though we hear everything around us we have to purposefully put on "ears" to hear God's still, small voice. Listening for and discerning when He is speaking is something we have to learn also. At first we are just like my granddaughter, unable to comprehend what it means to hear from God. In time we begin to understand when God is communicating with us. I wonder how often He has to use other forms of communication to talk to us because we don't have our "God-ears" on? I marvel at the miracle we have witnessed through my granddaughter and how different her world is now that she can hear. I wonder if our world would be amazingly different if we put on our "God-ears" more often and listened for His voice. Is it easy for you to discern when God is speaking to you?

"He who has ears,
let him hear."
Matthew 11:15

Learn how to say I love you in sign language.

> *"I've anchored my soul in the 'Haven of Rest,'*
> *I'll sail the wide seas no more;*
> *The tempest may sweep over wild, stormy, deep,*
> *In Jesus I'm safe evermore."*

The ministry of Love INC believes strongly in mentoring individuals into life-style changes that can transform their lives. But I have found, after years of managing our program, the best teachable moment is not in the throes of the crisis. If someone is out on the open sea in a capsized boat struggling for their very life, at that moment they need rescued, not taught. If I were to sail over to them and begin to teach them on what boat to buy, how to operate it, or lessons on when to sail, my instruction would fall on deaf ears. But if I focus on bringing them into safe harbor and addressing their basic needs first, I will be given opportunity to mentor them in how to plan for a safe journey in the future. Sometimes I think we're too quick to criticize and instruct individuals who are in difficult situations, knowing their choices have often caused the moment of crisis. But if we really want to impact their life, we must be willing to help them with their immediate need, while we begin the process of entering into a relationship

with them to teach and mentor them with future needs. When we are willing to invest in others, through relationships, we open the door for God to work transformation in not only their life, but our life as well. Have you ever mentored someone over an extended period of time as a volunteer?

"The wise in heart are called discerning, and pleasant words promote instruction."
Proverbs 16:21

Look into volunteer opportunities in your community that will help others.

February 9
Read 1 Corinthians chapter 1

I find it so encouraging that many of the Biblical giants were ordinary people. In fact Christ's twelve disciples were cast-offs from the religious teachers. They hadn't made the grade and were sent home to learn a trade. But God doesn't see in us what others see or even what we may see for that matter. He sees who He has created us to be, whether we're living out our potential or not. Much more important than our capabilities is our awareness of our great dependence on God. He can do the most through those who know Him best. It's not what we can do, but what we believe God can do through us that opens the door for miraculous and amazing things to happen. It's not how gifted we seem to be but how available we've made our gifts to Him that makes the difference. As I write these words I can't help

but wonder if God will use them to draw others close to Him? If you want to do something great for God spend time getting to know what a great God He is. Don't waste time trying to become all you can in your strength. But spend time asking God to strengthen and use you for His glory. Are you available to God for something bigger than yourself?

"But God chose the foolish things of the world to shame the wise;
God chose the weak things of the world to shame the strong. He chose the lowly things
of this world and the despised things—and the things that are not—
to nullify the things that are, so that no one may boast before Him."
1 Corinthians 1:27–29

"When we have exhausted our store of endurance,
When our strength has failed ere the day is half done,
When we reach the end of our hoarded resources
Our Father's full giving is only begun."

Start praying to be available for whatever God brings your way.

J was sitting in an airport one morning, waiting to board the plane. Flying is a great way to get to your destination quickly, but I find airports incredibly exhausting and boring. I was writing in my journal, not paying much attention, when soft sweet music started to fill the air. A man sitting in front of me had taken out his guitar and was strumming a sweet melodic song. The music swept through the air and I could see others glancing up, smiles twitching at the corners of their mouths, as they too listened to the soothing song. Pretty soon an elderly gentleman took a harmonica from his pocket and sauntered over to join the musician. Before long it was time to board the plane, but I believe everyone's spirits were lifted by the gift of music given by these strangers. Music is a universal language that encourages, uplifts, and binds even strangers together for a time. God has told us to make music in our hearts and that He inhabits our praises. I have found when my day seems drab and dull, if I hum an old familiar hymn and lift my thoughts in praise, my mood is lifted too. When's the last time you hummed a tune of thankfulness to God?

"Shout for joy to the Lord, all the earth, burst into jubilant song with music: make music to the Lord with the harp, with the harp and the sound of singing, with trumpets and the blast of the ram's horn—shout for joy before the Lord, the King."
Psalm 98:4-6

*"Jesus, Jesus, Jesus,
Sweetest Name I know,
Fills my every longing,
Keeps me singing as I go."*

Sing one of your favorite hymns or worship songs out loud.

February 11
Read Proverbs chapter 10

hen I was first married we moved to a remote farm and for several years lived without telephone service. About once a week we made the ten-mile drive to the one telephone booth in the small town near us. It was not convenient to sit beside a phone booth with small children, putting in quarters and trying to reach everyone on our list, or waiting for someone to call us back. But living without a phone was freeing in many ways. I never worried about missing a call or having our dinner or a conversation interrupted. Time spent on the phone was minimal, which left more time to enjoy family and other things in life. Impulsive conversations did not exist. I didn't have to apologize later for something I shouldn't have said in the first place. It's been many years since my phoneless days but I still find a ringing telephone intrusive. When I see people carrying their cell phone into a public bathroom, afraid to miss a call, I feel sorry for them. If people had to wait to communicate, what they thought they had to say would often become unimportant. Being able to speak our mind immediately may create problems that have to be repaired down the road. Who knows, we just might spend more time talking to God if we couldn't call someone else. Do you find yourself tied to your telephone?

"When words are many, sin is not absent, but he who holds his tongue is wise."
Proverbs 10:19

"Just when I need Him, He is my all,
Answering when upon Him I call;
Tenderly watching lest I should fall,
Just when I need Him most."

Try spending less time on the phone and more time talking to God.

Winter can appear harsh and dead looking, especially when the trees are bare, the ground is frozen, and most of the birds have flown south. The landscape looks cold and uninviting, and usually isn't pleasant to be out in. I find myself retreating within my house and only venturing out when necessary. I have met people whose exterior presence gave off the same vibes of harshness. They appeared cold, lifeless, almost frozen in their responses and communication, definitely not inviting to those around them. I try to look past their exterior, asking God to help me see the person inside. I have often found that life has been hard on them, sometimes due to their own choices, and their frozen exterior is a protection against further pain. But I think inside each of us is the desire to be loved and to love—to have purpose and meaning in our life, not a dormant, stagnant existence. When we meet someone who is hurting, it can be an opportunity to extend warmth, hope, and love into their lives. Many times this is not easy because they are difficult or guarded, but God can give us what we need to approach them. I have seldom approached someone who did not respond to genuine care and

love when offered. I try to simply and sincerely care for them in some small way and hope that God can use it to start thawing their frozen exterior and bring new growth into their life. Have you ever asked God to help you look beyond a cold exterior and see them through His eyes?

"An anxious heart weighs a man down, but a kind word cheers him up."
Proverbs 12:25

"Help somebody today,
Somebody along life's way;
Let sorrow be ended, the friendless befriended,
Oh, help somebody today!"

Offer some encouragement to someone who might be down and hurting.

When we get a small scrape we may put a bandage on it, but if we receive a deep cut, a Band-Aid won't be enough. We go to a care facility or doctor to receive proper treatment. If the wound is extensive it will take weeks or even months to heal and can leave a scar for the rest of our lives. Great care needs to be taken so the wound heals, or infection can set in and spread to other parts of the body causing major complications. When something major happens in our life we can become emotionally or mentally wounded. Unlike a physical wound the damage done to the mind, heart and emotions cannot always be seen. Often we try to cover our wounds hoping they will go away. We're hesitant to seek trained advice and don't even talk to God about it. Emotional wounds are just as real as physical hurts and we should not ignore them. Go to the Master healer, your Creator, and ask Him to help you. Sometimes it may require seeking help from a professional. The healing process won't happen overnight and we must be persistent in working through it. We can't afford to ignore deep hurts—they can fester and infect every part of our body. Have you hidden a hurt deep inside and know it's never healed correctly?

"O Lord my God, I called to you for help and you healed me."
Psalm 30:2

"There's not a friend like the lowly Jesus,
No, not one! No, not one!
None else could heal all our soul's diseases,
No, not one! No, not one!"

Give yourself a spiritual physical and make sure you're healthy.

*V*alentine's Day is for lovers. When you're in a loving relationship with someone it is a wonderful day to celebrate, but for many the day can be difficult and lonely. When I was going through my divorce it was a cold reminder of a love that was lost. For those whose loved one has passed on it is a stark reminder of how alone they now feel. For those who have yet to meet that special someone it only serves to further accentuate their singleness. Even in healthy relationships sometimes the day can be a disappointment if expectations are not met. But we are in a love relationship with One who will never let us down, never leave us or desert us. That person is Jesus Christ. No matter what your love life is like on earth your love life with Him is guaranteed and secure. If you feel lacking in the relationship it's not because of Him but because you've not accepted or entered into His deep and rich love. Spend this day wrapped in the gift of His love. Read His love letters in the Holy Bible and let them speak deeply to your heart. Share everything with Him—your fears, failures, hopes and dreams. Look around you and see all the beautiful blessings He has given you as a token of His love. Write yourself a letter and let the Holy Spirit guide your words then sign it, 'Love, Jesus.' He wants to be the love of your life. Do you have an intimate relationship with Jesus?

*"I love those
who love me,
and those who
seek me find me."*
Proverbs 8:17

*"Jesus loves me! This I know, For the Bible tells me so;
Little ones to Him belong; They are weak, but He is strong.
Yes, Jesus loves me! Yes, Jesus loves me!
Yes, Jesus loves me! The Bible tells me so."*

Write a love letter to Jesus listing all the ways you love Him.

February 15
Read Ephesians chapter 5

> *"He giveth more grace as our burdens grow greater,*
> *He sendeth more strength as our labors increase;*
> *To added afflictions He addeth His mercy,*
> *To multiplied trials He multiplies peace."*

Feminism was being redefined in the 60's and 70's when I was growing up. Women were being encouraged to stand up and be heard. I remember watching my parents' relationship and wondering why my mother didn't speak up more often. My father was the head of the house and I remember thinking I wouldn't be afraid to speak my opinion to him if I were my

mother. Now that I am older, and have struggled to be the godly wife the Bible talks about, I realize that my mother was not weak, she was being submissive to her husband. I was also unaware that no decision was made in our home without them conferring together privately before it was publicly announced. My father loves her deeply, showing her respect and honoring her as his wife. God has instructed us how to treat each other as husband and wife. I am fortunate that God gave me parents who modeled Christian behavior in their relationship. Have you struggled with submissiveness or honor in your marriage?

"Wives, submit to your husbands as to the Lord...Husbands, love your wives, just as Christ loved the church...however, each one of you also must love his wife as he loves himself, and the wife must respect her husband."
Ephesians 5:22,25, & 33

Think of a special way you could honor your mate today and do it.

> "Safe in the arms of Jesus,
> Safe on His gentle breast;
> There by His love o'ershaded,
> Sweetly my soul shall rest."

How long has it been since you slept like a baby? For many, sleep is elusive and difficult. A friend suffers from severe, chronic insomnia. He shared that when a person has very little sleep they have to be acutely aware that they are not as alert as they should be. When a person is tired they forget things, say the wrong things and find almost everything a struggle. Another friend who suffers from the same problem shared that as nighttime approaches the anticipation of another sleepless night creates enough anxiety to circumvent all efforts to fall asleep. So why is it babies can sleep so easily and deeply while many adults struggle? I'm no expert on the subject but it seems that infants aren't concerned about much—they don't worry, work too hard or have too much on their minds. They simply respond to their body's need to rest and enter into the deep refreshing sleep we all crave. There are many verses in the Bible that mention sleep and infer our ability to trust God. When we lay down to sleep we need to leave the worries and cares of this world with Him knowing He does not sleep and is watching over us. It's one thing to know this and quite another to convince your mind to let it all go—I know, I have struggled. Yet God wants us to sleep soundly and be refreshed for the new day. Let's come as a child and be tucked in by our Heavenly Father trusting Him to care for things while we rest—it's a gift He longs to give each of us. Do you struggle with getting enough sleep?

> "I will lie down
> and sleep in peace,
> for you alone, O Lord,
> make me dwell
> in safety."
> Psalms 4:8

Before you go to bed, give God your concerns
and thank Him for your blessings.

> *"Faith of our fathers, living still,*
> *In spite of dungeon, fire, and sword;*
> *Oh, how our hearts beat high with joy*
> *Whene'er we hear that glorious Word!"*

The people God brought out of Egypt witnessed and participated in miracle after miracle as He took them through the Red Sea, fed them with manna from heaven and guided them daily by a cloud. These same people abandoned God and their faith as they wandered in the wilderness for forty years. They forgot His miracles, forgot the hardships they had left behind and began to worship other gods as they pined for the good old days. I used to wonder how this could happen. How could they forget all the miracles and provisions God had given them? Then God reminded me that I often do the same thing. I forget how faithful He has been to me in the past. I forget the multitude of times He has moved in my life, sometimes miraculously. And I fail to thank Him for His daily provisions and often overlook His endless blessings. I am no different than my brothers and sisters of years ago. My faith can also be fickle at times. It is easy to look at others and criticize them but God wants me to look at myself first. He knows that if I concentrate on getting the plank out of my own eye, it will take the rest of my life and I won't have time to be picking slivers out of anyone else's eye. I need to focus on my own walk so I don't repeat history. Do you have a judgmental spirit?

"You hypocrite, first take the plank out of your eye, and then you will see clearly to remove the speck from your brother's eye."
Luke 6:42

Replace a spirit of criticism with praise.

A dry sponge is useless until it is moistened. But even though it's dry and brittle it doesn't quit being a sponge. On the other hand, sponges lose their effectiveness by becoming saturated. They are great for cleaning up spills but when full have to be wrung out. A Christian who is not filled with the living water of Christ is similar to a dry sponge. They are of little value in Kingdom work. They may be called Christian, but the purpose they were created for cannot be fulfilled as long as they are dry and brittle. A Christian who is only focused on taking in and is never being wrung out for others becomes saturated and useless. We need to be giving out as much as we are taking in or we lose our value to Christ. Either extreme is harmful to our productivity in Kingdom work. Dry and brittle or totally saturated are both conditions we want to avoid. Keep yourself soft and pliable by taking in the living water of Jesus Christ. But make sure you're being squeezed and emptied out in His work so you can continue to absorb and become all He has created you to be. If you compare yourself to a sponge what kind of shape are you in?

"As the body without the spirit is dead, so faith without deeds is dead."
James 2:26

"Deeper, deeper, blessed Holy Spirit,
Take me deeper still,
Till my life is wholly lost in Jesus,
And His perfect will."

Try using a dry sponge and see how worthless it is.

> *"Just where I am, oh, let me be*
> *A faithful witness, Lord, for Thee;*
> *While others seek a wider sphere,*
> *Oh, keep me faithful, Lord, just here!"*

Naaman was a commander in the army for the king of Aram. The Bible says he was a valiant soldier, but had the curse of leprosy. He heard that the prophet Elisha could cure him and sought him out. But when Elisha told him to wash himself seven times in the Jordan River he was outraged. He felt this simple solution was ridiculous making light of his situation and he went away angry. Naaman's servant questioned him. If he had been given a noble task would he not have done it? But because he was given a simple task was he not even going to try? Naaman decided to do what Elisha had said and he was cured of leprosy. We can be like Naaman and want to do great and mighty things for God but are put off when asked to do simple acts of service or obedience. God is looking at our heart not our capabilities. If we are prideful or arrogant and feel some things are beneath us He will often give us challenges that teach us humility and submission. I work with many volunteers and find their attitudes towards service very different. Some only want important tasks equal to their skills while others are willing to serve in any capacity and find nothing beneath them if it moves ministry forward. I have often seen these humble servants blessed in amazing ways by God. The Bible says, "Pride goes before destruction, a haughty spirit before a fall" (Proverbs 16:18). I want to be a servant who is quick to lend a hand no matter how small or trivial the task knowing God can be glorified in all types of work. What kind of servant are you?

"So he went down and dipped himself in the Jordan seven times, as the man of God had told him, and his flesh was restored and became clean like that of a young boy."
2 Kings 5:14

Serve someone today and examine your heart.

> "Out of my bondage, sorrow and night, Jesus, I come, Jesus, I come;
> Into Thy freedom, gladness, and light, Jesus, I come to Thee;
> Out of my sickness, into Thy health, Out of my want and into Thy wealth,
> Out of my sin and into Thyself, Jesus, I come to Thee."

My husband's parents were immigrants from the Ukraine. They were sponsored by a church and brought out of a German concentration camp. Coming to America meant hope and opportunity to the young family and they studied hard and became U.S. citizens shortly after arriving. They left all their belongings, except for one suitcase, and traveled for three weeks by boat and train to a new land they had heard about, but never seen. The Bible tells us that our citizenship is in heaven, but I wonder if we

have the same desire and determination to get there that my in-laws had. We seem to cling to our possessions, struggling to make the sacrifices necessary to embrace our new citizenship. They never returned to the Ukraine after arriving in America and had no desire to ever go back. I think we often look back at what we've been called to leave behind and we miss pieces of it. My in-laws knew that what they left behind could never compare to what they gained by coming to America. Becoming a citizen of heaven is the opportunity of a lifetime, literally, this life and the next. Have you ever thought about becoming a citizen of heaven, and what you need to leave behind as you enter into your new life with Christ?

> "But our citizenship is in heaven. And we eagerly await a Savior from there, the Lord Jesus Christ, who by the power that enables Him to bring everything under His control, will transform our lowly bodies so that they will be like His glorious body."
> Philippians 3:20-21

Thank God for our country and pray for its leaders.

*"Therefore, get rid of all moral filth and the evil that is so prevalent,
and humbly accept the word planted in you, which can save you."*
James 1:21

*"Take time to be holy, be calm in thy soul,
Each thought and each motive beneath His control.
Thus led by His Spirit to fountains of love,
Thou soon shalt be fitted for service above."*

My daughter called to say she was cleaning those hard to reach areas, such as behind the fridge and underneath the washing machine. It reminded me of my youth when every year my mother would spring-clean the house. She was a good housekeeper and our home was always clean but once a year we all had to pitch in and do the super-duty deep clean. She would plan a different room each day and we each had our assignments. It seemed I always had to vacuum the books and polish the wood furniture; things that certainly were not done on a weekly basis. The house always smelled and looked really clean when we were finished. Sometimes we need to do deep cleaning in ourselves. Many of us do the weekly things such as go to church, read our Bible, pray each day; all the stuff that keeps our surface looking clean. But what about those hard to reach areas like the inside of our soul and the dark recesses of our mind? Occasionally, we need to focus on getting under the skin and evaluating what needs a deep cleaning inside. In order to do this we'll have to set aside some down time with no intrusions or diversions and get alone with God. Through prayer and contemplation, He'll help us pull out the sin we've buried deep inside and get rid of it. The process won't be fun but once it's over we'll feel squeaky clean and ready for another year. Is it time to do some deep cleaning in your soul?

Plan a day to clean an area you've been putting off for a long time.

Who is Lord over your life? Whom do you answer to and seek direction from? Whom do you serve and accept in authority over you? It is common to hear people who call themselves a Christian say, "Jesus is my Lord and Savior." But is it just a name we give Him and not a title that carries weight in our life's decisions? Do we seek to do the things He has told us in the Bible or do we make excuses? I'm a complainer. It's mostly to my husband and I'll complain about little things—clothes left on the floor, cupboard doors left open, garbage not thrown away. I'll complain about the temperature, being tired, getting too much company, not getting enough company—I never run out of things to complain about. But in Philippians Chapter 2 it says to do everything without complaining or arguing. So, if Jesus is really Lord of my life, I need to quit complaining. Making Jesus Lord of our life isn't an on-again, off-again decision. We either obey Him or we don't—we can't pick and choose when we want to take His direction. Not everyone who calls Him Lord will enter the Kingdom of Heaven, but only those who do His will. Is Jesus Lord of your life or is it just a label you attach to Him?

*"Not everyone who says to me,
'Lord, Lord,' will enter
the kingdom of heaven,
but only he who does
the will of my Father
who is in heaven."*
Matthew 7:21

"Lord, take my life, and make it wholly Thine;
Fill my poor heart with Thy great love divine;
Take all my will, my passion, self and pride;
I now surrender, Lord, in me abide."

Seek to be obedient in every area of your life.

> *"Thou didst leave Thy throne and Thy kingly crown,*
> *When Thou camest to earth for me;*
> *But in Bethlehem's home was there found no room for Thy holy nativity.*
> *O come to my heart, Lord Jesus, There is room in my heart for Thee."*

I think I often romanticize the old days, but I do think there are some things we have lost as we've progressed. Homes were a lot smaller and families a lot larger in those days, so they had to share the space they lived in. Everyone shared a bedroom and sometimes even a bed. Usually there was just one large room where the family gathered. Circumstances forced people to share, get along with each other, and work through their disagreements. In today's world many of us live in large homes where we often share a house, but not our lives. We have our own space and if someone is bothering us, or we just want to be alone, we go to our own room. Entertainment is often in multiple rooms of the house, so if someone's doing something we don't like, we can find another room to do our own thing. We don't have to get along, we can just get away. We don't have to work through our difficulties, we can retreat into our own space and ignore them. We don't have to share our things or our lives but often end up struggling in our relationships. Self-indulgence is not taught anywhere in the Bible and shouldn't exist in our homes. Are there things you could change in your home to strengthen your family?

> *"You, my brothers, were called to be free. But do not use your freedom to indulge the sinful nature, rather, serve one another in love."*
> *Galatians 5:13*

Plan an activity your family could do together at home this week.

> *"There is a place of quiet rest,*
> *Near to the heart of God;*
> *A place where sin cannot molest,*
> *Near to the heart of God."*

ecently I was challenged packing for a trip I took. I wanted to get everything into one bag but the more I crammed and stuffed the more disorganized I felt. I took some things out but found myself putting other things in and eventually gave up and packed another bag. At times our lives can feel like an overstuffed suitcase. We just keep cramming more and more stuff into our schedules. The fuller it gets the more we try to rearrange it. Sometimes in frustration we'll take something off but almost instantly find something else to put in its place. Pretty soon we're bulging at the seams, ready to burst open and unable to enjoy anything because of all the pressure we feel. We find ourselves lugging our heavy suitcase around with us everywhere we go. Eventually our life will come apart like a broken bag or barely be held together with some temporary fix, like duct tape. We need to ask God what things we need in our life journey and unpack the extras. With God's help what is important will fit nicely and we'll be able to carry it with ease. Does your life resemble an overstuffed suitcase right now?

"What good is it for a man to gain the whole world, yet forfeit his soul."
Mark 8:36

List everything on your schedule and pray about what you should eliminate.

> *"The ax is already at the root of the trees, and every tree that does not produce good fruit will be cut down and thrown into the fire."*
> Matthew 3:10

> *"Fair are the meadows, fairer still the woodlands,*
> *Robed in the blooming garb of spring;*
> *Jesus is fairer, Jesus is purer,*
> *Who makes the woeful heart to sing."*

We have many orchards in our area and every February skilled pruners trim the trees in preparation for a harvest of fruit. As trees age they become less productive and eventually are cut down, rooted out, and burned. Often new trees are planted in their place. We should think of our lives as fruit trees and God as the master caretaker. He prunes, waters, fertilizes and protects us from the elements, preparing us to bear fruit in Kingdom work. When we choose to quit bearing fruit that honors God, our value as God's workers decreases. The Bible is very clear about the fate of those who become fruitless or produce diseased fruit. I believe that as long as we are willing, God will make us fruitful, but the choice is ours. Are you producing good fruit for the Lord?

Does your attitude resemble a sweet orange or a sour grapefruit?

I have always been intrigued by people who make pottery. It's fascinating to watch them take a lump of wet clay and start spinning a beautiful masterpiece from it. We are told that God is the potter, we are the clay and He is molding us into something beautiful for His service. But what if God had given us a catalog and asked us to pick the model we wanted to become? What if He had told us to pick the top ten personality traits we wanted? What if we had to pick our color of skin, eyes and hair and how tall we wanted to grow? It would have been a difficult if not impossible task for me to decide what I should look like and what character traits would be inherent in my personality. I'm so glad my Heavenly Father knew everything about me and didn't need my advice on how to create the perfect me. We have not been randomly crafted but knit together perfectly for the role we are to play. No one is a mistake or an accident but He sits at the potter's wheel working with us from creation to death perfecting the person He sees in us. We need to praise God for the qualities that make us unique and special. Often my favorite

pottery is not the perfectly shaped bowl but the one with character and color. Let's not spend time trying to remake ourselves but embrace what He has given us and develop it to its full capacity. Are you pleased with God's work or do you often wish you were a different "clay" pot?

"Yet, O Lord, you are our Father.
We are the clay, and You are the potter;
we are all the work of Your hand."
Isaiah 64:8

"Oh, how marvelous! Oh, how wonderful!
And my song shall ever be:
Oh, how marvelous! Oh, how wonderful!
"Is my savior's love for me!"

Thank God for how He made you.

*"I've found a Friend, oh, such a friend! He loved me ere I knew Him;
He drew me with the cords of love, and thus He bound me to Him.
And round my heart still closely twine those ties which naught can sever,
For I am His, and He is mine, forever and forever."*

Barnabas was an encourager. In fact his name means "Son of Encouragement." In Acts 4 we read that he sold his field and brought the money to the apostles. In Acts 9 Saul, after his conversion, tried to join the disciples but they were afraid of him, not believing he was really a disciple. But Barnabas stood up for him in front of the disciples. He related how he had seen Saul fearlessly preaching in the name of Jesus and asked them to give him a chance, which they did. Later in Acts 15 we read that Barnabas asked Paul to give John (also called Mark) another chance when Paul wanted nothing more to do with the deserter. Paul went his own way and Barnabas traveled with John to encourage him. Barnabas was often in the background paving the way for others who became well known in the Bible. His simple acts of obedience often required him to take an unpopular stance for others. He saw the best in people, even when they had failed, and came to their defense when they needed a second chance. He stayed behind the scenes but his role affected history. Every person has at least one Barnabas in their life—someone who has been there for them, encouraging and working beside them. They are the unseen heroes who have helped change the course of history. Who is a Barnabas in your life?

"But Barnabas took him and brought him to the apostles. He told them how Saul on his journey had seen the Lord and that the Lord had spoken to him and how in Damascus he had preached fearlessly in the name of Jesus."
Acts 9:27

Write a thank you to someone who has encouraged you.

*I*t's calving season and today we had our first spring calf. When a calf is born, the mother cow will immediately get up and start licking the calf to clean off the birth and stimulate the blood to flow, all the while talking to its new baby in soft low tones. Within an hour, a healthy calf will struggle to its feet and instinctively know to suckle the udder. The bond between the cow and calf has developed and the mother will go to almost any lengths to protect her new offspring. But when a cow is having difficulty birthing and we have to pull the calf, this can interfere with the natural bonding process. We've had cows not realize they've just calved and walk off to leave the calf to die or walk on it, not distinguishing it from the ground. At those times, we lock mother and calf up in a small pen and hope that in time the mother will accept her calf, to nurture and care for it. When God first created man, there was a natural bond between them. But when sin entered the picture, that natural bond was disrupted. Since that time man has walked away from God, ignoring his need

of Him, and at times even His existence. But God didn't lock us in a pen until we accept Him—He gave us our own free will. We can choose to walk away from God and struggle all our life, or return to Him and let Him nurture us into the person He created us to be; it's up to us. Do you have a special bond with your Heavenly Father?

"Those who live according to the sinful nature have their minds set on what that nature desires; but those who live in accordance with the Spirit have their minds set on what the Spirit desires."
Romans 8:5

"I would be nearer, my Savior,
Where I can hear Thy voice
Falling in tenderest whispers,
Making my heart rejoice."

Take a trip to the zoo or a farm and observe the relationship between the new offspring and parents.

February 29
Read 1 Corinthians chapter 15

I work with a lot of volunteers. When they offer to serve they expect their service will help someone. But I have been involved in service projects that did not meet the expectation we had at the beginning. Even though the volunteer did everything they could, sometimes the one being served seemed untouched and unchanged. The volunteer felt discouraged wondering if it was a waste of time. Any Kingdom work done to the best of our ability is not a waste of time. When a servant works for someone they need to realize the Lord is also working in them. He is teaching, molding, and accomplishing transformation in their life while they serve. Our focus is usually on those being served and we rate success by what we see in them. But God is looking at the complete picture and He places just as much importance on the servant as the one being served. No service is ever wasted—someone will be changed in the process. While you labor for others He labors for you and Kingdom work is done. Have you ever been disappointed in the outcome of a service you tried to do for someone else?

"Therefore, my dear brothers, stand firm. Let nothing move you.
Always give yourselves fully to the work of the Lord,
because you know that your labor in the Lord is not in vain."
1 Corinthians 15:58

"Rescue the perishing, duty demands it;
Strength for thy labor the Lord will provide;
Back to the narrow way patiently win them;
Tell the poor wand'rer a Savior has died."

Next time you serve someone thank God that He is also doing a work in you.

"The secret things belong to the Lord our God,
but the things revealed belong to us
and to our children forever,
that we may follow all the words of this law."
Deuteronomy 29:29

"I love to tell the story, 'tis pleasant to repeat,
What seems each time I tell it more wonderfully sweet;
I love to tell the story, for some have never heard
The message of salvation from God's own holy Word."

I recently put together a book of my family's history. I spent weeks interviewing my parents and gathering old pictures. I wanted to write their story as accurately as possible so it could be passed down from one generation to another. It was fascinating to hear the old stories of their ancestors and how their life had shaped my own. God has done the same thing for us. The Bible is the history of our past and the hope for our future. It's written to encourage us in our journey and to be passed from one generation to the next. The Old Testament is filled with the creation story and God's providence before Jesus came to earth. The New Testament, written by the disciples and inspired by God, records the history of Jesus' time on earth and the beginning of the church as we now know it. Everything we need to know about living is recorded in its pages. Have you taken the time, through the reading of His Word, to become intimately familiar with the God who created you?

The next time you read from the Bible, insert your name whenever possible and see if it becomes more personal.

"No discipline seems pleasant at the time, but painful. Later on, however, it produces a harvest of righteousness and peace for those who have been trained by it."
Hebrews 12:11

"Break Thou the bread of life, dear Lord, to me,
As Thou didst break the loaves beside the sea;
Beyond the sacred page I seek Thee, Lord;
My spirit pants for Thee, O living Word!"

We have a bowl in our house filled with a variety of nuts. Some nuts are easy to crack and get eaten quickly. Others are harder and the seed often gets damaged during the cracking process because it takes more force to get it open. Still others are really hard, and get thrown back in the bowl for someone else to try and open. Occasionally one of these hard-to-crack nuts is conquered, but often the seed has dried out because it was thrown to the side one too many times. We can be like a nut. Our seed lays inside of us and we have to be willing to be cracked so it can be used. If we don't resist being cracked our fruit will be juicy and good, useful in the Lord's work. If we resist, more pressure has to be applied, and there may be damage to the seed making us less useful than we might have been. And if we're one of those "tough nuts to crack" our seed may be all dried up before God can use us. A tough outer shell focused on keeping others out will harm us more than protect us. We need to be open to the Lord's discipline so we will reap a harvest of good works for the Lord. What kind of nut are you?

Crack a few nuts and notice the condition of the seeds inside.

There is a huge difference between religious activity and living for Christ. The Pharisees had mastered religious activity and followed every letter of the law. They knew how to appear religious and righteous yet Jesus could see into their hearts and knew they were hypocrites. His words were strong, condemning their behavior and warning them of the judgment awaiting them if they did not turn from their ways. Religious activity is not the same as intimacy with Christ. As a wife I could clean, cook, care for and attend functions with my husband and it would appear that we had an intimate relationship. I could do all the functions of a wife but withhold my love and devotion and our personal relationship would be non-existent. The things I did for him could never take the place of entering into a trusting, knowing and loving relationship. We can do the same thing with Christ. We can speak, act, attend functions and behave as Christians and yet withhold our love, devotion and submission to Him. We can appear to know Him but only really know of Him. God does not want a flurry of activity and show—He wants us. He wants permission to live in our hearts, to be our best friend and Master of our life. Does your life contain a lot of religious activity without any intimacy with Christ?

"Woe to you, teachers of the law and Pharisees, you hypocrites! You shut the kingdom of Heaven in men's faces. You yourselves do not enter, nor will you let those enter who are trying to."
Matthew 23:13

"Nearer, my God, to Thee, nearer to Thee!
E'en though it be a cross that raiseth me,
Still all my song shall be, nearer, my God, to Thee.
Nearer, my God, to Thee, nearer to Thee!"

Share your intimate feelings with Christ today.

In the Old Testament gatekeepers stood guard at the temple to prevent anyone unclean from entering. Today we still have guards posted at places of high importance, such as the White House in America or Parliament in England. No one is allowed inside unless they pass the guards and are deemed worthy of entry. Our heart is referred to as the dwelling place of Christ, the temple of the Lord. "Don't you know that you yourselves are God's temple and that God's Spirit lives in you?" 1 Corinthians 3:16. Nothing should be allowed inside unless it has been tested and deemed worthy, "for out of the overflow of the heart our mouth will speak" Matthew 12:34. The Bible gives us instruction on how to protect our hearts. In Philippians 4:6 & 7, we are told, "Do not be anxious about anything, but in everything, by prayer and petition, with thanksgiving, present your requests to God. And the peace of God, which transcends all understanding, will guard your hearts and your minds in Christ Jesus." Our heart is the temple of God where He resides and out of it flows all life. How much time do you spend protecting your heart from bad influences, evil thoughts and sinful ways? Have you let your guard down and allowed anyone or anything entry? The Scriptures place high importance on the condition of our heart and it's time we did too. What protective measures have you put in place to guard your heart?

"Above all else, guard your heart, for it is the wellspring of life."
Proverbs 4:23

"Though Satan should buffet, though trials should come,
Let this blest assurance control,
That Christ has regarded my helpless estate,
And hath shed His own blood for my soul.
It is well, with my soul, It is well, it is well, with my soul."

Ask God to reveal the condition of your heart
and see if you need to protect it better.

"Not a burden we bear, not a sorrow we share,
But our toil He doth richly repay;
Not a grief or a loss, not a frown or a cross,
But is blessed if we trust and obey."

My husband and I have a small herd of Hereford cattle. My husband spends time with them daily and they know him and respond to the sound of his voice. If they see him outside they call to him as if to remind him they have been waiting for his appearance. When he calls them they come running from wherever they are to greet him. They are not afraid of him and he can work with them as he needs to. I don't have this same relationship with them. They don't come when I call and they don't call to me when they see me outside. We're both uneasy around each other because trust has not been built between us. Our relationship with God is built on trust too. In order to know and hear Him we have to spend time with Him. Trust is built through relationship and proven over time. The cows know and trust my husband and they are responsive to him. I want to hear and respond to God when He calls, anticipating Him throughout my day. I want to spend enough time with God that I'll trust Him to take care of my every need. Do you trust God?

"But blessed is the man who trusts in the Lord, whose confidence is in Him.
He will be like a tree planted by the water that sends out its roots by the stream.
It does not fear when heat comes; its leaves are always green.
It has no worries in a year of drought and never fails to bear fruit."
Jeremiah 17:7 & 8

Think of a time you trusted God and He proved faithful.

"Dear friend, do not imitate what is evil but what is good. Anyone who does what is good is from God. Anyone who does what is evil has not seen God."
3 John 11

"I am a child of God,
I am a child of God;
I have washed my robes in the cleansing fountain,
I am a child of God."

When my children were little, we lived on a farm, and my boys loved to put on their daddy's irrigation boots and pretend they were going to change the water. Even though the boots were huge and they could hardly walk, they felt all grown up. They were walking in their daddy's shoes and that's what mattered.

Do we have that same desire to walk in the shoes of our Heavenly Father? We've been created in His likeness and we need to spend time learning of Him and growing into His image. My boys spent time with their daddy every day, and the more they were around him the more they were learning from him. The best way to get to know our Heavenly Father is to spend daily time with Him and His Word. If we don't desire to walk with Him we'll never get to know Him in the intimate way my sons bonded with their daddy. Is God the role model in your life?

Did you walk in your daddy's shoes when you were little?

"There is pow'r, pow'r, wonder-working pow'r
In the blood of the Lamb;
There is pow'r, pow'r, wonder-working pow'r
In the precious blood of the Lamb."

I love to sit on my porch and watch the birds fly. I have noticed when the wind is gusting hard, the large hawks and eagles spread their wings and fly directly into the wind, catching a draft. Then they no longer have to flap their wings for the wind lifts them and they soar higher and higher, riding the wind currents. I have watched them play in the wind for hours effortlessly floating in the air. God has told us we too can soar but it's not going to happen when everything is still and calm. In order to soar we have to face an adversity or challenge that is coming at us threatening to knock us down. Only then, through His power and might, can we rise and soar above our problems. When we feel overwhelmed and inadequate we have the greatest potential to soar, for when we are weak He is strong. When we quit trying to flap our tiny wings and allow Him to pick us up and carry us above the adversity we can soar under His strength and through His might. Have you been soaring lately, or do you need to be pushed out of the nest?

"But those who hope in the Lord will renew their strength.
They will soar on wings like eagles;
they will run and not grow weary, they will walk and not be faint."
Isaiah 40:31

Watch the birds soar the next time the wind blows.

March 8
Read Psalm 96

J stepped out the door this morning and was greeted by a chorus of song unequaled anywhere. The robins were chirping, the geese were honking, a rooster was crowing, the blackbirds were singing, the meadow larks were trilling, and the doves were cooing. It was as if they had joined together in beautiful harmony, singing spring is coming, spring is coming! The celebration is evident in nature all around that winter is passing and spring is on its way. Tiny little buds have started to appear on the bushes, spring bulbs have pushed through the ground and are ready to burst into glory, and the perennials are venturing forth in the new year to shine their glory for another season. All of God's creation is tuned into the dawning of a new season and the enthusiasm exhibited is evident to all. Do we celebrate the change of seasons in our lives with joy, or do we cower in fear of letting go of the old to welcome the new? Let us shake off the cold, stretch out our limbs and burst forth in song—a new day is dawning, let us rejoice and be glad in it! Let us join with all of creation and celebrate all that change offers, the hope that comes from another season of opportunity and growth. Praise the Lord! Praise the Lord! Are you celebrating the change of season in your life or are you mourning the passing of the old?

"Sing to the Lord a new song; sing to the Lord, all the earth.
Sing to the Lord, praise His name;
proclaim His salvation day after day."
Psalm 96:1 & 2

"Praise Him! Praise Him! Jesus, our blessed Redeemer!
Sing, O Earth, His wonderful love proclaim!
Hail Him! Hail Him! Highest archangels in glory;
Strength and honor give to His holy Name!
Like a shepherd, Jesus will guard His children,
In His arms He carries them all day long."

Go for a spring walk and notice the earth awakening for another year.

"Sow for yourselves righteousness, reap the fruit of unfailing love,
and break up your unplowed ground; for it is time to seek the Lord,
until He comes and showers righteousness on you."
Hosea 10:12

"Since Jesus came into my heart,
Since Jesus came into my heart;
Floods of joy o'er my soul like the sea billows roll,
Since Jesus came into my heart."

When a farmer gets ready to plant he does not go to an unprepared field and throw seeds from the edge, hoping they'll be blown into the field and take root. There is much soil preparation before it is ready for planting. The ground will have to be cleared of all debris, broken open by plowing or disking, and the hard clods crushed until the soil is loose and refined ready to receive the seed. Then the farmer takes great care in how he places the seed in the soil—not too deep, not too many, and not too early or too late in the season. A well planted field that is taken care of produces an abundant harvest in due time. As Christians we often want to see new growth in our lives but don't realize all the preparation that must happen before our hearts are ready to receive the seed. We must rid ourselves of any known sin.

We must plow deeply into our heart, turning over the old in preparation for the new. We must allow everything left to be crushed and refined through pressure and trials until the soil of our soul is ready. Then we must not randomly place new seeds into our mind and heart. We must be selective in what kind, when, how many and how deeply we plant the desired crop. If we take time preparing our hearts and planting the seeds of faith correctly we will reap an abundant harvest in due time. Have you tried to plant random seeds without proper preparation beforehand?

What is the soil condition of your heart?

March 10
Read Psalm 119

During my senior year of high school my boyfriend was in college. He wrote me often and I remember how excited I was to get his letters, savoring every word over and over again. He often included clippings from things he had read that would encourage and lift my spirits. Those letters made the year bearable as I found myself falling deeper and deeper in love with him. I wanted to spend every moment with him and the love letters made me feel a part of his life—despite our distance. The Bible is God's love letter to us. It contains words of love, encouragement, hope and instruction. He inspired those who wrote the words, creating the most beautiful love letter of all time.

The Bible speaks of His love for us in a personal way that can encourage and uplift us each time we read it. Yet do we savor every word and read it over and over again with excitement and feelings of love? I would never have dreamed of not opening one of the letters I received from my boyfriend—it was the first thing I sought out when I came home from school. God wants us to look at His Word, the Bible, in the same light. His words are waiting for us to read and enjoy as an affirmation of His great love for us. Have you ever thought of the Bible as God's personal love letter written just for you?

"Open my eyes that I may see wonderful things in your law."
Psalm 119:18

"Wonderful story of love; Tell it to me again;
Wonderful story of love; Wake the immortal strain!
Angels with rapture announce it, Shepherds with wonder receive it;
Sinner, oh, won't you believe it? Wonderful story of love."

Write a love letter to Jesus listing all the ways you love Him.

For seven years our well water was undrinkable. It contained a lot of sulfur, smelled like rotten eggs and turned everything black. During those years we had two choices: to haul all of our drinking and cooking water, which we did for the first few years; or to run it through a purification system, which we did for the last few years. The system removed the impurities and made the water useable. Since that time I have been grateful for good, pure water. The Bible tells us to purify ourselves from anything that contaminates the body and spirit. We can't expect pure thoughts and words to come from a mind and soul that have been contaminated by things of the world. We need to filter what we watch on TV and movies, the kind of magazines and books we read and what we do on the internet. If we don't let the Holy Spirit filter what we are putting into our body and mind we may become polluted and deadly to ourselves and others. Is your internal well polluted or pure?

"Since we have these promises,
dear friends,
let us purify ourselves
from everything
that contaminates body and spirit,
perfecting holiness
out of reverence for God."
2 Corinthians 7:1

"The cleansing stream I see, I see!
I plunge, and, oh, it cleanseth me!
Oh, praise the Lord, it cleanseth me!
It cleanseth me, yes, cleanseth me."

Enjoy a cool refreshing glass of pure water.

March 12
Read Isaiah chapter 43

As spring approaches, the grass starts to grow, telling of the coming summer. It soon becomes a mixture of old and new, brown and green, as the new blades push up through the old. The spring rains bring refreshment and I can almost daily watch it change. Along with the water, the lawn is fertilized and sprayed, preparing it for the summer. I will mow it soon, removing the old and exposing the new spring green color, helping my yard take on a vibrant and fresh appearance. New growth is important in our lives as well, and we need to take steps to help it develop. There are many ways to give your spiritual growth a fresh start. Recommit to attending church on a regular basis. Attend a Bible Study group or read a new study book at home that will stretch and expand your thoughts. Commit to memorizing Scripture and set aside daily devotional time in the Word and with the Lord. And as the new habits and ideas take hold, be sure and mow off any of the old ones that are holding back your walk. Our walk with the Lord needs to be encouraged to grow, but with commitment and regular application, we can be as fresh and vibrant as spring grass.

"See, I am doing a new thing! Now it springs up; do you not perceive it?
I am making a way in the desert and streams in the wasteland."
Isaiah 43:19

"More about Jesus let me learn,
More of His holy will discern;
Spirit of God, my teacher be,
Showing the things of Christ to me."

Take a stroll and notice the spring growth in the world around you.

We live in a fast paced world. Everything is geared to get us what we want quickly. There are fast food restaurants on almost every corner and at home we have microwaves so we can eat quickly and get on to something else. Instant communication is a must. Everyone carries cell phones and has access to internet and e-mail no matter where they are. We can be reached at any time, anywhere and become impatient if we can't reach someone. We travel on freeways, pay for our gas at the pump and shop on the internet, all to save time. It's no wonder we lose patience with God. He definitely doesn't work in our timeframe. In fact the Bible says that one of His days is like a thousand of our years. Many of the people in the Old Testament spent 40 days here or 40 years there, waiting on the Lord. So why do we lose all hope when God doesn't answer our prayers the minute we pray? We want Him to join our world and respond pronto so we can move on to other things. But He's got something else in mind—it's called building character. Building character is a slow process that can't be hurried. God knows what He's doing. We just need to slow down and wait for His timing—after all it is perfect. Do you struggle with patience?

"Moses was there with the Lord forty days and forty nights
without eating bread or drinking water. And He wrote on the tables
the words of the covenant—the Ten Commandments."
Exodus 34:28

"Peace, peace, wonderful peace!
Flowing so deep in my soul;
Peace, peace, sweet peace,
How it maketh the sad heart whole."

Leave your cell phone in the car when you go somewhere.

I love sunflowers and display them throughout my kitchen and family room. Their bright cheery faces make me smile. But the main reason I've decorated with them is because of the way they grow. A sunflower follows sunlight. It turns its large yellow head toward the sun following it from sunrise to sunset. They remind me to keep looking up and follow the "Son" through my day. I also keep some smooth stones on my kitchen counter. They remind me that Christ is the rock and my foundation. These smooth and polished stones also remind me their beauty did not come easily. They were smoothed by falling around and around with other stones and sand until all their rough edges were worn off. I like to think that life is polishing my rough edges, making me into something precious in God's sight. At work we have bells at every work station. When we believe God has answered a prayer we ring them for all to hear and give thanks. I think it's good to choose some tangible reminders to help us along the way. Do you have any reminders to help you in your daily walk?

*"So that people may see
and know, may consider
and understand,
that the hand of the Lord
has done this,
that the Holy One
of Israel has created it."
Isaiah 41:20*

*"Happy day, happy day, when Jesus washed my sins away!
He taught me how to watch and pray, and live rejoicing every day:
Happy day, happy day, when Jesus washed my sins away!"*

Put something in your kitchen to remind you of Christ.

"But the seed on good soil stands for those with a noble and good heart,
who hear the word, retain it, and by persevering produce a crop."
Luke 8:15

"Softly and tenderly Jesus is calling,
Calling for you and for me;
See, on the portals He's waiting and watching
Watching for you and for me."

We have a grandfather clock sitting in our foyer that chimes deeply and beautifully every quarter hour. I love the sound ringing through our house, and yet most of the time I am oblivious to its sweet music. It amazes me that something so rich and loud could become so common and everyday that I don't even hear it chiming out the hour. Often I will find my subconscious registering the last few chimes and realize I have missed it again. I wonder how often I do the same thing to God. I believe He is speaking to us all day long, but if we're not listening for His voice, we may not hear it. The gentle prodding in our spirit goes unnoticed and the things He wants to share with us pass by without a pause. It seems I'm quick to ask things of Him, or question why and voice my concerns. But I wonder how often He wants to say something to me and I'm too distracted to hear His voice. Have you ever felt you might have just missed a blessing God was trying to give you, but it passed before you noticed?

Find a quiet place and daily spend at least five minutes there
seeking to hear God's voice.

"Rock of ages, hide my soul,
Keep me while the billows roll;
When the threat'ning waves I see,
Let me ever hide in Thee."

The eye of the storm is at the center of a hurricane. Here the barometric pressure is much lower than the area around it and often the sky is clear and beautiful with a light breeze—it is pleasant and enjoyable. But surrounding the eye is the eyewall where the most severe weather is happening. Horrendous thunderstorms, terrific winds and extreme weather conditions exist in the eyewall. It's amazing that hurricanes are so destructive and extreme and yet contain this area of serenity and calmness at the core of their being. Life often feels like a hurricane—out of control, with horrific circumstances bearing down on us and destroying things in its path. Yet in the center of every storm is God who promises peace and joy in spite of the extreme conditions surrounding us. I have known people who have faced incredible trials and obstacles and yet they seem at peace. They have learned the secret of living a joyful life is to stay centered in God in spite of the conditions around them. They know if they stray from Him they will find themselves unprotected, where the hard things of life can get to them. Staying centered in Christ is extremely important if we want to have a life filled with peace. Are you riding out life's storms centered in Christ and enjoying the peacefulness that comes from knowing Him?

"And the peace of God, which transcends all understanding, will guard your hearts and your minds in Christ Jesus."
Philippians 4:7

What image comes to mind when you think of peacefulness?

t. Patrick's Day has its roots in Christian history. Saint Patrick was kidnapped at the age of sixteen from Britain and taken to Ireland as a slave. He tended sheep until his escape six years later. After returning to his homeland he felt a call to become a priest and return to Ireland to preach. March 17th, the day he died years later, was declared a holiday in remembrance of him and his Christian faith. In modern culture very little is known about the real origin of the holiday. Secular customs have taken precedence and the celebration now involves pinching people if they don't wear green and eating corned beef and cabbage at the local pub. I wonder how St. Patrick would feel if he saw how the holiday, initiated in his honor, is observed today? I want to leave my grandchildren a legacy of my faith and love for God. I share my personal stories of God's faithfulness and miracles so they can pass them on to their children. When I pass on, I want any remembrance of me to include that I loved God with all my heart and sought to serve Him faithfully in my life. I want my life to be a lasting legacy of my deep love for God. What do you hope people will remember about you after you have gone?

*"I will sing of the love
of the Lord forever;
with my mouth I will make
Your faithfulness known through
all generations. I will declare
that Your love stands firm forever,
that You established
Your faithfulness in heaven itself."*
Psalm 89:1 & 2

*"I will sing the wondrous story
Of the Christ Who died for me;
How He left His home in glory
For the cross of Calvary."*

Reflect back on memories of your grandparents
and thank God for your heritage.

andom people were asked what words came to mind when they heard the word Christian. For most, 'hypocritical,' 'judgmental,' 'critical' and 'exclusive' were some of the adjectives used. But when asked what they thought of when they heard the word 'Christ' their comments were very different. 'Loving,' 'gentle' and 'caring' were some of the adjectives used to describe Him. If Christians are Christ followers why doesn't the world see both alike? One day my granddaughters gathered tadpoles in the pond. They kept them in a jar and watched their transformation into frogs. Their appearance and name changed as they matured. The caterpillar becomes a butterfly, a tadpole turns into a frog, and a saved sinner should become Christ-like. While there is a visual transformation in the butterfly and frog, sometimes there is not a dramatic change in the life of a Christian. We are to take on the image of Christ and bear His likeness, but apparently the world often can't see the resemblance. Many times the terms used above to describe Christians are accurate. What we preach and profess is not consistent in our life. We behave one way around church friends and another way around the rest of the world. Transforming into the image of Christ means everything in our life must change. The finished product should not resemble who we were before. Do you bear the image of Christ in your life?

"Do not lie to each other,
since you have taken off
your old self with its practices
and have put on the new self,
which is being renewed in knowledge
in the image of its Creator."
Colossians 3:9 & 10

"Blest be the tie that binds
Our hearts in Christian love;
The fellowship of kindred minds
Is like to that above."

Strive to be consistent in your Christian walk.

"Let Him do the planning, let Him use our days,
Victory, victory, all the way along;
Yielding to His Spirit, His shall be the praise;
Victory all along through Jesus."

Wind farms are becoming popular as an alternate energy source. Quite a few have sprung up in southern Idaho especially on high desert ridges where the wind blows consistently. A wind farm's power is created through the unseen force of wind turning the blades. We have an unseen source of power available in our lives too in the presence of the Holy Spirit. We cannot see Him, but can see the effect He has on a life by the amazing works that are produced. One of my favorite sayings is, "The difference between a good work and God's work is prayer." Prayer is the real work of a Christian's life for it is through prayer the Holy Spirit's power is engaged in our lives. Anything that happens after we pray is the result of our prayers not the result of our efforts. Once we have prayed we can accept whatever the answer is knowing God is in control. If a windmill is erected in an area where the wind does not blow the blades will not turn and create power. This same principle applies when attempting to do God's work. If you haven't prayed about it first imagine yourself blowing on the huge blades of the windmill trying to create enough wind to turn them. It's impossible and so is attempting God's work without prayer. Do you pray before you work or only when your own efforts fall short?

"After they prayed, the place where they were meeting was shaken.
And they were all filled with the Holy Spirit and spoke the word of God boldly."
Acts 4:31

Visit a wind farm in your area or online and learn about this energy source.

March 20

Read 2 Corinthians chapter 3

I have been told quite often that I resemble my mother. I've always taken it as a compliment because I think she is a beautiful woman. While people's comments usually refer to our physical likeness, I believe we share some character traits too. It's common for children to resemble and behave like their earthly parents, but the Bible tells us that we have been created in the image of our God. We have His Word, the Bible, as an instruction manual to teach us how to live, so we can be transformed into His likeness by a renewing of our minds, not our bodies. How much we resemble God is directly related to how intimately we get to know Him. We have to purposely rid ourselves of those practices which are not of God and "put on the new self, which is being renewed in knowledge in the image of its Creator" (Colossians 3:10). Growing into God's likeness does not happen by chance, it's a choice we make and seek after all our days here on earth. Has anyone told you lately you resemble your Heavenly Father?

"And we, who with unveiled faces all reflect the Lord's glory, are being transformed into His likeness with ever increasing glory, which comes from the Lord, who is the Spirit."
2 Corinthians 3:18

"Living for Jesus, a life that is true, Striving to please Him in all that I do; Yielding allegiance, glad-hearted and free, This is the pathway of blessing for me."

Look internally and see if you can see some of God's characteristics in your life.

"But I know Whom I have believed,
And am persuaded that He is able
To keep that which I've committed
Unto Him against that day."

rom our porch we can watch a dust storm approaching long before it arrives. The blowing dirt fills the air and obscures everything as the huge wall of dust particles advances. Even after the wind has died, everything in the valley is shrouded in a cloud of dust. It takes a long time for the dirt to settle and the view of the valley to become clear again. My life can get just like a dust storm. Everything can begin to swirl at a crazy pace and I feel like I'm butting against a huge wall. All the commotion and activity leaves me in a fog. Nothing seems clear and life feels confusing and out of control. When I feel like this I need to sit still and wait for the dust to settle. I know God is in the middle of all the activity but if I don't withdraw and wait I won't see Him through the haze of commotion. Once things settle down the fogginess disappears and I can see His light shining through, bringing clarity out of my confusion. Does your life seem to swirl at a crazy pace feeling out of control?

"When Jesus spoke again to the people, He said, 'I am the light of the world.
Whoever follows me will never walk in darkness, but will have the light of life.'"
John 8:12

Plan some down time and enjoy some rest and relaxation.

> *"Let not your heart be troubled, His tender word I hear,*
> *And resting on His goodness, I lose my doubts and fears;*
> *Though by the path He leadeth, but one step I may see;*
> *His eye is on the sparrow, and I know He watches me;*
> *His eye is on the sparrow, and I know He watches me."*

We live in a world of instant gratification. My father came out of the Depression and like so many others of that era he always paid cash and saved or invested the rest. Very few people of my generation live that way. Taking out loans, buying with credit, spending every penny that's earned are common practices in today's culture. Our Love INC long-term relational program is focused on helping families get a handle on their money using Biblical principles as their guideline. After six years of running the program I have found there is one major concept that makes all the difference in the families' success. It is not the classes they must take, even though the classes are good. It is not the mentor who monitors their every financial decision, even though it helps to have someone guiding them. It is not that we hold their checkbooks, credit and debit cards, which forces them to make all their decisions one night a week in front of us. And it is not the multitude of incentives they receive to motivate them to stick with the program allowing them to pay off more debt. The thing that makes the most difference is when they grasp the concept that it is all God's to begin with, not theirs. Once they understand *whose* it is and that they are just stewards of what God gives them, their motivation, priorities, and focus become completely different. It's no longer about the money; it's about honoring God. That makes all the difference in the world. Do you honor God with your financial choices?

> *"No one can serve two masters.*
> *Either he will hate the one and love the other,*
> *or he will be devoted to the one and despise the other.*
> *You cannot serve both God and money."*
> *Matthew 6:24*

Look at your budget and see if you're making wise choices.

*"But we have this treasure in jars of clay to show that this all-surpassing power
is from God and not from us. We are hard pressed on every side,
but not crushed; perplexed, but not in despair, persecuted;
but not abandoned; struck down, but not destroyed."*
2 Corinthians 4:7-9

"Count your blessings, name them one by one,
Count your blessings, see what God has done!
Count your blessings, name them one by one,
Count your many blessings, see what God has done!"

When my boys were little we lived on a farm. Weather permitting they would spend almost every day outside collecting treasures from around our farm yard. At night when they came in to take their baths and get ready for bed, I would find their pockets stuffed with those treasures. I would empty their pockets and they would beg me to let them keep all they had gleaned from their day. So beside the bed stand it would go and, after they had fallen asleep, I would gently remove the broken glass, rusty nails and anything else that might hurt them. In their innocence they were unable to tell the difference between a real treasure and something harmful. We often

go through our days picking up stuff around us—a comment here, an overheard conversation there, a disappointment in our job, and on and on. At night we need to empty our hearts and minds and lay the contents at the foot of Jesus' cross. We need to ask Him to sort through it while we sleep and take away those things which could be harmful, leaving only what is beneficial in growing us into His likeness. If we would get in the habit of handing our day over to Christ at night, the burdens we carry from day to day would become manageable not overwhelming. We often carry needless trash around thinking it has value and yet it weighs us down. Are you feeling burdened? Do you need to ask God to clean out your pockets?

Carry something shiny in your pocket to remind you God's love is your treasure.

My father had a problem with his heart a year ago and had to have a stint put in it. Before the surgery he was having difficulty doing everyday tasks but didn't know what was wrong. Once it was determined that he was getting insufficient blood flow to his heart, the correction was made and he's feeling much better. When our heart is not working correctly it affects everything else in our body. A healthy spiritual heart is just as important. All spiritual problems start in the heart and affect other parts of our life. The Bible is filled with Scriptures related to the heart. Several verses in Proverbs refer to the heart; "An anxious heart weighs a man down...before his downfall a man's heart is proud...all a man's ways seem right to him, but the Lord weighs the heart... guard your heart, for it is the wellspring of life." In Matthew we are reminded that the words we speak come from the overflow of our heart. And God reminds us again and again that He looks at our heart. In 1 Samuel 16:7 we read, "The Lord does not look at the things man looks at. Man looks at the outward appearance, but the Lord looks at the heart." If you feel anxiety, envy, fear, anger, jealousy, pride, deceit, criticism, or a multitude of other sinful emotions, take a look inside your heart. You may have something blocking the flow of the Holy Spirit to your heart and all these outward signs are pointing to an inward problem. Do you have a heart problem?

*"The lamp of the Lord
searches the spirit of a man,
it searches out his inmost being."*
Proverbs 20:27

*"Holy Spirit, full of love,
Coming like a gentle dove,
Come, baptize our hearts anew,
Sweetly, gently, like the dew."*

Read through Proverbs and count how many Scriptures refer to the heart.

My son and his wife are youth group leaders. They recently asked if I would help them prepare a special event for the girls in their group. I set out my finest china and crystal, along with flowers and candles to show our guests they were special. They arrived, all dressed up, and were given seats of honor with picture place settings and a Scripture picked specifically for them. As the five-course meal was served great care was taken to treat them with respect and dignity. During the evening they were each given a china plate and long-stemmed red rose, symbolizing their value and worth. Several of the girls do not have a positive father figure in their lives and therefore may not feel valued, loved, or worthy of respect. But they hold a seat of honor in their Heavenly Father's sight. My prayer is that the evening remains etched in their minds forever, and when they feel pressured by the world to make compromising choices, they will make the right choice because they have been shown love and respect. God values each of us beyond our ability to understand. We need to make choices that will not compromise our self-worth or minimize how much God values us, for we are worthy to be called His children. How do you see yourself—valuable and priceless, like fine china, or chipped and scarred, like a broken plate?

"How great is the love the Father has lavished on us, that we should be called children of God!"
1 John 3:1

"God is my Father, and Jesus my Brother, Since I'm adopted by heavenly love; I am an heir in the kingdom of glory, And have a crown that is waiting above."

Write an encouraging note to a young woman reminding her of her great worth to God.

March 26
Read 1 Kings chapter 19

> *"Open my ears, that I may hear. Voices of truth Thou sendest clear;*
> *And while the wave notes fall on my ear, everything false will disappear.*
> *Silently now I wait for Thee, ready my God, Thy will to see,*
> *Open my ears, illumine me, Spirit divine!"*

Learning to hear the Lord has been a growing process for me. I have never audibly heard His voice but have learned to recognize when He is speaking to me personally. In the past if I was seeking direction I would retreat to a quiet place and start praying fervently for His leading. Then I would pause to see if I felt anything yet. If it seemed nothing had changed I would go back to my fervent prayers then pause and listen. This could go on for a while with my searching and pleading becoming more desperate as the silence intensified. One time after one of these sessions, feeling discouraged, abandoned and worn out, I found myself just sitting quietly. It was then as I calmed down and quit begging Him to respond to me that I clearly felt direction in my soul. This happened more than once before I put it together and realized I couldn't hear Him when I was desperate and begging. I needed to place my request before Him and settle into a quiet attitude of praise knowing in His time the answer would come. It often doesn't come the same day that

I pray for direction and I find myself continuing to praise Him for the coming answer, believing He has heard my prayer. In His time and if I'm not frantic I will receive His answer and it has never been too late. Have you ever felt desperate in searching for an answer from God?

> *"Then a great and powerful wind tore the mountains apart and shattered the rocks*
> *before the Lord, but the Lord was not in the wind. After the wind there was*
> *an earthquake, but the Lord was not in the earthquake. After the earthquake came a fire,*
> *but the Lord was not in the fire. And after the fire came a gentle whisper."*
> *1 Kings 19:11 & 12*

Have an empty chair in the room when you pray, visualizing Jesus in it.

"Oh, how I love Jesus,
Oh, how I love Jesus,
Oh, how I love Jesus,
Because He first loved me!"

Have you ever watched a young child look at an insect or small bug? They get really close to look intently and express delight in what they see. I see pesky insects but they see something exciting and unique. When I walk with my grandchildren they go slowly stopping to look at anything that catches their eye. I love these walks together as they open me up to see the world through their eyes, and I experience fresh joy in my surroundings. A new believer experiences joy and child-like delight when they are first saved. They look at the world differently and are filled with wonder and are in awe of the God who created it. They are in a new love relationship with God and find delight in living life. Many times as we mature in our faith we become filled with head knowledge and move from wonder of His grace to a spirit of criticism and judgment. We leave our love affair with God and enter into a religious relationship with the world. The joy we first felt is replaced with a "do this" and "don't do that" attitude as we strive to walk our talk. All of us are prone to this. We must work hard at remembering the joy and wonder of being in love with God. Are you in love with God?

"Because your love is better than life, my lips will glorify you."
Psalm 63:3

Take a walk with a child and see the world through their eyes.

March 28
Read 1 Corinthians chapter 7

oday we went to a farm auction, which is very common in farming communities. People bring a variety of things ahead of the auction day and register what they have to sell. On auction day, there will be rows and rows of stuff, from equipment all the way down to nuts and bolts. A couple of auctioneers will work up and down the lines selling each item to the highest bidder. Lots of people attend these auctions, some in hopes of getting a bargain and others to see if their item brings their hoped for price. By day's end, most everything has been sold to someone, and trucks and trailers are loaded with the new-found treasures and taken home. When walking around an auction yard, it often resembles a junk yard, with bits and pieces of everything. Some things are sold as is and the buyer is well aware they may be broken when they buy it, but believe they see value in it anyway. God sees value in each one of us, no matter what we look like or how smoothly we are running at the moment. Satan may have tried to convince you that you are of little worth and so you've lined yourself up to be auctioned off to the highest bidder. You may

even have a broken-down sign stuck to your back, but it doesn't matter. God's at every human auction, pulling people from the line and reminding them that the price has already been paid. He's the highest bidder, having purchased you at great cost. You're His treasure and He's taking you home to live with Him, if you'll let Him. Do you believe you're of great worth in God's eyes?

"You were bought at a price;
do not become slaves of men."
1 Corinthians 7:23

"Jesus paid it all,
All to Him I owe;
Sin had left a crimson stain,
He washed it white as snow."

Don't put a value on God's love, it's priceless.

"Standing, standing,
Standing on the promises of God my Savior;
Standing, standing,
I'm standing on the promises of God."

Has God given you a specific task to do but you wait to see His provision before you step out? I have often found myself at a crossroad and had to make a choice. A choice to step out in faith and do what He laid on my heart, or hold back and wait until I saw a way to accomplish it. In Joshua Chapter 3 the priests had to set foot in the Jordan before the Lord held back the water so they could cross. I think God often requires us to do the same thing. Each time we are willing to get our feet wet He is there to meet our needs and open every door. He is preparing the harvest field, calling His workers and His purpose will be accomplished. If the priests had refused to step into the flood waters the nation of Israel waiting behind them would have been stopped from crossing. We must not be an obstacle that blocks the way for others but rather a vessel He can work through to accomplish His purpose. If we stay close to Him we will be free to move in His power as He wills. Let us hold nothing back as we seek to do our best and glorify Him each step of the way. It is a mighty and humbling thing to be used of the Lord in Kingdom work. Are you willing to get your feet wet?

"And as soon as the priest who carry the ark of the Lord—
the Lord of all the earth—set foot in the Jordan,
the water flowing downstream will be cut off and stand up in a heap."
Joshua 3:13

If there is something holding you back from doing the Lord's work,
give it up and move forward.

March 30
Read 1 Corinthians chapter 12

> *"Back to the one foundation, from sects and creeds made free,*
> *Come saints of every nation to blessed unity.*
> *Once more the ancient glory shines as in days of old,*
> *And tells the wondrous story—One God, one faith, one fold."*

I love music and enjoy listening to an orchestra or choir perform. Playing in perfect harmony takes practice and commitment. When my children were little and learning to play instruments their concerts were not always beautiful. Initially everyone seemed to be doing their own thing, some going too fast and others too slow. There were those who had not practiced and were challenged by their instruments, making squeaks and squawks a part of the song. Then there were those who didn't watch the conductor and played to their own beat, almost as if they were alone. But through the years the children who were dedicated improved, and the concerts became pleasant to attend. Working on a team is similar to being part of the orchestra. We all have different roles to play. There will be times when our part is resting and other times when we may be the soloist. But if we don't work together and recognize there is a conductor who is tying it all together, we will create discord and confusion. It takes dedication and commitment, with everyone working together, to do great things for the Lord. We need to be on the same page doing everything to the best of our ability. Then our lives will bear witness to the masterpiece God creates when we work together in perfect harmony. Are you a good team player or a soloist who struggles when playing with others?

"The body is a unit, though it is made up of many parts; and though all its parts are many, they form one body."
1 Corinthians 12:12

Listen to your favorite music and notice the harmony
of the different instruments.

"Marvelous, infinite, matchless grace,
Freely bestowed on all who believe!
You that are longing to see His face,
Will you this moment His grace receive?"

One of the things I love about the ocean is the endless waves washing up against the shore. Since God set the boundaries of the seas, the waves have rolled in and out without effort. I can sit for hours and watch the water, feeling God's love and peace wash over me as the cares of the world are carried away. I once heard an analogy that God's grace is like the rolling waves of the ocean and I can't think of a better way to visualize it. It's without effort—we can't earn it and we don't deserve it. And yet it flows upon us, wave after wave, washing away our sins and imparting life. There is nothing we have done, are currently doing, or will ever do that can separate us from God. It's His free gift to us because He loves us and wants to spend eternity with us. We have to accept His gift of grace and confess Him as our Lord and Savior. We are imperfect humans and will struggle with the temptation of sin all our life. Satan would like us to believe that God is unable to extend forgiveness and grace for some sins but that's a lie. God's grace is unending just like the waves of the ocean. Have you let God's restoring love and forgiving grace wash over you?

"The grace of our Lord was poured out on me abundantly,
along with the faith and love that are in Christ Jesus."
1 Timothy 1:14

Thank God for His unending grace.

April 1
Read Jude

My oldest son likes to play April Fool's jokes on me. He usually comes up with something believable and, even though it is April Fool's day, I find myself falling for it until I hear him laugh. Then I know I've been tricked again. Many people live as if the salvation message is an April Fool's joke. It's almost as if they think that on Judgment Day the reality of hell will be denounced as a bad joke. I wonder if they think God is going to say, "April Fool's, I was just joking and there is no hell. Everyone is going to live with me in Heaven." The sad thing is there is a heaven and a hell and there will be a Judgment Day. It is the truth, not a fabricated story, and those who are living their lives pretending it's not going to happen are going to be very upset come Judgment Day. " 'As surely as I live,' says the Lord, 'Every knee will bow before me; every tongue will confess to God.' So then, each of us will give an account of himself to God." Romans 14:11 & 12. Are you ready to stand before the Lord?

*"To Him who is able
to keep you from falling
and to present you
before His glorious presence
without fault and with great joy—
to the only God our Savior be glory,
majesty, power and authority,
through Jesus Christ our Lord,
before all ages, now and forevermore!
Amen."*
Jude 24 & 25

*"To the old rugged cross I will ever be true;
Its shame and reproach gladly bear;
Then He'll call me some day to my home far away,
Where His glory forever I'll share."*

Call someone you know and let them know Jesus loves them.

The pasture where our cattle graze is surrounded by a single or double strand of electric wire. All that stands between the cows and their freedom is this small strand of wire and when the wire is "hot" the cattle will not touch it or cross over it. Occasionally, something will short the wire out, causing it to lose its power and the cows are able to sense this and eventually will break through and get loose. When this happens we have to walk the fence, find the short and correct the problem so the fence will once again keep the cattle inside. Our conscience should serve as our hot-wire and shock us if something is against God's will. He has given it to us, through the gift of the Holy Spirit, so that we will know where our boundaries are and stay away from sin. If we allow the world to dull our senses, the ability to feel shock at things around us might short out and we could venture into what we perceive as new freedom, and wander away from God. We fence our cattle in so we can care for

them, protecting them from harm and providing for their every need. God's commandments are there for the very same reasons—to protect and care for us. Let's make sure we stay connected to our heavenly source of power and constantly check that we're at full voltage all the time. Have you ever ignored your conscience because you wanted to do something you knew you shouldn't?

"But the Counselor, the Holy Spirit, whom the Father will send in my name,
will teach you all things and will remind you of everything I have said to you."
John 14:26

"Holy Spirit, keep us still,
Help us do the Father's will;
Give us grace and strength each day,
Keep us in the living way."

Check out your heart and make sure you
have a full connection to the Holy Spirit.

April 3
Read Matthew chapter 5

ave you heard the saying, "I'll scratch your back if you scratch mine"? Horses often do scratch each others' backs. It's common to see them nibbling on the back of each other, both receiving satisfaction. Most of us are eager to help someone if we know they will return the favor. But the Bible instructs us to give to those who have no way to repay us. I find people are willing to help when the need is real and their efforts are appreciated. But what about those times when we're taken advantage of and mistreated? Turning the other cheek, especially when I'm pretty sure it's going to get slapped, is really hard. But who said being a Christian is easy? As Jesus said, "If you love those who love you, what reward will you get? Are not even the tax collectors doing that? And if you greet only your brothers, what are you doing more than others? Do not even pagans do that?" Christ has called us to live and behave differently than the rest of the world. He wants us to scratch the backs of those who don't have arms to return the favor. Are you willing to help someone who can't repay you or is unappreciative of your efforts?

> *"Do not resist an evil person. If someone strikes you on the right cheek,*
> *turn to him the other also."*
> Matthew 5:39

> *"I want to work for Jesus,*
> *His cheerful servant be;*
> *To show I truly love Him*
> *Who did so much for me."*

Help someone who cannot return the favor.

> *"Joyful, joyful, we adore Thee, God of glory, Lord of love;*
> *Hearts unfold like flow'rs before Thee, Op'ning to the sun above.*
> *Melt the clouds of sin and sadness; Drive the dark of doubt away;*
> *Giver of immortal gladness, Fill us with the light of day!"*

The crocuses are blooming outside our office door, signaling spring is on its way. These bright, colorful flowers push their tender shoots up through the dirt well before the weather is truly warm. It's not uncommon to see them covered with a late snow fall, their warm colors starkly contrasted to the cold winter white. I find it amazing that their bulbs lie frozen in the dirt through the frigid temperatures. With the first warming of the ground they push through the soil and burst into vibrant color announcing another new season of opportunities. Sometimes life can resemble the cold, frozen atmosphere of winter. It seems that everything within us lies dormant, suppressed by surrounding difficulties. When I feel that way just getting through each day is tiring and draining, and I wonder where my joy has gone. Then someone or something will come my way and I feel a small tug of hope, a crack in the hard surface suffocating me. If I draw close to God and sit in His warmth and wait, new growth will shoot through that small crack. As I bask in His presence something beautiful will emerge from within, springing forth hope for a new season. Spring's flowers are God's reminder that all things are cyclical. Whatever is in your life right now will one day pass and you'll bear blossoms for His glory once again. Are you lying frozen in the ground, or can you feel the surface starting to crack in preparation for new growth?

"See, I am doing a new thing!
Now it springs up;
do you not perceive it?"
Isaiah 43:19

Take a spring walk and enjoy the budding flowers.

*"I am still confident of this; I will see the goodness of the Lord in the land of the living.
Wait for the Lord; be strong and take heart and wait for the Lord."*
Psalm 27:13 & 14

*"More love to Thee, O Christ, more love to Thee!
Hear Thou the prayer I make on bended knee;
This is my earnest plea: More love, O Christ, to Thee;
More love to Thee, more love to Thee!"*

When my daughter-in-law wants to be sure her children hear her she will say, "Stop and look at me." She waits until she has their full attention before giving them instruction. She has found that if they are preoccupied with other things, they don't really hear her and usually don't follow through with what was said. They respond like they heard but it hasn't registered and is forgotten almost immediately. As I go about my day I find myself communicating regularly with God. I'm sharing a thought, asking Him a question or crying out for help. It's usually a steady flow heading heavenward. But I wonder if I'm really listening to God or if I'm preoccupied and not giving Him my full attention. We tend to think God doesn't answer or answers slowly when we pray to Him. But maybe He's trying to get our attention before He responds. Maybe He's saying, "Lois, stop and look at me." Continual chatter on my part doesn't mean we're communicating it means I'm communicating. I would have more clarity of what God wants me to do if I would just stop and give Him my full attention. Being still and waiting to hear God is something we have to purpose in our heart or it doesn't happen. Do you stop and look up when you're asking God something?

Still yourself before the Lord.

"And let us consider how we may spur one another on toward love and good deeds. Let us not give up meeting together, as some are in the habit of doing, but let us encourage one another—and all the more as you see the Day approaching."
Hebrews 10:24 & 25

"There is not a friend like Jesus,
Patient, tender, kind, and true;
If you'll be a friend of Jesus,
He will be a friend to you."

Sometimes life can get really big, like a huge rock wall and I am unable to see over. I lose perspective and feel bogged down. When it happens at work the challenge of ministry weighs on me and I feel personally responsible for it. I wonder how I'm going to get it all done, and if I'm even capable of the task. I normally don't say a word to anyone as I struggle under the load, but God knows I need encouragement. It's at those times I am grateful my staff is tuned into the Lord's leading. He nudges

them to come and give me a pick-me-up at just the right time. They share a recent blessing and remind me of all the ways He has provided for our needs. Often they encourage me through prayer, helping me remember that this work is His responsibility not mine. I'm just one of His many servants. The boost is exactly what I need to help me see over the wall. It helps take my gaze off myself and my circumstances and places it back where it belongs. My Heavenly Father cares for me and He sends help when I need it most. Can you remember a time when someone lifted you when you really needed the boost?

Call and encourage someone today.

> *"That heavenly Teacher, in words that are plain,*
> *This truth declared to men,*
> *If ever they would to His kingdom attain,*
> *They must be born again."*

Whenever possible we corral heifers when they are ready to have their first calf in case they need help. One was getting ready to birth so we got her into the pen and the grandkids took their place on the fence waiting to see the calf born. Even though they have seen cows give birth before each time there is anticipation as they wait to witness the miracle of new life. I never tire of seeing God's miraculous design and feel blessed that our grandchildren can witness it at such a young age. We have been told that unless we are born again we will not see the kingdom of God. Nicodemus, a Pharisee and member of the Jewish council, heard Jesus' teaching and wanted to know more. But when Jesus tried to explain it Nicodemus was confused and unable to understand. This second birth is just as much a miracle as our first birth. We must willingly lay aside our old life and ask Jesus to come into our heart for us to be born of the Spirit. We do not have a say in our first birth but this second birth does not happen unless we desire it. I imagine the heavenly realms wait in anticipation for each of us to be born again. In Luke 15:7 we are told "there is . . . rejoicing in heaven over one sinner who repents." Birth is exciting whether it's of the flesh or the Spirit and both are miraculous. Have you been born again?

"I tell you the truth, unless a man is born again, he cannot see the kingdom of God."
John 3:3

Share your testimony of when you accepted Jesus into your life.

*L*ittle children and older adults have a lot in common. Neither one of them are out to impress anyone, so they let you know how they feel and what they think, whether you want to know or not. They are not concerned with fashion and don't care if it's new or used as long as it is comfortable. Usually family is the most important thing to them and they enjoy the simple pleasures in life like sharing time together. They show their emotions freely, offering love quickly and expressing dislike loudly, not feeling a need to hide how they feel. So why is it, from teens through middle-age, we seem to get it all messed up as we set out to impress others? Climbing the ladder of success becomes important and we'll do almost anything to achieve it. We'll wear clothes that are in fashion even though they are uncomfortable and impractical. We fake how we feel and often hide our real emotions, not wanting to make a fool of ourselves or upset someone else. We sacrifice relationships and family to do what others have said is important while feeling guilty and torn. Jesus says that what others think about us is not important and being highly esteemed by our peers holds no value with Him. Paul states that if he were still trying to please men he would not be a servant

of God (Galatians 1:10). We seem to start out right and often end right, so maybe it's those middle years we need to get figured out. What's high on your priority list— being successful in the eyes of others or being right with God?

"As for those who seemed to be important—whatever they were makes no difference to me; God does not judge by external appearance."
Galatians 2:6

"I'd rather have Jesus than men's applause;
I'd rather be faithful to His dear cause;
I'd rather have Jesus than worldwide fame;
I'd rather be true to His holy name."

List your current activities and it will show you what's really important to you.

"Father, the time has come. Glorify your Son, that your Son may glorify you.
For you granted Him authority over all people that He might give eternal life
to all those you have given Him. Now this is eternal life: that they may know you,
the only true God, and Jesus Christ, who you have sent.
I have brought you glory on earth by completing the work you gave me to do."
John 17:1–4

> *"Christ the Lord is ris'n today, Alleluia!*
> *Sons of men and angels say, Alleluia!*
> *Raise your joys and triumphs high, Alleluia!*
> *Sing, ye heav'ns, and earth, reply, Alleluia!"*

There are many Easter traditions. Coloring boiled eggs, Easter egg hunts, bunny rabbits, ham dinner with family, malted Easter eggs, buying that special Easter dress, an Easter bonnet are all things many of us participate in to some extent. It's wonderful to create memories with our loved ones but the reason we celebrate Easter has little to do with any of these traditions. Recently at a church I attended the pastor mentioned getting ready for the CEO's they were expecting at the Easter service. I was confused with what he meant and then he clarified his statement. CEO stood for 'Christmas and Easter Only' attendees—those people who only show up twice a year because it's part of their holiday tradition. Church services are carefully planned hoping that the CEO's in the audience will hear, see or experience something that turns their twice a year attendance into something more than just a tradition. Christmas and Easter aren't just nice holidays to plan traditions around. They celebrate the three most significant events in the history of our world—the birth, death, and resurrection of our Lord and Savior, Jesus Christ. Do you know any CEO's and have you shared the real reason for the season with them?

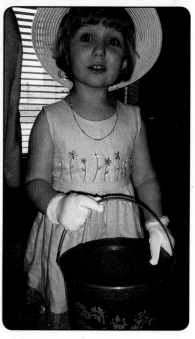

Invite someone to your Easter service who doesn't normally attend church.

> "When we walk with the Lord in the light of His Word,
> What a glory He sheds on our way!
> While we do His good will, He abides with us still,
> And with all who will trust and obey.
> Trust and obey, for there's no other way.
> To be happy in Jesus, but to trust and obey."

If you earnestly seek to serve and follow God do not be surprised if you are asked to do something that doesn't make earthly sense. Can you imagine being Noah when God asked him to build an ark in a desert in preparation for a flood? He must have endured incredible ridicule as he worked for many years building a huge boat and I'll bet his neighbors, and maybe even some of his family, wrote him off as a crazy religious zealot. Noah's faith was strong and time proved that God was faithful. It's not hard to be a Christian when my walk is sensible and doesn't draw a lot of attention to itself. But when He's asked me to believe in and respond to something that seems utterly impossible and totally improbable, it gets a little

harder to stay the course. It's not easy to be exposed to our peers in that way, but if we're going to be a Christ-follower, we have to be willing to believe and do what He calls us to, in spite of how it looks to those around us. Has God ever called you to a task that seems ridiculous or odd and what was your response?

"So God said to Noah, 'I am going to put an end to all people . . . so make yourself an ark . . . everything on earth will perish, but I will establish my covenant with you.' Noah did everything just as God commanded him."
Genesis 6:13-22

Think of a time when God was faithful in helping you
do something which seemed impossible.

April 11
Read Ecclesiastes chapter 3

ake a moment to write down the five things most important to you. Our list may include God, family, work, health, friends—things many of us treasure. Now take a minute to list where you spend your time during an average day. For many of us work and sleep take a good share of our twenty-four hours. But we all have some hours and minutes in the day we get to choose how to spend. Do you spend any of your time on the things that made your important list? All of us struggle with having enough time in our day to do the things we want to do. Sadly, if we're not careful, we will squander what precious time we have on things that are not on our important list. If I wait until I find time for the important things I may never find it. I have to make time for the people and things that are important to me. We all have the same number of hours in our day; it just seems some people are better at using their hours than others. Don't let your life waste away with unimportant things. Manage your time so the things on your important list are included. Do you manage your time wisely?

"He has made everything beautiful in its time. He has also set eternity in the hearts of men; yet they cannot fathom what God has done from beginning to end."
Ecclesiastes 3:11

"All to Jesus I surrender;
All to Him I freely give;
I will ever love and trust Him,
In His presence daily live."

Plan a family outing or date night with those close to you.

"And when they had mocked Him, they took off the purple robe and put
His own clothes on Him. Then they led Him out to crucify Him."
Mark 15:20

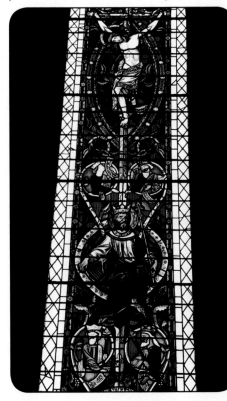

Have you ever contemplated what part of the crowd you would have been in if you were living when Jesus walked on earth? Would you have joined those who lined the streets waving palm branches and shouting, "Blessed is the King who comes in the name of the Lord!"? Would you have been in the throngs who shouted, "Crucify Him! Crucify Him!" as He stood before Pilate to be tried? Would you have followed Jesus as He carried the cross up the hill to Golgotha, weeping and wailing as you mourned the coming death of your Savior? Would you have been one of the women who went to the tomb and found it empty after He was buried? Would you have been in one of the groups to whom Jesus appeared after His death as He comforted and affirmed that the Holy Scriptures were being fulfilled? Jesus came to earth not just for them but for us too. Our sins nailed Him on the cross also. In whose steps have you followed and have you personally heard Him say, "Go into all the world and preach the good news to all creation"? What part of the crowd are you in today?

"Up from the grave He arose, with a mighty triumph o'er His foes,
He arose a Victor from the dark domain,
and He lives forever, with His saints to reign.
He arose! He arose! Hallelujah! Christ arose!"

Read the account of Jesus' crucifixion and resurrection in all four gospels.

April 13

Read Proverbs chapter 1

*L*ittle children want to do what they see others doing. They imitate daddy shaving or mommy putting on make-up. They watch intently, picking up behaviors we may not even be aware of. My husband, upon hearing one of the grandchildren say something, will jokingly say to me, "I wonder where she heard that from?" knowing that I say the same thing. Our example influences how they will live, talk and respond to life. If a child lives in an environment that is critical, chances are they will become critical and judgmental of others. If they hear those around them gossiping, they may participate in gossip when they grow up. If expressions of love are absent or rare, they may have difficulty expressing themselves when they become an adult. Our actions speak much louder than what we say. Grown children either want to be like their parents or spend the rest of their lives trying to be different than their parents were. Are you setting an example the children in your life will want to follow when they become adults?

"Listen, my son, to your father's instruction and do not forsake your mother's teaching. They will be a garland to grace your head and a chain to adorn your neck."
Proverbs 1:8 & 9

"J have decided to follow Jesus;
J have decided to follow Jesus;
J have decided to follow Jesus;
No turning back, no turning back."

Serve as a role-model for a young person in your life.

When I want to stress a point I often repeat it several times. I will even ask the listener to repeat back to me what they have heard to make sure I've made myself clear. After Jesus was crucified and resurrected He returned several times to different audiences confirming that He had conquered death and was alive. One of those times was when Peter and others had been fishing and just returned to shore after a fruitless night. Jesus commanded them to throw their nets out the other side and they caught so many fish they could not haul them in. He prepared a meal for them and after they had eaten He gave very personal and important instructions to Peter. He didn't just say it once but three times He asked Peter to affirm his love for Him, commanding him to feed His sheep. Peter, broken and ashamed for having denied knowing Jesus three times, was now at a turning point in his life. He was being chosen to do important work and Jesus wanted to make sure he understood the depth of the call. Read the verses in John Chapter 21, 15 through 17 and insert your name in the place of Simon Peter. Jesus has something important to say to you and He wants to make sure you understand. Have you answered the call upon your life?

"When they had finished eating, Jesus said to Simon Peter, 'Simon son of John, do you truly love me more than these?' 'Yes Lord,' he said, 'You know that I love You.' Jesus said, 'Feed my lambs.'"
John 21:15

"Savior, like a shepherd lead us, much we need Thy tender care;
In Thy pleasant pastures feed us, for our use Thy folds prepare.
Blessed Jesus, blessed Jesus! Thou hast bought us, Thine we are.
Blessed Jesus, blessed Jesus! Thou hast bought us, Thine we are."

Donate to a local food bank and help feed His sheep.

April 15

Read Ezekiel chapter 34

> "Have Thine own way, Lord! Have Thine own way!
> Thou art the Potter, I am the clay.
> Mold me and make me after Thy will,
> While I am waiting, yielded and still."

We recently planted a small fruit orchard beside our house. Each spring we wait to see the beautiful blossoms, and their potential for an abundance of fruit. But sometimes we experience a late frost and, if the fruit blossoms are tender and new, they freeze ending the chance for fruit from that tree for the year. I think the same thing can happen to Christians in their spiritual growth. We may have new blossoms of potential fruit budding in our lives, but the blossom is tender and can be easily crushed or killed. A careless word, a critical judgment, or a negative attitude can cause us to lose our blossom before the fruit can take hold. Care must be taken to protect and nurture it until the tiny blossom is replaced with the budding fruit. Just as a bare fruit tree doesn't produce mature fruit overnight, neither do we grow spiritually mature in a day. It's a process which starts with a tiny bud that blossoms into a beautiful flower, and if nurtured under the right conditions, will grow into new spiritual fruit. Do you have any new blossoms you need to nurture into a fruitful harvest?

"I will bless them and the places surrounding my hill. I will send down showers in season; there will be showers of blessing. The trees of the field will yield their fruit and the ground will yield its crops; the people will be secure in their land."
Ezekiel 34:26 & 27

Select one of the fruits of the Spirit
and find opportunities to nurture it today.

When Love INC clients are ready to be matched with a mentor I interview them. The interviews are extremely important as I try to get to the heart of their situations. I rely on prayer and God's strength to give me discernment, but still find them very draining emotionally. One couple I interviewed had deep-set problems including addictions, deception, financial woes and a marriage that was about to end. Getting to the heart of the matter meant straight talk and a lot of tough love. First the husband was Mr. Nice Guy, lying through his teeth. Then he switched to tears saying, "How can you hurt me like this?" He then moved to anger with the attitude, "How dare you—who are you to talk to me that way?" Finally there was the breaking point with deep sorrow and anguish as the ugly truth spilled out. Going home that night I questioned myself. What right did I have to get so deeply involved in someone else's life? But God used me to touch that couple and later the wife confided that after sixteen years this was the first time her husband had responded to help. I praise God but it was not without cost. When God works through me it is often out of my comfort zone. I have to rely totally on Him and fill up in order to be poured out. As I am emptied I feel bruised and torn in the process. We can't pretend we can do God's work and remain untouched. It's not easy to be broken so He can spill out onto another but it's worth it. Have you allowed God to use you to touch another?

"But even if I am being poured out like a drink offering on the sacrifice and service coming from your faith, I am glad and rejoice with all of you."
Philippians 2:17

"Take time to be holy, be calm in thy soul,
Each thought and each motive beneath His control.
Thus led by His Spirit to fountains of love,
Thou soon shalt be fitted for service above."

What are you full of—God or yourself?

April 17
Read Colossians chapter 4

> *"Oh, how praying rests the weary*
> *Prayer will change the night to day;*
> *So when life seems dark and dreary,*
> *Don't forget to pray."*

We are told to take everything to God in prayer and many of us do a good job of placing our requests before Him. The problem is that after we've given them to Him, we take them back and try to handle them ourselves. If we place a letter in the mailbox, but take it back out it will never reach the intended recipient. When we go before God with our requests we need to trust Him enough to leave them with Him. I have been told we must believe that God will answer our prayers or we shouldn't pray. If we pray in disbelief it makes the prayer ineffective because "according to our faith will it be done to us" Matthew 9:29. After we have prayed, believing God will answer the prayer, we need to enter into an attitude of praise. We continue to bring the request before Him but with a grateful heart that He has heard and is answering. We also need to prepare our hearts to receive His answer, whatever it may be. God gives us the best answer, not necessarily the answer we have wanted or expected. If we prayed in faith believing and praised Him while we waited we have the assurance that His answer is best for our lives. How are you doing with presenting and leaving your requests with God? Do you accept His answer with a grateful heart?

"Devote yourselves to prayer being watchful and thankful."
Colossians 4:2

Start praising God for the answer you will receive for a prayer request.

108

Children often talk to and play with imaginary friends. I like to imagine I have a guardian angel who watches over me. When I pray for protection I imagine God's angels surrounding the ministry, guarding our doors from anything intending to harm us. In my imagination these angels almost appear comical with their blackened-eyes, bandages, slings and crutches, but they're out there fighting the battle for me. When I stumble or fall I picture a squashed angel lying beneath me softening the blow and I thank God for him. Throughout the Bible there are references to God's angels. In Luke Chapter 15 we are told the angels rejoice when a sinner is saved. Hebrews Chapter 1 tells us there are ministering angels and Psalm 91 says they protect us from harm. In Ephesians Chapter 6 we are told "our struggle is not against flesh and blood, but against the rulers, against the authorities, against the powers of this dark world and against the spiritual forces of evil in the heavenly realms." I don't know what the spiritual realm is like and I'm not aware that I've ever met an angel but I believe God when He tells me they're around. I find comfort in knowing His angels surround and protect me wherever I go. Do you believe in angels?

"And there was war in heaven. Michael and his angels fought against the dragon, and the dragon and his angels fought back. But he was not strong enough, and they lost their place in heaven. The great dragon was hurled down— that ancient serpent called the devil or Satan, who leads the whole world astray. He was hurled to the earth, and his angels with him."
Revelation 12:7—9

"When we all get to heaven,
What a day of rejoicing that will be!
When we all see Jesus,
We'll sing and shout the victory!"

Look up angel in a concordance and read different Scriptures about them.

> *"My Jesus, I love Thee, I know Thou art mine;*
> *For Thee all the follies of sin I resign;*
> *My gracious Redeemer, my Savior art Thou;*
> *If ever I loved Thee, my Jesus, 'tis now."*

If we want to know more about God we just need to look at the diversity in His creation. God has placed unique natural instincts in the animal kingdom. The raccoon was given a robber mask around his eyes because he steals food from others yet never eats anything without washing it first. The skunk has the distinctive white stripe down his back almost as if to warn us that if he lifts his tail we're in trouble. The possum lays down and plays dead when threatened and the killdeer fakes a broken wing to lead predators away from her nest of young. Geese fly in formation so they can go great distances without getting tired and honk encouragement to those behind them. Robins know that worms are easier to pull from the ground in the dew of the morning. Male birds know to puff up their chests when courting a female to impress her. A squirrel knows to store nuts for the long, cold winter so he has plenty to eat. Animals embrace their instincts but we often fight against the natural instinct God placed in our souls to commune with Him. We battle the inner desire we feel for Him and try to fill it with a multitude of other things. Perhaps it's time to follow our natural instincts and draw close to Him. Have you drawn close to Him lately?

"How many are your works,
O Lord! In wisdom
You made them all;
the earth is full
of your creatures."
Psalm 104:24

Take a walk in the country and enjoy God's creation.

"Perfect submission, all is at rest,
I in my Savior am happy and blest,
Watching and waiting, looking above,
Filled with His goodness, lost in His love."

Have you ever had someone call or drop in with no reason except to see you? My life is so busy that usually I don't call or see someone unless I have a specific reason to contact them. There have been a few occasions when someone has dropped by my house unexpectedly and with no apparent reason. My first thought was to question why they had come; what did they want or need? But once I realized they just wanted to see me and share life with me, I was warmed and encouraged by their gift of friendship and time. I think God is delighted when we do the same thing with Him. When I have a need, concern or worry I'm quick to take it to the Lord. It's less often that I approach Him with no purpose except to be in His presence, and yet that's when I find I am most blessed and uplifted. I think God loves it when we show Him how much we love Him by stopping in for a visit just to know Him better. Have you made an unannounced visit to God recently with no other purpose than to spend time with Him? I know you'll be blessed if you do.

"I have loved you with an everlasting love;
I have drawn you with loving kindness."
Jeremiah 31:3

Spend some time with God today
for the sole purpose of loving Him and being loved back.

> *"Will you come to Him, the Lord of all?*
> *Will you come to Him, for mercy call?*
> *Will you come to Him and prostrate fall?*
> *Will you come?"*

Do you feel like you've wandered into the world's playground and can't find your way out? Do you find yourself on a slide climbing the ladder of success and feeling pushed from behind? Are you sitting on the teeter-tooter going up and down at the mercy of the person sitting opposite you? Perhaps you're in a swing going back and forth headed nowhere. No matter how hard you work the swing only goes so high and you feel stuck. Then there's the wonderful merry-go-round. You find yourself going around in circles hanging on for dear life all the while someone else is pushing you faster and faster until you start to feel sick. All the fun and joy the world promised you is falling short and your life seems meaningless. Perhaps it's time to walk away and join the race God has called you to. There's a starting spot reserved just for you. No one can run in your place. It's not going to be easy but you've never been told it would be. You have the assurance you won't run alone. You're equipped with everything you need, and the finish line is worth reaching. So how about it—is it time to quit playing around and get in the race of your life?

"Therefore, since we are surrounded by such a great cloud of witnesses,
let us throw off everything that hinders and the sin that so easily entangles,
and let us run with perseverance the race marked out for us."
Hebrews 12:1

Go for a walk or run and enjoy being outside.

*"Yes, I'll sing the wondrous story
Of the Christ Who died for me,
Sing it with the saints in glory,
Gathered by the crystal sea."*

For many believers witnessing about their faith can be unsettling. I know what I believe and what I want to say, but sometimes I find my words getting jumbled as I try to speak them. My ten year old granddaughter came to stay a weekend with me and we went to church together. After church, while driving home, she asked me what baptism was. I felt my stomach do a little jump. Her family doesn't attend church regularly and I wanted to give a clear answer. I told her we would chat when we got home, giving myself some time to pray. I didn't want to say too much or too little and wanted God to give me just the right words. Once home we sat together and I shared about inviting Jesus into your heart and that baptism is the outward sign of accepting Christ as your Savior. She listened very intently and then said, "Jesus lives in my heart. I know He does. I'll ask my dad if I can get baptized." I shot another prayer upward thanking Him for the words and asking Him to continue knocking at the door of her heart. God wants us to speak boldly and fearlessly when proclaiming the Gospel message. We don't need big, fancy words, we just need to speak honestly from our heart and He'll take care of the rest. Do you get tongue-tied when asked to share about your faith?

*"At that time you will be given what to say, for it will not be you speaking,
but the Spirit of your Father speaking through you."*
Matthew 10:19

When an opportunity arises, share your faith with someone.

> *"On Christ, the solid Rock, I stand;*
> *All other ground is sinking sand,*
> *All other ground is sinking sand."*

One of my favorite stories in the Bible is when Peter saw Jesus walking on the water and called out to Him. When Jesus said, "Come!" Peter quickly jumped onto the water and started walking toward Him. But when he looked down and realized he was doing the impossible he started to sink and called out to be saved. Jesus words to Him were, "You of little faith, why did you doubt?" I used to think that Jesus was referring to Peter doubting Him, but I think now that Jesus was referring to Peter doubting himself. Peter demonstrated he had faith in Christ but lacked faith in himself to do the impossible through Christ's strength. Often in my own walk I have been quick to say, "Yes, Lord!" and jump out of the boat. But once in the impossible situation, I've started to doubt my ability to do what I felt convicted by God to attempt. As I doubt I waver and start to sink. Our faith needs to grow not only in believing that God can do the impossible, but that God desires to do the

impossible through us. When we find ourselves walking on water with unsure footing, let's keep our eyes on Jesus, the source of all our strength. Have you ever started something big for Christ, then quit because you became afraid you couldn't do it?

> *"Then Peter got down out of the boat and walked on the water to Jesus.*
> *But when he saw the wind, he was afraid and, beginning to sink, cried out,*
> *'Lord, save me!' Immediately Jesus reached out His hand and caught him.*
> *'You of little faith,' he said, 'why did you doubt?'"*
> *Matthew 14:29-31*

If you got back in the boat out of fear,
perhaps it's time to climb over the edge again.

*H*ave you been praying for something for a long time and have yet to receive an answer? Have you become discouraged while waiting and feel as if your prayers are bouncing off heaven's walls? Draw encouragement from the Scriptures. In the Bible the prophet Habakkuk cried to God wondering why He was not listening to him. In Chapter 2 we see him decide to station himself and watch for the Lord's answer. The Lord tells him that "though it linger, wait for it; it will certainly come and will not delay." In 1 Kings Chapter 18 Elijah prayed to the Lord for the promised rain. Six times he sent his servant to see if it was approaching but nothing was on the horizon. Elijah continued to believe and pray and the seventh time he sent his servant a small cloud was forming in the distance. Both of these Old Testament servants continued to believe and watch for the Lord's answer. They did not quit praying and in God's time the answer did arrive. Don't give up hope. God is hearing your prayers and He knows how and when to answer them. Continue to believe and take up a watchful position yourself—His answer is forthcoming. Have you grown discouraged over an unanswered prayer?

"For the revelation awaits an appointed time; it speaks of the end and will not prove false. Though it linger, wait for it; it will certainly come and will not delay."
Habakkuk 2:3

"O Jesus, blest Redeemer,
Sent from the heart of God;
Hold us, who wait before Thee,
Near to the heart of God."

Thank the Lord for a forthcoming answer you've yet to receive.

"So God created man in His own image, in the image of God He created him;
male and female He created them . . . God saw all that He had made,
and it was very good."
Genesis 1:27 & 31

"Open my eyes, that I may see
Glimpses of truth Thou hast for me;
Place in my hands the wonderful key
That shall unclasp and set me free."

I recently met a young woman who was using her gift of photography as a ministry. She shared with me how she takes pictures of women caught in the cycle of domestic violence and helps them see themselves in a different light. She related how one woman she photographed saw her picture and exclaimed, "That isn't me; it's too beautiful." She had been so beaten down that she couldn't see any beauty in herself. But the photographer kept reassuring her, "That is you; you are beautiful both inside and out." As the young woman started to see herself differently she started to believe in herself and her future. She and her then-abusive husband, through counsel-

ing and the Lord's healing, were able to save their marriage, and now have four beautiful children they are raising in the Lord. God often sees us differently than we see ourselves. We see our mistakes, our sins, our failures and our life scars. God sees who He created, not who we might be at the moment. If we draw near to God He will show us who we really are, giving us a snapshot of how He views us. There is beauty in everything God created, including you. What snapshot do you carry around in your mind and do you need to exchange it for the one God has of you?

Put a photo of yourself on your bathroom mirror
and remind yourself you are uniquely created.

> *"Holy, holy, holy! Lord God Almighty!*
> *Early in the morning our song shall rise to Thee;*
> *Holy, holy, holy, merciful and mighty!*
> *God in three Persons, blessed Trinity!"*

Sometimes I am asked for a work or spiritual reference for a former employee or acquaintance. References are easy to give when I have had a long-lasting relationship with someone. But when I've not worked closely with them over a period of time I feel less adequate to give an honest appraisal of their work ethic or character. People usually try to list references from people who know them well and who will give them a good recommendation. As Christians we are told to bear testimony and give witness of our Lord Jesus Christ. The deeper our relationship with Him the better able we are to speak intimately of Him. If we have spent time with Him and walked closely beside Him we will be able to relate what He has done for us and our testimony will be deep and personal. If our relationship with Him is shallow and based only on what we have read or been told, but not experienced personally, our testimony will lack depth and validity. We need to grow in our relationship with Christ until we can stand up and boldly proclaim all that He has done for us, giving a strong witness for all to hear. Do you think you would be a good reference for Christ and would He list your name on His application as someone to call?

"The life appeared; we have seen it and testify to it, and we proclaim to you the eternal life, which was with the Father and has appeared to us. We proclaim to you what we have seen and heard, so that you also may have fellowship with us. And our fellowship is with the Father and with His Son, Jesus Christ."
1 John 1:2 & 3

When was the last time you gave testimony of what Christ has done for you?

117

April 27
Read Genesis chapter 45

"And now, do not be distressed and do not be angry with yourselves for selling me here,
because it was to save lives that God sent me ahead of you . . .
So then, it was not you who sent me here, but God."
Genesis 45:5 & 8

> *"Just a closer walk with Thee,*
> *Grant it, Jesus, is my plea,*
> *Daily walking close to Thee,*
> *Let it be, dear Lord, let it be."*

oseph's life seemed unfair and beyond his control. His father loved and favored him more than his brothers. His brothers were jealous and sold him into slavery to get rid of him. For many years Joseph's life was not his own but he was blessed by the Lord and excelled in everything he did. When he ran from the advances of Potiphar's wife he was punished for doing what was right. It seemed that life was beating him up but Joseph didn't view it that way. No matter who owned him or whether he was free or imprisoned he continued to find ways to serve God and was blessed because of it. His life was orchestrated by God to put him in a position of authority that would eventually save others. What if Joseph had fought against his conditions, becoming hard-hearted and embittered? Could God have used him if he had become a vindictive, angry person, ready to get back at those who had wronged him? We don't know why bad things happen to good people. We don't know why sometimes our best efforts aren't good enough and people betray us. But God knows what He's doing and we need to trust Him and do the best we can despite our situation. Who knows, we just might be part of a much grander plan than we could ever imagine! How do you respond when someone treats you unfairly?

Reflect on a time when good came from something seemingly bad.

good friend of mine was recently diagnosed with stage four cancer. The news hit hard for everyone, especially her husband and their five children. The world ceased to exist as they had known it and they readjusted their lives to see if she could beat it. As she started down the long road of chemo and experimental nuclear treatments the attention had to be focused on her, something she was not used to. After the initial shock I saw a transformation take place inside her that was more dramatic than the physical ravages caused by the chemo. She began to live each day with delight and praise, regardless of sickness, weariness or the unknown future. She celebrated every small victory and found good in every challenge. She touched us all as we watched her surrender and embrace each day as a gift from God. Then, after many months, she was given the miraculous news that the cancer was in remission—she had been given her life back, at least for a time. It was then, for the first time, that I saw her stumble a bit as she tried to make sense of it all. She had come to such peace with her illness that she wasn't sure how to re-enter the world of the living. The old fears, challenges, and expectations came rushing back as she tried to figure out what God wanted from her now. She soon realized that God wanted just the same attitude of praise she had

given Him while sick. Yes, she's different now. She's found peace that doesn't depend on living or dying—peace that knows whether the sun is rising or setting. God is still there and we have much to give Him thanks for. Have you experienced God's peace in your life or does it fluctuate with your circumstances?

"Peace I leave with you; my peace I give you. I do not give to you as the world gives. Do not let your hearts be troubled and do not be afraid."
John 14:27

"A wonderful Savior is Jesus my Lord,
He taketh my burden away,
He holdeth me up and I shall not be moved,
He giveth me strength as my day."

Visit and encourage someone who is struggling with illness.

April 29
Read Matthew chapter 9

ow we pray makes all the difference in the world. A simple prayer of faith anticipating His answer with a grateful heart is the most powerful tool we have at our disposal. An unbelieving prayer with little expectation of an answer is ineffective because God moves according to our faith. We are the open road or the blocked freeway to the answer. I hate getting stuck in a traffic jam on the freeway. I feel trapped, powerless to move, unable to see the obstacle and at the mercy of those in front of me. My attitude is the only thing I can control when I'm trapped in a traffic jam. I can be peaceful in the wait or become angry and anxious, but I cannot change the circumstances. A faithless prayer is just as immobilizing and powerless. But believing prayers empower us to soar above our circumstances. All obstacles seem unimportant. The need to see ahead is diminished and our spirit is peaceful knowing all is in His hands. Believing prayers are based on faith with eyes fixed on Him and a thankful, receiving spirit. What kind of prayers do you pray?

"According to your faith will it be done to you."
Matthew 9:29

"Faith is believing, simply receiving
What in His promise God has revealed;
Trust Him forever, doubt Him, no, never,
Till thy petition His Spirit hath sealed."

Soar above your situation believing God answers prayers.

*U*mbrellas protect us from the rain during a storm. But when it is raining on the farm and we need to work it's impossible to carry an umbrella around and accomplish much. Instead we put on rain coats that protect us from the elements, but allow us to work with both hands. The Word of God should cover us like a coat, protecting from all spiritual attacks. We are told never be unprepared, but arm ourselves so we will be able to stand against the enemy, Satan. There are times when it is difficult to carry our Bible in one hand and do the work we have to do. That is why we need to memorize Scripture. We will never be caught off guard and unarmed if we have God's Word tucked away in our heart where nothing can steal it. It is good to spend time reading the Bible every day but it is also important to memorize Scripture. We never know when we might find ourselves in a dangerous predicament and need to take out the Sword of the Spirit to defend ourselves. Have you taken time to commit Scripture to memory and do you reflect upon it throughout your day?

"Therefore put on the full armor of God, so that when the day of evil comes, you may be able to stand your ground, and after you have done everything, to stand."
Ephesians 6:13

"A mighty fortress is our God, a bulwark never failing;
Our helper He, amid the flood of mortal ills prevailing:
For still our ancient foe doth seek to work us woe;
His craft and pow'r are great, and, armed with cruel hate,
On earth is not his equal."

Memorize today's Scripture.

> *"What a friend we have in Jesus, All our sins and griefs to bear!*
> *What a privilege to carry everything to God in prayer!*
> *Oh, what peace we often forfeit, Oh, what needless pain we bear,*
> *All because we do not carry everything to God in prayer."*

I often eat a bowl of cold cereal in the morning to start my day. One morning as I was eating I found myself reading what was on the cereal box and started thinking. Lots of children eat cold cereal in the morning and read the boxes while they eat. In fact, this is probably some of the first information their brain processes for the day. Is this how we want them to start their day, with cold cereal advertisements? Wouldn't it be great if we could convince the cereal companies to put positive messages on their boxes—messages that would reinforce a child's value and worth. What if the first thing they read was how loved and important they were—that they were created uniquely special and there was a purpose and a plan created with them in mind? What if they were told they wouldn't be alone and that Jesus wanted to be their special friend? I believe it would make a huge difference in our world if we focused more on feeding positive thoughts to our children. Is there something you can do to encourage a child in their self-worth and value?

"Therefore encourage each other with these words."
1 Thessalonians 4:18

Write a positive note to someone and place it
where they will see it first thing in the morning.

I like all kinds of flowers and plant them all around my house every year. I try to plant varieties that, if watered and cared for correctly, will bloom all summer long. But I have to admit I also love cutting a fresh bouquet of flowers. Even though I know they're not going to last long there is something about a bundle of beautifully arranged flowers that lifts my spirit. If I take really good care of them they may last a week or more, but eventually the beauty is gone. They've lost their usefulness and I throw them away. Our lives can be like a flower. If we are planted in the soil of the Lord we can grow and produce blossoms all our life. But some of us more closely resemble a freshly-picked bouquet. At first we are extremely beautiful and fragrant doing vibrant and meaningful work. But since we are not rooted in God, we quickly wear out, our blossoms fade and our ability to produce quality work is over. I want to make sure I stay rooted in Christ, grounded in His life-producing Word, so I can continue to work for Him all the days of my life. What kind of flower do you most resemble—potted or picked?

"The grass withers and the flowers fall, but the Word of our God stands forever."
Isaiah 40:8

"I come to the garden alone,
While the dew is still on the roses,
And the voice I hear falling on my ear
The Son of God discloses."

Pick a fresh bouquet and thank God for the beauty He has created.

> *"Standing on the promises that cannot fail,*
> *When the howling storms of doubt and fear assail,*
> *By the living Word of God I shall prevail,*
> *Standing on the promises of God."*

When I was going through my divorce I felt alone and scared. Even though I had family and friends supporting me I had lost my best friend of twenty-two years and I wasn't sure how to go it alone. I remember lying on my bed at night, clutching my Bible to my chest and crying out to God to protect me. There was so much uncertainty washing around me and it seemed new decisions had to be made every day. I had lost faith in my judgment and doubted every choice I made. Some days I felt so confused and alone I wondered if life could go on this way. Then one day a friend gave me a Scripture card and the verse became my rock for the next few years. I claimed the promise as my own and repeated the verse whenever fear and anxiety attacked me. As the months passed my fear and dread for the future started to diminish and I know it's because I had clung to God's hand, believing that He would uphold me at all times. God's promises are there for us in good or bad times. He is faithful to His Word and His promises are sure. When life seems too large to live find a Scripture that promises His strength, direction and protection and store it in your heart. Repeat it often and insert your name in it wherever possible. God is our rock and we can cling to Him when everything is crashing in around us. Do you have a favorite Scripture memorized for those difficult days?

"So do not fear, for I am with you, do not anxiously look about you, for I am your God. I will strengthen you and help you; I will uphold you with my righteous right hand."
Isaiah 41:10

Commit a Scripture to memory that gives you a promise from God.

s a parent we will do almost anything to protect our children even putting ourselves in danger if it means saving them from harm. When my children were hurt, I often wished I could trade places with them to spare them the pain. As I read the story of when God tested Abraham by asking him to sacrifice Isaac I cannot imagine the emotions Abraham must have felt. He loved God but he also loved his son and must have felt confused over God's instructions. For three days they traveled to the place God had instructed them to go—three days to anguish over what he was going to do to his son. As they walked the final distance Isaac asked his father where the lamb was for the burnt offering. Can you imagine how torn Abraham must have felt as he replied that God would provide? When they reached the spot, with no other sacrificial lamb in sight, Abraham continued in his obedience to God and tied Isaac to the altar. What terror Isaac must have felt as his father raised the knife to kill him. It was only then, seconds before he was to kill his only son, that God provided another sacrifice—the ram. Abraham

had passed the test and shown allegiance to God over everything else, even his precious and only son. Would I pass the test—would you? We are to put God before anything else in our life and be obedient to Him even unto death. Is God first in your life?

> *Then God said, 'Take your son,*
> *your only son Isaac, whom you love,*
> *and go to the region of Moriah.*
> *Sacrifice him there as a burnt offering*
> *on one of the mountains*
> *I will tell you about.'*
> *Genesis 22:2*

> *"So I'll cherish the old rugged cross,*
> *Till my trophies at last I lay down;*
> *I will cling to the old rugged cross,*
> *And exchange it some day for a crown."*

Journal your activities for the next week and let it reflect your priorities.

May 5
Read John chapter 21

*S*ervice motivated by any other reason than to glorify God becomes disappointing to the servant at some point. If we focus on the people we serve we will face a multitude of conflicting emotions depending upon their attitudes. Some people are not grateful and have an "I deserve it" attitude. When Jesus healed the ten lepers only one returned to tell Him thanks. Others are never satisfied always asking for more no matter how much they receive. Some people can be critical and abrasive making you want to run away rather than finish the job. Others do not want to take ownership for any part of their need and are satisfied to have others do all the work. The only way we can continue to serve people day after day is to be motivated simply to please and glorify God. Serving God can also become disappointing if we look at other servants and start comparing ourselves to them. When the servants hired to work in the vineyard saw those hired last were paid the same as them, they were dissatisfied and upset. There was a time when another ministry seemed to be competing with what we were doing. I found myself focusing more on what they were doing and less on what we were doing. A wise volunteer pulled me back on track by asking what was my motivation; doing the best I could for God or doing more than the other ministry? There is only one way to be a satisfied servant and that's to remember who we're working for. Nothing else matters. Have you ever been disappointed when you served someone?

"What is that to thee,
follow thou me."
John 21:22

"O Jesus, Thou hast promised to all who follow Thee
That where Thou art in glory there shall Thy servant be;
And Jesus, I have promised to serve Thee to the end—
Oh, give me grace to follow, my Master and my Friend."

Give someone a helping hand today.

126

ell phones have changed how we communicate. Before I had a cell phone I never thought about being in the car and not being accessible by phone. I knew people could call me when I got to my destination or leave a message at home. Now it seems everyone has a cell phone with them all the time so they can be reached no matter what they are doing—if they choose to take the call. Because we can see who is calling before we answer the phone we don't have to talk to anyone we don't want to. This feature is sometimes abused allowing us to ignore people if we don't want to be bothered. I'm glad God is not like that. He isn't sitting up there choosing when He wants to take my call and when He doesn't feel like it; He's willing to hear my prayers anytime I turn to Him. Because He is omnipotent He can do all things at once and never be too busy for us. The world would probably be a better place if we spent more time on the direct line to God and less time on our cell phones with others. Have you ever ignored a call because you didn't feel like talking to someone?

"In my distress I called to the Lord; I cried to my God for help.
From His temple He heard my voice; my cry came before Him, into His ears."
Psalm 18:6

"I must tell Jesus! I must tell Jesus!
I cannot bear my burdens alone;
I must tell Jesus! I must tell Jesus!
Jesus can help me, Jesus alone."

When driving talk to God instead of using your cell phone.

I shared during prayer time that the ministry had been difficult over the last few weeks. We were on the verge of opening a new ministry and Satan's attacks were coming full force in an effort to discourage and wear us down. Later that day I received a rose and card from one of the couples who regularly attend the prayer time. They were praying for me and had asked that I be anointed with the oil of joy, like God anointed Jesus. As I read their words I felt God's love pour over me as if oil were running down my body penetrating deeply and spreading through my being. God's joy started to bubble in my soul and I was overcome with emotion. These faithful prayer warriors had been His messengers to encourage me. This same couple

confided that later that night, during intercessory prayer, they had become deeply moved and wept. As I started to say, "please don't cry for me," they interrupted and said, "Oh, it wasn't you it was the Lord moving in us as we held you up in prayer. It's doing the Lord's work." Intercessory prayer is one of the most powerful acts we can engage in. When God calls His people to pray for others and they are obedient it opens the gates of Heaven and power from on high pours down on those lifted up. I truly felt anointed with the oil of joy that day. Has God ever moved you to intercede in prayer for someone and were you obedient?

"Your throne, O God, will last for ever and ever; a scepter of justice will be the scepter of your kingdom. You love righteousness and hate wickedness; therefore God, your God, has set you above your companions by anointing you with the oil of joy."
Psalm 45:6 & 7

"Oh, how praying rests the weary!
Prayer will change the night to day;
So when life seems dark and dreary,
Don't forget to pray."

Pray for someone who works in full-time ministry today.

"More like the Master I would live and grow;
More of His love to others I would show;
More self-denial, like His in Galilee,
More like the Master I long to ever be."

My deck needs repainting. The sun has peeled up the old paint and it's in dire need of attention. Before I can paint it, I will need to scrape all the old peeling paint off and prime the wood again, making it ready to take on a new coat of paint. If I don't prepare the surface before I apply the new paint, it won't be long before the old will erode the new paint job and I'll be back to where it was before I started. When I have an area in my life that I want to change, it will require me to get rid of the old, before I adapt the new too. I can cover up my old ways for awhile with a fresh start, but if the old is lurking just under the surface, it won't be long before it will erode the new and expose the sin beneath it. This getting rid of the old requires a lot of work and self-evaluation—it isn't easy to change old ways. I have to be committed to the change and know that, without God's help, my strength will be insufficient. I need to call upon Him to help me identify and rid myself of those things which are making me unattractive on

the surface. Keeping my home in good repair requires constant upkeep and so do I. I'm just a work in process and I'll be fixing things up on the inside and the outside until God calls me home. Is there anything in your life that needs a fresh coat of paint?

"Search me, O God, and know my heart; test me and know my anxious thoughts.
See if there is any offensive way in me, and lead me in the way everlasting."
Psalm 139:23 & 24

Think of something you want to change and ask God
to give you the strength to do it.

*"For, before the harvest, when the blossom is gone and the flower
becomes a ripening grape, he will cut off the shoots with pruning knives,
and cut down and take away the spreading branches."*
Isaiah 18:5

*"I need Thee every hour; teach me Thy will;
And Thy rich promises in me fulfill.
I need Thee, oh, I need Thee; every hour I need Thee;
Oh, bless me now, my Savior, I come to Thee."*

I love to grow flowers and find tending them therapeutic for my soul. In the spring I fill my flower boxes with petunias, alyssum, geraniums and other annual flowers that will bloom all season. But the blossoms are fleeting and in no time dead ones hang from the stems. If I don't "dead-head" the plant it will not bloom as profusely as if I care for it. I regularly pull or cut the dead blossoms to keep the plants vibrant. This constant caring reminds me of my relationship with God. I bear fruit, but if I don't allow God to prune and trim me the fruit will grow old and useless and I'll quit producing new fruit. This pruning process is essential to my spiritual growth. Sometimes it's just a matter of pulling something off my schedule. Other times He may close doors and remove me from active service for a while. Sometimes it's almost as if He cuts me all the way back so I have to start completely over. God is the master gardener and I need to trust that He knows what He's doing and allow Him to care for me on a regular basis. Have you asked God to see if you have any dried blossoms that need removing?

Plant a flower box and care for the flowers throughout the summer.

> *"Sweeter as the years go by,*
> *Sweeter as the years go by,*
> *Richer, fuller, deeper, Jesus' love is sweeter,*
> *Sweeter as the years go by."*

As a young child I lived near my grandparents. Almost every day while I lived at home I would run down the road and see them. They were a huge influence in my life, helping shape me into the person I've become. They had time for me, listening to my stories, and teaching me things like sewing and cooking. They loved me and I loved them—we mutually enjoyed each other's company. Because of my relationship with my grandparents I developed a deep respect for the elderly. Older people have a wealth of wisdom to share with those who will listen and they often tell it like it is, having no need to impress anyone. I feel children who don't get to experience these relationships miss out on something special. There's a richness in multi-generational bonding that cannot be replaced by anything else. The young learn to value the elderly, and the elderly enjoy life

through the eyes of a child. In today's mobile society families often don't live close to one another, and grandparents and grandchildren may not have the opportunity to grow together. I have friends who serve as adoptive grandparents to children whose own live far away and I think it's a wonderful blessing to both parties. Do you have childhood memories with your grandparents?

> *"Children's children are a crown*
> *to the aged, and parents*
> *are the pride of their children."*
> *Proverbs 17:6*

Take a child whose grandparents don't live close for ice cream.

When my mother-in-law lived with us her mobility diminished with each passing month. At first she used a cane and eventually a walker in the house. If she went anywhere outside the home we pushed her in a wheelchair. While it was good to have these options to help her get around they made her rely on others. Sometimes our faith seems handicapped. We limp around as if wounded and often require crutches to lean on. Our lack of faith can become a disability, hindering our spiritual growth and diminishing our ability to soar above our problems, as if confined to the wheelchair. We find ourselves unable to do much without relying on others. The Bible tells us to throw off everything that hinders and the sin which so easily entangles us. So let us throw our crutches to the side and push our weak faith out of the wheelchair. God has promised that He will help us be strong and we can run our race with victory if we keep focused on Him. Our only crutch needs to be our unending need for God—all other crutches just keep us from leaning on Him, the source of all our strength. Is your faith crippled and weak?

"Do you not know? Have you not heard? The Lord is the everlasting God, the Creator of the ends of the earth. He will not grow tired or weary, and His understanding no one can fathom. He gives strength to the weary and increases the power of the weak."
Isaiah 40:28 & 29

"Standing on the promises I cannot fall,
List'ning every moment to the Spirit's call,
Resting in my Savior as my all in all,
Standing on the promises of God."

Exercise your faith by doing something new in ministry.

One morning I looked out of my house and noticed a band of sheep moving down our road. I quickly ran outside to watch, fascinated by how they would move hundreds of sheep without fencing or other boundaries. I noticed there were several sheep out front wearing bells. They were following the shepherd who was in front calling to them. They responded to His call and their eyes were focused on him alone, oblivious to the world around them. A herdsman protected the lead sheep from being pushed by the rest of the herd trailing after them. These sheep were following the ringing bells of those in front, unable to hear the voice of the shepherd themselves. Sheep dogs helped keep the band tightly together and moving forward. Jesus is our Shepherd and we are to hear and follow His voice. If we've spent time with Him we will recognize and respond to His call keeping our eyes focused on Him as we move through life. There will be others behind us who do not know Him yet, or cannot hear Him due to the roar of their own life. They will follow us and we have the huge responsibility of leading them to the Shepherd, not away from Him. Can you recognize the Savior's call and are there others following you?

"You my sheep, the sheep of my pasture, are people, and
I am your God, declares the Sovereign Lord."
Ezekiel 34:31

"Following Jesus day by day,
Following Him—His will obey,
Following Him, I cannot stray,
I'll follow Him all the way."

Study sheep and see why Jesus compared us to them.

> *"Sunlight, sunlight in my soul today,*
> *Sunlight, sunlight all along the way;*
> *Since the Savior found me, took away my sin,*
> *I have had the sunlight of His love within."*

I once thought that as I matured in my Christian walk I would feel more worthy, better about myself. But I have found the opposite to be true. The closer I get to God, the deeper my relationship grows, the more sin I see in myself—a sinner in need of grace. It's almost as if the closer I get to His light the more it shines into me and reflects those areas where I need to grow. If I look in a mirror in a dimly lit room I look better than if all the lights are on. And if I look in a magnified make-up mirror with lights all around the edges I get downright depressed. Everything I couldn't see in the dimly lit mirror is now magnified and then spotlighted. It's humbling to say the least. But that's how I feel when I stand in the presence of God. He seems to illuminate and magnify everything about me. The wrinkles and blemishes in my life stand out as ugly blotches. Using a make-up mirror helps me become more presentable to the rest of the world and standing in God's light helps me become a better reflection of Him. Have you let God's light magnify and illuminate you? How do you look?

"Now we see but a poor reflection as in a mirror; then we shall see face to face.
Now I know in part; then I shall know fully, even as I am fully known."
1 Corinthians 13:12

Study your reflection in a mirror—do you like what you see?

When I first started doing ministry work I thought I would see a lot of people come to know Christ through our efforts. It didn't take long for me to realize I was mistaken and I quickly grew discouraged. One night, in a dream, God spoke to my need to see results, which He showed me was all about me, not about trusting what He was doing. Sometimes we plant seeds, sometimes we weed out sin, other times we fertilize through encouragement and often we water with prayers. We have work to do, but after we've done our task, the results need to be left with Him. Seeds planted in the ground do not instantly burst forth. Much time passes between when the seed is covered with dirt and the first sign of growth appears. The farmer continues to water, fertilize, weed and nourish knowing that, in due time, the seed he has planted will sprout and eventually produce a harvest. I am no longer concerned about seeing the harvest of my efforts. I focus on doing my part to the best of my ability and leave the results in God's hands. Are you willing to serve God in any capacity even if it means you don't get to see the end result?

"So neither he who plants nor he who waters is anything, but only God, who makes things grow. The man who plants and the man who waters have one purpose, and each will be rewarded according to his own labor."
1 Corinthians 3:7 & 8

"I'll go where You want me to go, dear Lord,
O'er mountain, or plain, or sea;
I'll say what You want me to say, dear Lord,
I'll be what You want me to be."

Plant a bean seed and see how long it takes to sprout.

> "*Bringing in the sheaves, bringing in the sheaves,*
> *We shall come rejoicing, bringing in the sheaves;*
> *Bringing in the sheaves, bringing in the sheaves,*
> *We shall come rejoicing, bringing in the sheaves.*"

We have a small cattle ranch and grow some of our own feed for the cows including alfalfa hay. Alfalfa seed is very small and the plants are tender and tiny when they first sprout. Once established, alfalfa is a very hardy crop sending its roots down as deep as 10 or 12 feet into the soil, allowing the crop to withstand the harvest without dying. Alfalfa is harvested several times in a season. During each harvest, the hay is cut and then left to dry so, when it is baled, it will not mold and smolder into a fire. The farmer will withhold water so he can cut the hay, allow the rows to dry, and then bale and stack the crop. This can take a few weeks, and the plants are not irrigated during this entire time. Because the roots go deep into the soil it can withstand this dry time and spring back to life once it is irrigated again. Our faith needs to resemble an alfalfa plant, rooted deep in our soul through the Word of God. Then when life's challenges assail us and we feel dry and parched, cut down and left to wither, we know that we will withstand the test of time and spring back to life as God pours His refreshing Spirit down upon us. What do you draw your strength from during your "dry" times?

"Still other seed fell on good soil, where it produced a crop—
a hundred, sixty or thirty times what was sown."
Matthew 13:8

Turn on your favorite worship music and
quench your thirsty soul by reading from the Psalms.

often hear people say they want to grow in their faith but are unsure how to do it. God has given us very clear directions in Romans Chapter 10 where it says, "Faith comes by hearing and hearing by the Word of God." One way to grow our faith is by reading the Bible. Many times people attend church but they do not study God's Word. Their knowledge of God comes second hand but God wants us to have a first person relationship with Him. He wants us to study His Word and allow it to speak to us personally. The Bible reveals God's character, heart and mind. The more you know God the more you will trust Him and your faith will grow. The stories in the Old Testament teach us of His faithfulness. The Psalms give us a glimpse of His deep love for us. In Isaiah we are reminded of His power and might through all of creation. As we move into the New Testament we study the life and death of Jesus. We find our purpose for living in the letters of Paul. Hebrews is filled with stories of great faith and encouragement. The book of James warns us that we must walk the talk. Revelation tells of a time yet to come. Reading God's Word is not optional if you want to deepen your relationship with Christ. The more you know Him, the more you will trust and believe Him to be Who He says He is—and your faith will grow. Do you spend time in God's Word every day?

"Now faith is being sure of what we hope for and certain of what we do not see."
Hebrews 11:1

"More about Jesus let me learn,
More of His holy will discern;
Spirit of God, my teacher be,
Showing the things of Christ to me."

Commit to reading daily from your Bible.

A cow got out of our pasture and was headed toward the main road. She couldn't remember how to get back in. The rest of the herd, inside the fence, was following her and calling to her. My husband and I walked her back along the fence until she found the opening she had crawled through and was able to get back with the rest of the herd. Without our help she would have ended up on a main road and in danger. Sometimes we can get on the wrong side of the fence and can't remember how we got there. We know we're in territory the Bible has told us to avoid but without help we find ourselves wandering further into danger. It's not uncommon when someone gets off track to have others yelling at them from a distance. We can be quick to judge their behavior and criticize what they are doing but keep our distance because we don't want to get involved. My husband and I could have yelled at our wandering cow forever and it would not have brought her back to the herd. We had to go where she was and walk her back to safety. That's what we need to do for our lost or confused brothers and sisters. When someone's made a poor choice and headed down the wrong road go to them and guide them back on track. That's what Jesus always did. He walked with the sinners and those who were lost, pointing the way to the Father. Should we do any less? Do you know someone who needs help getting back on track? Are you willing to help them?

"My brothers, if one of you should wander from the truth and someone should bring him back, remember this: Whoever turns a sinner away from his error will save him from death and cover over a multitude of sins."
James 5:19 & 20

"He leadeth me, He leadeth me,
By His own hand He leadeth me;
His faithful foll'wer I would be,
For by His hand He leadeth me."

Call someone who you know is struggling and pray with them.

s we got ready to build our home there was much preparation before any building could take place. Our contractor asked us to decide where the cornerstone would be. It seemed like such a huge decision to make—it would determine which direction, at what angle and how the house would sit forever. I can still remember driving the stake into the ground knowing everything connected to the house would center around that stake. We are told to drive our stake in the ground and choose Christ as our cornerstone. We are to measure everything else in our life against Him and build our life on Him. The enemy will try to confuse us and fill us with doubts and fears about the direction of our life. We need to stand firm, point to the cornerstone of Jesus Christ and be immoveable in Him. Ban Satan from your life and cling to the sure foundation of Christ. Nothing can move you outside His will if you are standing on the rock of Jesus Christ. Have you claimed Christ as your cornerstone?

"See, I lay a stone in Zion, a tested stone, a precious cornerstone for a sure foundation; the one who trusts will never be dismayed."
Isaiah 28:16

"How firm a foundation, ye saints of the Lord,
Is laid for your faith in His excellent word!
What more can He say than to you He hath said—
To you who for refuge to Jesus have fled?"

Examine your faith and see if you have any cracks in the foundation.

> *"Come, poor sinner, yield to Jesus,*
> *At His throne of mercy bow;*
> *Oh, the Spirit bids you welcome,*
> *Come, and He will save you now."*

Have you ever been around a child that needed a nap or was undisciplined? They are difficult to deal with because no matter what happens they remain unhappy. They might be appeased briefly by getting their own way but very soon become dissatisfied and want something different. Their emotions ricochet around the room like a bouncy ball, one minute up and the next minute down. They blame everything on someone else and become more unruly with each passing moment. Adults act out their emotions differently but often display inappropriate behavior when they don't get their way. God is our Heavenly Father and the Bible says He disciplines those He considers His children. But just like an overtired child we often resist what we need the most. We fight against what the Lord is trying to teach us, doing everything we can to blame others or run away and escape. But God disciplines us for our own good just like we do our children. We will either bend in submission to His teachings or break in rebellion. The choice is ours but God is not going to give in. The next time you find yourself wanting your own way, stop and consider if God is trying to teach you something and you're behaving like a child. Can you think of a time when God was disciplining you and you resisted?

"Know then in your heart
that as a man disciplines his son,
so the Lord your God disciplines you."
Deuteronomy 8:5

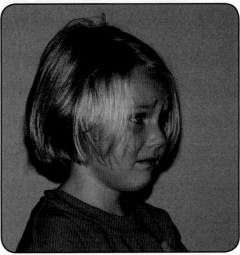

Reflect on a time when God disciplined you.

Have you ever faced a project or job that seemed almost insurmountable? I have many times, and one of those was after we built our new home. I wanted to put in a large yard, but didn't have the money to plant sod or hire help. To top it off we had built on rocky soil, so I had to first remove the rocks and haul in top soil before I could even start the process of designing, leveling and hand-seeding a yard. It was a slow process but I found that by focusing on one section at a time and working on a regular basis, I was able to make headway. After a few years my yard was complete and I felt a sense of accomplishment. These same principles can be applied to our Christian walk when we need to make a change in lifestyle or habit but find it overwhelming at first. I've found when I feel that way the first step is to pray and ask God to show me the way. Then I try to break the process into manageable pieces, removing any known sin that might get in the way. Once I've prepared myself I can start planting the new concept and then apply the water of the Spirit; as I pray it takes root and grows. It's just one step at a time but if I stay with it, eventually I'll be able to look back and see something new growing in my life. Is there something you've been putting off because it seems overwhelming? Ask God to show you how, and just start moving one step at a time.

*"Not that I have already
obtained all this,
or have already
been made perfect,
but I press on to take hold
of that for which Christ
Jesus took hold of me."*
Philippians 3:12

*"Step by step, every day,
He will lead us all the way;
Nothing can our hearts dismay,
While we follow, follow Jesus."*

Write down the steps required to begin something you've been putting off.

"And I pray that you, being rooted and established in love, may have power, together with all the saints, to grasp how wide and long and high and deep is the love of Christ, and to know this love that surpasses knowledge—that you may be filled to the measure of all the fullness of God."
Ephesians 3:18 & 19

"Wide, wide as the ocean, high as the Heaven above;
Deep, deep as the deepest sea is my Savior's love.
I, though so unworthy, still am a child of His care;
For His Word teaches me that His love reaches me everywhere."

Oh, how Jesus loves you and me! The Bible is filled with words of His love written personally for each of us. In John 15:13 I read that He laid down His life for me but has not left me alone. In John 14:26 I am told the Holy Spirit, the Counselor, has been sent to teach me all things and to remind me of everything He said while on earth. In Hebrews 4:15 &16 I am reminded that He is a compassionate Savior who is able to sympathize with me. I can approach the throne of grace with confidence and receive mercy and grace in my times of need. In John 17:11 He prays to the Holy Father for my protection through the power of His name. In Hebrews 6:19 He assures me He is my hope having entered into the inner sanctuary on my behalf. In Romans 8:34 He tells me He is sitting beside the Father interceding for me and assures me nothing can separate me from His love. In John 15:15 He reminds me I am His friend and He has shared the Master's business with me. He instructs me in John 15:16 to remember I have been chosen to bear fruit that will last and He will give me what I need if I ask in His Name according to His will. And in John 14:2 &3 He talks of the place He is preparing for me and how He has promised to come back and take me to be with Him one day. Yes, He loves each of us intimately and completely. Do you fully comprehend the depth of His love for you and have you opened wide your heart to Him?

Insert your name in the above texts and let Jesus speak personally to you.

"Lord Jesus, let nothing unholy remain,
Apply Thine own blood and extract every stain;
To get this blest cleansing, I all things forego—
Now wash me, and I shall be whiter than snow."

Planting a garden or flower bed is just the first step in growing something fruitful or beautiful. The weeds come up just as readily as the planted seed so the weeding begins. We don't just pull the weeds once and be done. It becomes a regular task if we want to keep them under control. New weeds sprout almost daily and if left to grow they become too large and deeply rooted to be pulled without killing the plant also. Sin grows just as readily in our lives. When we first accept Christ one of the steps to salvation is to confess our sins and get rid of the things in our life that are contrary to Christian teachings. But once will not be enough. On a regular basis we need to pull additional sin and bad habits that have sprouted. This confessing and turning from our sinful ways will be done for the rest of our lives. If we neglect ridding ourselves of sin on a regular basis, it can take root and become so deeply embedded that we will not be able to get rid of it easily. The fruit we bear for Christ or the beauty we show in our lives will be stunted or damaged if sin is left to grow uncontrolled. When was the last time you did some serious weeding in your life?

"The kingdom of heaven is like a man who sowed good seed in his field. But while everyone was sleeping, his enemy came and sowed weeds among the wheat and went away. When the wheat sprouted and formed heads, then the weeds also appeared."
Matthew 13:24 & 25

Spend time in reflection today ridding yourself
of any sin that may have sprouted.

> *"Oh, the beautiful garden, the garden of prayer,*
> *Oh, the beautiful garden of prayer;*
> *There my Savior awaits, and He opens the gates*
> *To the beautiful garden of prayer."*

I used to garden a lot and really enjoyed it. In the spring when I first put out the young tomato seedlings I would cover them with a cap to protect them from the elements until they took root and became stronger. As they grew I would uncover them in the day but put the cap back on at night. Eventually, they would become strong and able to withstand the weather so the cover would be removed completely. Then I would make a cage and put it around them so they would have something to anchor to as they grew. If a tomato plant is not staked, the fruit may become buried beneath the foliage and not mature completely, or rot due to lack of air and sun. New faith is like a tender tomato plant and God often shelters it from the storms of life nurturing it as it takes root. As it starts to mature He will allow more trials to come against it, but continue to be close to protect it when needed. As our faith matures, God lets the elements of life beat down upon us knowing that we are firmly rooted and planted in Him and can withstand the tests. He is like the stake beside us always there for us to grab onto, helping us reach upward so our fruit will mature and not be hidden and unpicked, eventually rotting. If we resist anchoring to Him we can be weighed down by the trials of life and hide any developing fruit. Are you staked to Christ and growing mature fruit for His service?

"I am the vine;
you are the branches.
If a man remains in me
and I in him,
he will bear much fruit;
Apart from me
you can do nothing."
John 15:5

Buy a tomato seedling and nurture it into a mature and fruit-bearing plant.

Have you ever tried to wear a pair of shoes that didn't fit? For me, finding a pair of shoes that is comfortable is almost impossible. It seems everything hurts when my feet hurt. I lose my desire to do anything and just want to get home so I can take off my shoes. Occasionally I've purchased a pair I thought I could make fit. I've tried to stretch, loosen or adjust them to no avail and soon I just give up and give them away. I think the same thing happens when we try to be someone we're not. It's as uncomfortable as a pair of shoes that don't fit. It feels awkward and you soon find yourself losing enthusiasm to do anything. You just want to stay home and be barefoot. You might think that in time you can adjust, stretch and twist yourself into what others want, but it will never feel right. It's always going to be uncomfortable and will limit your potential. So the next time you're trying to squeeze yourself into being someone you're not—quit it. God made you a perfect fit and you are the only person you can wear comfortably. Do you try to change to please others?

"Before I formed you
in the womb I knew you,
before you were born
I set you apart."
Jeremiah 1:5

"Oh, how marvelous! Oh, how wonderful!
And my song shall ever be:
Oh, how marvelous! Oh, how wonderful!
Is my Savior's love for me!"

Put on a comfortable pair of shoes and go for a walk.

May 25
Read Ecclesiastes chapter 12

I find old cemeteries intriguing with row after row of headstones and beautiful monuments in honor of those who have passed on. Often several generations of a family are buried together. My husband and I have discussed where we should be buried and feel it's not as easy a decision as when families lived in the same community for generations. Our families are buried in different cemeteries and neither of us live where either family is buried. Our children don't live in our town and are even further removed from where their ancestors are buried, so our final resting place has not been fully resolved. While it's nice to see families buried in one place, my burial place is not as important as the assurance of knowing where my soul will live eternally. Once I have died my physical body will return to dust, but I know that my destiny is to live with Christ eternally. I want those left behind to celebrate my life with them and rejoice that it was just the prelude to life everlasting. Do you have assurance of life eternal after this life is over?

> *"And the dust returns to the ground it came from,*
> *and the spirit returns to God who gave it."*
> *Ecclesiastes 12:7*

> *"Will the circle be unbroken*
> *By and by, by and by?*
> *In a better home awaiting*
> *In the sky, in the sky?"*

Buy some fresh flowers in memory of someone
in your family who has passed on.

When a seed is planted it sends a root underground securing the foundation for the seedling that will appear above ground. As the plant matures it is important that the root grows so it can support the foliage above ground. If something damages the root the plant will not be able to sustain life and will become stunted or die. When we become Christians we send down a root into the foundation of our Lord and new growth will start to appear in our life. As our faith grows and we engage in more and more activities it becomes easy to focus on the new growth and start to neglect making sure we are firmly rooted in the Lord. If our personal relationship, the root of our faith, does not grow as steadily as the fruit of our faith we will eventually become worn out in Christian work and the fruit we once had may even die. It is easy to get distracted "doing" and quit "being" in the presence of the Lord. The busier I get the more I need to take time alone with Him and His Word. Are you rooted in the Lord or have you been so busy "doing" for Him that you've neglected "being" in Him?

"So then, just as you received Christ Jesus as Lord, continue to live in Him, rooted and built up in Him, strengthened in the faith as you were taught, and overflowing with thankfulness."
Colossians 2:6 & 7

"Jesus is all the world to me, My Friend in trials sore;
I go to Him for blessings, and He gives them o'er and o'er.
He sends the sunshine and the rain, He sends the harvest's golden grain;
Sunshine and rain, harvest of grain, He's my Friend."

Spend time each day resting in the presence of the Lord.

abies in all of the animal kingdom, including humans, do not worry about being cared for. A nest of baby robins is filled with activity as feeding time draws close. Little heads and beaks stretch upward waiting for the fresh worm mother is bringing them. As these baby birds grow they jump from the nest and land on the ground. The mother bird continues to care for them until they develop enough strength to fly. As God's children we need the same confidence that He will feed and care for us. We worry about things He has promised to provide for us. God wants us to be dependant on Him as we grow and mature. Most of our life we are like a baby robin—out of the nest but not able to fly on our own. In this life we'll always be a human "being" made in His image and for His purpose. Do you trust God to feed and care for you?

"Look at the birds of the air; they do not sow or reap or store away in barns,
and yet your heavenly Father feeds them. Are you not much more valuable than they?"
Matthew 6:26

"I sing because I'm happy,
I sing because I'm free,
For His eye is on the sparrow,
and I know He watches me."

Claim God's promise to meet your daily needs.

*"Let the fire fall on me,
Let the fire fall on me;
The fire of Pentecost, consuming sin and dross,
Let the holy fire from heaven fall on me."*

We've all heard the saying where there is smoke there's fire and that is true in most cases. In the spring we spend considerable time burning the weeds which have died through the winter, getting things prepared for spring planting. As we burn along the ditch banks, a trail of smoke will follow even after the fire has died down. If we look back and see smoke billowing, it usually means the fire has reignited itself and we need to go back and make sure it doesn't spread. Gossip, like smoke, can be a warning sign that something is wrong deep in our soul. Usually gossip stems from feelings of inadequacy, fear, control, competitiveness, anger, or other sinful emotions. It may start as a very small comment, but can quickly escalate into a raging fire if not controlled and put out. Whenever I find myself making a comment that borders on gossiping, I need to take a good look inside myself and see what's going on. I need to identify and confess my sin, apologize if I have spoken wrongly to someone, and address the real issue burning deep inside of me. The sin of gossip can be excused as sharing a concern for another or just wanting to tell others our perceived truth, but it's all gossip to God, no matter how we describe it and needs to be doused with a heavy washing of the Holy Spirit the minute we see it smoking. How do you handle gossip in your life?

*"He who guards his lips
guards his soul,
but he who speaks rashly
will come to ruin."*
Proverbs 13:3

Ask God to help your words build others up, not cause destruction.

May 29
Read Psalm 19

Last week we were invaded by the miller moth migration. They started hiding on our screen doors. I discovered the problem when I opened the door unaware they were there and they flew inside the house before I could close the door. Needless to say I've been swatting millers each night as they come out from their hiding places. They prefer dark places and I continually find them in closets, in the folds of bedding or curtains and other hidden areas. The migration season usually lasts a couple of weeks and I'm hoping they move on soon. But in the meantime I am persistent in exposing and getting rid of them in my home. Sin in our life can be similar to a miller. In the daylight of public life sin can be hidden and unexposed to the naked eye. But just because you can't see it easily doesn't mean it isn't there. When things become quiet and less public it often flares up coming out from the dark recesses of our mind where it's been hiding. It can take us by surprise and we wonder where that thought, behavior or comment came from. We have to be persistent in getting it out of our life, exposing whatever might be lurking in some hidden closet of our mind. I've been very careful before opening my outside doors lately and I also need to be careful what I open my mind and soul to. Do you have any hidden sins in your life that seem to fly out at the most unexpected times?

"Who can discern his errors?
Forgive my hidden faults.
Keep your servant also from willful sins;
may they not rule over me.
Then will I be blameless,
innocent of great transgression."
Psalm 19:12 & 13

"Search me, O God, and know my heart today,
Try me, O Savior, know my thoughts, I pray;
See if there be some wicked way in me;
Cleanse me from every sin, and set me free."

Pray for God to expose hidden sin you are not aware of.

"Hallelujah! What a Savior,
Who can take a poor, lost sinner,
Lift him from the miry clay and set me free!
I will ever tell the story, shouting glory, glory, glory,
Hallelujah! Jesus lifted me."

Mountain top experiences are wonderful and invigorating. When I was young my family took yearly pack trips into high mountain lakes. We would hike all day up long, steep, narrow paths until we reached the summit where in the draw the lake would rest. The air was thin making it hard to breathe. The soil was sparse and rocky with little vegetation. But the view was spectacular, the peacefulness unequaled. My memories of these mountain trips are precious. Our spiritual journey needs mountain top experiences also. Whether it's a week-end retreat, a long sought-after vacation, a successful and uplifting event or a power-packed seminar, we will find ourselves renewed and refreshed in our relationship with Christ after the experience. As wonderful as these times are, we can't live on the mountain tops. The atmosphere restricts long-term growth, the rocky soil produces sparse fruit and our area of service is limited. We have to return to the valley where we can go the distance. It's there that the rich soil allows abundant growth and harvest. It's there we find the crowds needing our help. It's there God wants us to live and work. When you find yourself wearing down and getting tired, go to the mountain top and refresh your perspective. We need a balance of both worlds to be healthy and vibrant. When was the last time you refreshed your spirit?

"For the Lord
is the great God,
the great King
above all gods.
In His hand
are the depths
of the earth,
and the mountain peaks
belong to Him."
Psalm 95:3 & 4

Plan a weekend get-away.

May 31
Read Daniel chapter 3

The story of Shadrach, Meshach and Abednego has always amazed me. They refused to worship the golden image King Nebuchadnezzar had set up. Instead, they continued to worship God and were brought before the King to defend themselves. I've often wondered what my conversation with God would have been like had this happened to me. I probably would have cried out in despair questioning why God was allowing this to happen. Hadn't I stood my ground and continued to worship Him? Was this my reward for being faithful? Why was He turning His back on me in my greatest time of need? But the response the three men gave was nothing like that. They continued to proclaim the sovereignty of their God claiming He could save them, but if He chose not to they would still worship Him. And we know that God not only saved them, but walked with them in the fire and they came out without a single hair burned and no smell of fire on them. God was glorified because they had

the faith to trust Him no matter what happened. We often spend too much time questioning, rather than trusting God. I want my faith to grow until it praises God, not questioning Him for whatever life brings me, believing He's in control. Do you ever question what God is doing and feel angry or confused by it?

"If we are thrown into the blazing furnace, the God we serve is able
to save us from it . . . but even if He does not . . .
we will not serve your gods or worship the image of gold you have set up."
Daniel 3:17 & 18

The next time you want to question God praise Him instead.

> "On Christ the solid rock I stand,
> All other ground is sinking sand,
> All other ground is sinking sand."

I love going to the coast, sitting on the rocks, and watching the crashing waves. The roaring sound of the ocean is almost deafening. I often see moss, sea life, and small pebbles washing onto the rocky surface, moved by the flow of the tide. But the rocks stay grounded, not moved by the force of the water, secure in their footing. It seems they can withstand almost anything that comes against them, enduring through the ages regardless of the constant beating of the waves. In contrast, sand is carried with each ebb and flow of the tide. It is carried on my feet when I walk across it, and moved by almost everything that comes in contact with it. My faith needs to resemble a rock, built on our Lord Jesus Christ, solid and sure. It should not be unstable like sand, blown from here to there, or swept away by every new fad that comes along. What does your faith resemble; a rock, a grain of sand or something in between?

"Do not tremble, do not be afraid. Did I not proclaim this and foretell it long ago?
You are my witnesses. Is there any God besides me?
No, there is no other Rock; I know not one."
Isaiah 44:8

Find a smooth stone and carry it with you to remind yourself
to stand upon the Rock Jesus Christ.

June 2
Read Isaiah chapter 14

Many of us try to stay informed about local and national events by reading the newspaper or listening to the news. We want to be informed about what is happening around us. But much of the news is spun to reflect the commentator's perspective. Facts are twisted or left out and we have to sift through it to find the truth. God has given us the best newspaper in the world through His living Word, the Bible. If we want to know what's going to happen and what our future holds we just need to read it. He's recorded life from the beginning to the end and we have the opportunity to be as informed as we desire. It is up to us. His perspective is not warped. It's His eternal plan that will unfold just as He has said. As I watch and read the news I see so much happening that we have been warned about in the Bible. God has recorded both our history and our destiny in the Bible and it's a must read for those who want to be informed. Do you see events taking place that you have read about in the Bible?

"The Lord almighty has sworn,
Surely, as I have planned, so it will be,
And as I have purposed, so it will stand."
Isaiah 14:24

Thank God that His Word is accurate and true
and we have the freedom to read it.

ave you ever seen pictures that are really two in one? There is the obvious one which you see at first glance but a completely different picture is hidden in the artwork that requires more contemplation to identify. Life is like that too. We often form our opinions of people or situations on our first impression. If we react at that moment we may miss something and find later that our initial evaluation was incorrect. Many people present a good first impression, but underneath is a hidden side. We must be wise and discerning, not hasty and foolish. Jesus told us that many false prophets will come to us disguised in sheep's clothing, but inwardly they are ferocious wolves and we will be able to recognize them by their fruit. Time is our ally and we need to be slow in forming new alliances and friendships. Anyone can fool someone for a moment but very few can fool anyone for a long time. Eventually what they say and pretend to be doesn't match other areas of their life and their true colors start to show. So just like studying the picture to find the hidden image, let's step back and study new acquaintances to see if there is a hidden side to them. Have you ever been deceived by someone who pretended to be someone they weren't?

"Watch out for false prophets. They come to you in sheep's clothing, but inwardly they are ferocious wolves. By their fruit you will recognize them."
Matthew 7:15 & 16

"'Tis so sweet to trust in Jesus, just to take Him at His Word;
Just to rest upon His promise, and to know, "Thus saith the Lord!"
Jesus, Jesus, how I trust Him! How I've proved Him o'er and o'er;
Jesus, Jesus, precious Jesus! Oh, for grace to trust Him more!"

Invite someone you'd like to get to know for dinner or dessert.

June 4
Read Psalm 104

We have amazing sunrises and sunsets and watching them is a great way to start and finish my day. But I have to make a conscious effort to get up, open the blinds or go outside if I want to see the morning sun peak over the horizon. At night I have to leave whatever I'm doing and go out on my back porch or it will pass before I realize it. Every day is filled with the Lord's blessings but if we've not tuned into His world we'll miss most of them. I have so much to thank Him for. The hot shower in the morning reminds me there are those who don't have this luxury. When I step outside and the birds are singing their masterpiece I need to thank Him I have ears to hear the symphony. As the rain bathes the earth, falling gently on my skin and the fresh smell tingles my senses, I should thank Him I can smell and feel. God's colorful display is all around me, deep rich hues of color enhanced by soft delicate splashes of light. Thank you, Lord, for eyes to see. My cupboards

have food, I have a safe place to lay my head at night, my feet can take me where I want to go, I have people who love me and whom I love. Oh, how very blessed I am! God is so good to us. We need to slow down and reflect on how blessed we are. When was the last time you counted your blessings?

"I will sing to the Lord all my life; I will sing praise to my God as long as I live.
May my meditation be pleasing to Him, as I rejoice in the Lord . . .
Praise the Lord, O my soul. Praise the Lord."
Psalm 104:33–35

"Count your blessings, name them one by one,
Count your blessings, see what God hath done!
Count your blessings, name them one by one,
Count your many blessings, see what God hath done."

Spend time counting your blessings and praising God.

> *"What have I to dread, what have I to fear,*
> *Leaning on the everlasting arms?*
> *I have blessed peace with my Lord so near,*
> *Leaning on the everlasting arms."*

Today we sat under our covered porch to watch a spring storm coming as we have many times before. It's fascinating to see the storm gather momentum as it approaches and often it will become calm just before the winds bear down on us. Wrapped in a blanket we prepare to watch God put on a dazzling display. The thunder roars, lightning flashes, the wind howls, the heavens open and the angels drop buckets of fresh heaven-sent water our way. All our senses become engaged as we sit protected and watch the magnificent show. Once it passes the sun peeks out, the birds return to their post and the flowers lift their rain-laden heads to drink it all in. A storm in our life can happen much the same way. Sometimes it's unexpected but often we know it's approaching before it hits. What if we faced it head on nestled under the Lord's protective arm instead of trying to run away? Retreating in fear or reacting in anger could mean we will miss something wonderful He has prepared to teach us. Perhaps we should take our seat beside our Master and engage all our senses as we go through it. Once the storm has passed—and it will—we can peek out from under His watchful care, see if it's safe to return to our post

and lift our heads to drink in everything He wants us to learn. The earth receives much refreshment from these storms and our lives are enriched after we've endured and learned through a trial. Do you embrace the storms in your life?

> *"The Lord does whatever pleases Him, in the Heavens and on the earth, in the seas*
> *and all their depths. He makes clouds rise from the ends of the earth;*
> *He sends lightning with the rain and brings out the wind from His storehouses."*
> *Psalm 135:6 & 7*

The next time it rains find a protected spot outside and enjoy it.

June 6
Read Matthew chapter 5

> *"So be careful, dear ones, what kind of seeds you sow,*
> *Lest some day there will be sad regrets and misery;*
> *Be careful, I say, what kind of seed you sow today,*
> *Lest some day you will weep when you reap what you sow."*

I don't like to shop and usually only go when absolutely necessary. Occasionally, I go window shopping with a friend and I'm amazed at how often I find something to buy. I'm not sure why it's called window shopping because if I go looking I'm probably going to buy. Sometimes after seeing the newest styles, I find my closet looking drab and boring, and am enticed to buy new things I don't even need. The same thing can happen in our relationship with our spouse. We can be happy with who we have at home until we start window shopping in our mind. If we start looking at the newer merchandise we can become disenchanted with our mate and before we know it want to try something new. We get so caught up in this new relationship that we dump the old only to find too late it's a terrible mistake. God told us to keep our eyes focused and not to swerve to the right or the left (Proverbs 4:27). When it comes to our marriage we can't afford to go window shopping even once. What steps can you put in place to keep your marriage healthy and alive?

"But I tell you that anyone who looks at a woman lustfully has already committed adultery with her in his heart."
Matthew 5:28

If you are married share with your mate five things you love about them.

My six-year old granddaughter was walking around the yard with pen and paper in hand. Occasionally she would stop and write something. This continued for quite a while before Grandpa asked her what she was doing. "Oh, I'm writing something to help Grandma with her book," she said and then went back to her work. She knew I had been working on the devotional and she wanted to help me write it. It brought a smile to my face as I thought how cute. She is just learning to read, so couldn't be writing much I could use. And then God caused me to pause. I wonder how many times I try to help Him when He hasn't asked me to because the task is way beyond my abilities. In my naivety I am no different from my granddaughter who thought she could help me write. God probably smiles a lot at my efforts and must shake His head at all my attempts to do His work. One day my granddaughter may be an author and one day I may be able to do more difficult tasks for Him. But right now I need to focus on the things He has called me to and equipped me for. My time would be best spent doing those things and leaving His work alone. Are you attempting to do God's work for Him?

"The Lord will fulfill
His purpose for me;
Your love, O Lord,
endures forever—
do not abandon the works
of your hands."
Psalm 138:8

"Take my moments and my days,
Let them flow in endless praise;
Take my intellect and use
Every pow'r as Thou shalt choose."

List what ways God has equipped you for His work.

June 8

Read Ephesians chapter 4

Planting a garden takes a lot of work, but planting is just the beginning. After it starts to grow, weeding, fertilizing, and watering are also needed to produce a crop. Then there's the harvest to reap what you've grown. Lettuce is one of those crops that keeps reproducing if it's picked. Lettuce is tender and sweet if cut when it's young. If the leaves are left too long they become bitter and tough, and the plant goes to seed and becomes inedible. We go to church to have seeds of service planted in the soil of our hearts. If we continue to go these seeds will take root, grow and mature. Gathering with other believers can help weed out sin seeds and encourage new growth. If we only go to church to receive, and do not begin to harvest, we may go to seed, so to speak. We need to use the gifts and talents the Lord has equipped us with in service for others. We should not be afraid to give away what has grown inside us, for just like a lettuce plant, we will continue to produce good fruit if we are picked and ready for service. I want the garden in my life to feed many around me, sharing the blessings God has given me. Is there a crop in your life ready to be picked?

"It was He who gave some to be apostles, some to be prophets, some to be evangelists, and some to be pastors and teachers, to prepare God's people for works of service, so that the body of Christ may be built up . . . and become mature, attaining to the whole measure of the fullness of Christ."
Ephesians 4:12 & 13

"Give of your best to the Master;
Give of the strength of your youth;
Clad in salvation's full armor,
Join in the battle for truth."

Pick or buy fresh vegetables and make a delicious salad thanking God for good food.

"Just as I am, poor, wretched, blind;
Sight, riches, healing of the mind,
Yea, all I need in Thee to find,
O Lamb of God, I come, I come."

Our old dog, Sammy, and our young cat, Paws, make an odd pair but they are best of friends. Paws loves to go everywhere Sammy goes, following her to the field to sniff out gophers, snuggling against her when it's nap time, guarding our house and sleeping together at night. An odd couple but very happy with each other. My husband and I are an odd pair also. He likes to sleep in; I get up at the crack of dawn and go to bed early. He has several projects started at the same time; I like to work on one thing at a time. He likes things out where he can see them; I like everything tucked away in a drawer or closet. He's a patient man who doesn't let things disrupt his peace. I lose patience and get edgy when things don't go as I planned. He indulges himself with goodies when the urge hits; I deny myself and am disciplined. Yes, we're opposites in so many ways, but we both love God, family and our home. We're simple people with simple pleasures and together we make a good blend. God knew I needed some of the qualities inherent in Basil and He knew I would bring excitement and depth to Basil's home. Our differences complement one

another, enhancing our good qualities and toning down those less appealing characteristics. My life is more rounded, I've much more depth in my soul and I've even started to cultivate a few of the characteristics I like so much about my husband. Do you have a relationship with someone who is very different than you are and does it complement both of you?

"There are different kinds of gifts, but the same Spirit.
There are different kinds of service, but the same Lord.
There are different kinds of working, but the same God works all of them in all men."
1 Corinthians 12:4–6

List and reflect on the differences and similarities of someone close to you.

161

June 10
Read Psalm 104

I live on a rim overlooking a valley, facing west. Night after night as the sun sets in the sky I am treated to the most amazing color displays. What seems like an ordinary sky turns into something extraordinary as the sun works its magic in the closing hours of the day. It bounces off the clouds and mountains and almost seems to shout God's magnificent glory. What's really interesting about a sunset is that you are not seeing the sun, but a reflection of the sun. I want my life to bear witness of the "Son's" light shining within me. I pray God will take my ordinary life and turn it into something extraordinary for His glory. When people look at me, I hope they see a reflection of the "Son" in my life. Have you ever met someone who radiated Christ's love in their life?

"O Lord my God, you are very great;
You are clothed with splendor and majesty.
He wraps Himself in light as with a garment;
He stretches out the heavens like a tent and
lays the beams of His upper chambers on their waters.
He makes the clouds His chariot and rides on the wings of the wind.
He makes winds His messengers, flames of fire His servants."
Psalm 104:1-4

"Now the day is over,
Night is drawing nigh,
Shadows of the evening
Steal across the sky."

Try to watch the sunset tonight and thank God
for taking you through another day.

*T*hroughout the Old Testament, we see God placing people in circumstances where He could use them for a specific purpose. The story of Esther is one beautiful example of this. Esther's life started with hardships. She was orphaned and raised by her cousin Mordecai. Through a series of events orchestrated by God she eventually was chosen by King Xerxes to become his queen. This placed her in a position that later helped save the Jews from unjust persecution. Our lives are not random happenings. God is behind the scene placing people where He needs them for His purposes. These situations may require hardship and challenges or abundance and blessing but God knows what He is doing. If you have been blessed with wealth or authority it is because God has allowed it. It should be used to promote Kingdom growth, not personal gain. If you find yourself suffering and struggling in your life it may not be to burden or crush you, but might have a far-reaching, eternal purpose not yet realized. The important thing is that wherever we

find ourselves we are focused on living for Christ and using our resources, whether few or many, to honor and glorify Him. Do you believe your life's circumstances have been orchestrated by God and are part of a much bigger plan?

"Do not think that because you are in the king's house you alone of all the Jews will escape. For if you remain silent at this time, relief and deliverance for the Jews will arise from another place, but you and your father's family will perish. And who knows but that you have come to royal position for such a time as this?"
Esther 4:14

"Living for Jesus, a life that is true,
Striving to please Him in all that I do;
Yielding allegiance, glad-hearted and free,
This is the pathway of blessing for me."

Think of how to use what God has given you to bless others.

June 12
Read Proverbs chapter 18

> *"Jesus calls us! By Thy mercies,*
> *Savior, may we hear Thy call,*
> *Give our hearts to Thine obedience,*
> *Serve and love Thee best of all."*

My deaf three-year-old granddaughter has Cochlear implants in both ears and we communicate with her as if she were a hearing child. Recently when I was watching her, she repeatedly ignored me when I asked her to do or stop doing something. She had her hearing devices on, and I assumed she was choosing not to hear me, something she has learned to do. I finally had to sit her down and discipline her. I felt bad and couldn't understand why she was being so difficult that particular night. I received a call from her mother shortly after they took her home saying they had lost one of her hearing devices and wondered if it was at the house. After an extensive search I found the device hung around a kitchen cabinet. She had taken it off because it quit working. Her other device's batteries had run low and it was not working correctly either. I then realized she had not been hearing that night which was why she had ignored me. The reality that I had disciplined her unfairly brought tears to my eyes. I chastised myself for not inspecting her devices to see if they were working. Sometimes we can be quick to judge and criticize others when their behavior seems inappropriate. Perhaps if we knew the underlying cause we might feel more compassion for them. I learned a lesson from my granddaughter which I hope helps me respond differently when I'm frustrated. Have you ever been quick to judge someone only to find out your judgment was incorrect?

> *"The first to present his case seems right,*
> *till another comes forward and questions him."*
> *Proverbs 18:17*

Take time before God and see
if there is anything in your "eye" that needs removed.

164

When I first started writing this devotional book I was confident God had placed the desire on my heart and I was responding in obedience. Now, several months into writing I find myself wondering if this is really what God wants me to do or if it was what I wanted to do. I've had to lay many other things aside as I work at getting it completed. I often question whether the finished product will bring God glory or become a dusty book on my family's shelf. I don't know the answers today but I do know I must persevere and finish the work I felt called to begin. What happens after I complete it will be up to God not me. Finishing what we begin for the Lord is most important. Persevering is hard especially when one is past the exciting beginning and quite a distance from the finish line. It's the middle part that can bog us down and we may even feel drawn to move on to new and more exciting things. God wants our faith to grow beyond constant prodding and encouragement. He wants us to do the work at hand even when it seems really quiet from above and the end results are unknown. Is there a task you felt called to begin that you've yet to complete? Are you committed to finishing it to the glory of God?

"So do not throw away your confidence; it will be richly rewarded. You need to persevere so that when you have done the will of God, you will receive what He has promised."
Hebrews 10:35 & 36

"Day by day, and with each passing moment, strength I find, to meet my trials here;
Trusting in my Father's wise bestowment, I've no cause for worry or for fear.
He Whose heart is kind beyond all measure gives unto each day what He deems best
Lovingly, its part of pain and pleasure, mingling toil with peace and rest."

Pray for strength to complete an unfinished task.

or over 200 years the American flag has been a symbol of strength and unity, a source of pride and inspiration for American citizens. We celebrate all that it stands for on Flag Day, reflecting on our rich heritage. The flag is symbolic of what the American people have achieved through hard work, sacrifice and patriotism but in and of itself it is not these things. It is the people of America who make up the characteristics it stands for. Christianity is represented by such symbols as the cross, the crown of thorns and a fish. Churches and individuals often display these symbols in their homes, in jewelry or on their bodies to represent their faith in Christ. While there is nothing wrong with displaying Christian symbols they do not make one a Christian. We can wear a cross necklace and have no relationship with Christ. We can display a Bible in our home, but never open it and consider it just a book in our library. Many people have fish symbols on their vehicles but drive inappropriately. Symbolic displays may not involve much thought or connection. They are pretty, attractive or popular, so we display them. Let's make sure if we display Christian symbols that our behavior honors Christ. Does your walk line up with your talk?

"Be very careful, then, how you live—not as unwise but as wise."
Ephesians 5:15

"On a hill far away stood an old rugged cross,
The emblem of suff'ring and shame;
And I love that old cross where the dearest and best
For a world of lost sinners was slain."

Reflect on each Christian symbol in your home and its personal significance.

I think living life is similar to a bike ride. Sometimes it's all uphill and I'm not sure I can make the climb. Other times, I find myself flying down hill hanging on for dear life and feeling out of control. I love it when the road levels out and I find myself just traveling along taking in the scenery. Occasionally, I might get the wind at my back, which pushes me onward and helps ease the ride. And other times I find myself headed into the wind fighting every inch of the way just to keep going. I've had barking dogs nip at my heels and all I wanted was to get away fast. Sometimes a car comes too close or too fast and I have to get off the road. But through it all, I've learned that the most important thing is to keep pedaling, because I'll never reach my destination if I quit. What kind of bike ride are you on today and are you still pedaling?

"The Lord is my strength
and my shield;
My heart trusts in Him,
and I am helped.
My heart leaps for joy
And I will give thanks
to Him in song."
Psalm 28:7

"Little feet, be very careful where you go, as in life you daily travel to and fro;
Never for a moment stray, from the straight and holy way;
Oh, be careful, be careful, little feet."

Journal where you are today, relating it to a bike ride,
and thank God for His promise to always be with you.

June 16
Read Colossians chapter 1

"Jesus is all the world to me, and true to Him I'll be;
Oh, how could I this Friend deny, when He's so true to me?
Following Him I know I'm right, He watches o'er me day and night
Following Him by day and night, He's my Friend."

Our apricot tree is heavy with fruit and I'm looking forward to picking and eating it once it is ripened. It would be foolish of me to harvest it right now. The apricots are undeveloped, small in size and hard as a rock. A premature harvest would waste the complete crop and I would have to wait until next year for another chance to harvest apricots from my tree. Sometimes we get anxious to harvest spiritual fruit prematurely. We see something new growing in our life and we get in a hurry to use it for the Lord. But it's not mature yet; there's more to learn and more growth required before it's ready. An early harvest would damage or destroy what is growing and we would have to start over. Trying to use a new gift or talent before it's ready is like trying to pit and eat an unripe apricot. You can't get to the seed without ruining the hard shell of fruit covering it and it tastes bitter. Don't get in a hurry to use something new in your life. Let God mature it completely and then the harvested fruit will be soft and sweet, pleasant to all who eat it. Are you hasty to accomplish something for God before you're fully prepared?

"We pray this in order that you may live a life worthy of the Lord and may please Him in every way: bearing fruit in every good work, growing in the knowledge of God, being strengthened with all power according to His glorious might so that you may have great endurance and patience and joyfully giving thanks to the Father Who has qualified you to share in the inheritance of the saints in the kingdom of light."
Colossians 1:10-12

Identify a new fruit growing in your life and consider how to cultivate it.

The years before my first marriage ended were ones of deceit and hypocrisy. My husband and I were active in our church. He served as a deacon and I was on the worship team and even led a women's retreat. We attended regularly and our children were actively involved in their youth activities. But behind closed doors our lives were dramatically different. We led separate lives, argued when we were together and did not honor God. I tried to hide the ugly reality from our children and family but I'm sure everyone knew something was wrong. The stress was unbelievable and eventually when everything crumbled around us I almost felt relieved. At least I no longer had to pretend that everything was perfect. I knew that God was not pleased and I needed to make a change in my life. I confessed my sins, sought forgiveness and committed to living the rest of my life in accordance to His Word and His Will. We can't live with our feet in both campgrounds. We have to choose if we will serve God or not and no choice is a choice not to serve Him. I've not been perfect since I chose to serve Him but now I don't live a double standard. I try to honor God in public and behind closed doors. He's given me another chance to make the right choice and I know that, with His strength, I can do it. Do you have any hypocrisy in your life you need to confess and turn from?

"In the same way, on the outside you appear to people as righteous but on the inside you are full of hypocrisy and wickedness."
Matthew 23:28

"Amazing grace! How sweet the sound
That saved a wretch like me!
I once was lost, but now am found;
Was blind, but now I see."

Seek good counsel if you are struggling in your life.

survey on religious practices among adults divided Christianity into two categories. The "Casual Christian" was the largest group comprising almost two-thirds of all adults. Less than sixteen percent were labeled "Captive Christian." The Casual Christian was someone who believed in God and the principles taught but was minimally involved. Christian living was not integrated into their everyday life. They tended to practice religion but did not have a personal relationship with Christ. The Captive Christians were so named because they chose to be volunteer slaves to Christ and were fully committed to living in obedience to God. Their devotion to Him was extreme. They sought to serve Him in all aspects of their lives producing fruit and showing they were His true disciples. In John Chapter 15, Jesus explains that unless we bear fruit to His Father's glory we will be cast aside and burned. There is no place in Heaven for the Casual Christian. Only those who fully commit and show themselves to be His true disciples will spend eternity with Him. Are you a Casual or a Captive Christian?

"This is to my Father's glory, that you bear much fruit, showing yourselves to be my disciples."
John 15:8

"Ye seed of Israel's chosen race, Ye ransomed from the fall,
Hail Him Who saves you by His grace, and crown Him Lord of all;
Hail Him Who saves you by His grace, and crown Him Lord of all."

Would those around you, outside of your church, know you are a Christian?

"Let us fix our eyes on Jesus, the author and perfecter of our faith,
who for the joy set before Him endured the cross, scorning its shame,
and sat down at the right hand of the throne of God.
Consider Him who endured such opposition from sinful men,
so that you will not grow weary and lose heart."
Hebrews 12:2 & 3

"Be Thou my Vision, O Lord of my heart;
Naught be all else to me, save that Thou art;
Thou my best Thought, by day or by night,
Waking or sleeping, Thy presence my light."

Whenever I feel overwhelmed it is usually because I've taken my eyes off Jesus. As I look at everything that needs to be done and all the provision it will take it seems impossible and I want to give up. I think it is one of the reasons we live in a world where miracles are rare and mediocrity is the norm. To attempt great things for God we have to narrow our vision until we're only focused on Him, not the situation around us. If we need to see that it is possible before we begin, we'll never begin. Faith requires us to believe

and hope for things which are unseen (Hebrews 11:1). God delights in taking the ordinary and doing something extraordinary with it. He doesn't need great people—He needs people who desire to show the greatness of their God. If we've got our eyes on ourselves or the world around us, we'll find great things beyond our reach. But if we've got our eyes on Jesus we'll move in obedience and accomplish more than is humanly possible. It's time to look heavenward with excited anticipation of being part of something much bigger than ourselves. What are you looking at, Jesus or the world around you?

Start praying for God to do something extraordinary
with your ordinary talents.

June 20
Read Matthew chapter 18

I love how free children are to enjoy life. It's no wonder God tells us that unless we become as little children we will not enter the Kingdom of heaven. I share my life with three children and many grandchildren. It really is true that being a grandparent is special. As a young mother in difficult times, I don't think I enjoyed my children as much as I am enjoying my grandchildren. They seem to remind me daily that life is full of special moments that need to be enjoyed. Often what delights a child and brings pure joy to their face, would be seen as an interruption or complication to my day. My first reaction to a cascade of water pouring down my face would probably not be delight, but why shouldn't it be? A little refreshing water might be exactly what I need to wash away a heavy load and lighten my mood. Do you need to ask God to give you a child-like spirit?

"And He said, I tell you the truth,
unless you change and become like little children,
you will never enter the kingdom of heaven."
Matthew 18:3

"I'm a child of the King,
A child of the King:
With Jesus my Savior,
I'm a child of the King."

Remember the last time you let go and laughed like a child
and thank God for it.

> *"Faith of our fathers, we will love*
> *Both friend and foe in all our strife;*
> *And preach thee, too, as love knows how*
> *By kindly words and virtuous life."*

What an important role fathers play in their children's lives. I like the country song about a little boy who wants to grow up and be just like his daddy. Children model behavior they see in their homes. In the Bible fathers are instructed not to provoke or discourage their children, but rather to encourage them whenever possible. They are to honor God and love their wives as they love themselves. Godly traits fathers should strive for include being honest, hardworking, quick to lend a hand to others in need and not greedy. Other Christian attributes include self-control, a gentle spirit, and slowness to anger. Fathers are the spiritual leaders of their homes and should pray openly with and around their children, modeling daily communication with their Heavenly Father. Most of all they need to be quick to give and receive love, openly displaying and communicating affection to their families. Being a good father is a high calling, but fathers have the best model in all the world to draw from—their own Heavenly Father. He has promised to give them all they need to do the job right. What attributes did your father model when you were growing up?

"Fathers, do not exasperate your children; instead,
bring them up in the training and instruction of the Lord."
Ephesians 6:4

Write a letter of gratitude to a father figure in your life.

$\mathcal{S}$omebody planted a seed in my soul that took root, sprouted and eventually grew. Others came around me to water, encourage and care for the tender young plant. Still others pulled out the bad seeds that also were trying to grow and some pruned me so my foundation would become unshakeable. Eventually I became a tree and after a year or two I started to bear fruit of my own. As I matured, I grew more fruit, much of which was picked and given to others who didn't yet have their own fruit. As they tasted the fruit and found it to be good, they took the seed and planted it in their souls where it took root, sprouted and eventually grew. We don't become mature Christians just to bear fruit and eat what delights us, letting the abundance drop to the ground and go to waste. No, we become fruit-bearing Christians so the seeds of our faith can be planted in others. The cycle of new life is passed from believer to non-believer, a never-ending circle. We all have the potential to be a fruit-bearing tree. Remember what Jesus did when He came upon the fig tree without fruit? Share the good fruit and plant seeds of eternal life in all who cross your path. Are you producing and sharing the fruit of your faith with others?

"Seeing a fig tree by the road,
he went up to it but found
nothing on it except leaves.
Then He said to it,
'May you never bear fruit again!'
Immediately the tree withered."
Matthew 21:19

"I'll live for Him who died for me,
How happy then my life shall be!
I'll live for Him who died for me,
My Savior and my God!"

Plant a cherry seed and see if it sprouts.

ells Canyon is a deep gorge cut through western Idaho that starts in the lower part of the state and extends north to the Columbia River in northern Idaho. It's a favorite tourist attraction and much of it is only accessible by boat due to the deep canyon walls carved out by the flowing river. It took hundreds of years to create this beautiful gorge which is one of Idaho's more spectacular sights. The Word of God is like a river flowing through our lives. At first it may only be cutting through the surface of our heart. But if we stay in the Word and study it over and over again it will continue to cut deeper and deeper into our very core. Christ longs to dwell deep within us, in those hidden and hard-to-reach places. His living water will cut through all the sin, garbage and pain in our life into the very core of our being and dwell there. Let the Word of God flow in your life on a regular basis until it reaches the deep places of your soul and creates a spectacular witness for others to see. Do you read your Bible regularly and hear it speaking deep into the recesses of your heart?

"The word of God is living and active. Sharper than any double-edged sword, it penetrates even to dividing soul and spirit, joints and marrow; it judges the thoughts and attitudes of the heart."
Hebrews 4:12

"Deeper, deeper in the love of Jesus
Daily let me go;
Higher, higher in the school of wisdom,
More of grace to know."

Think of a passage in the Bible that revealed new insights you didn't see the first time you read it.

I grew up fishing. Our summers were filled with camping trips in the beautiful mountains of Idaho. My father taught us to fly fish at an early age and I loved wading the streams and rivers hoping to catch my limit. Fishing is a quiet sport with long periods of waiting between fish bites. But when you feel the tug of your line the sport is on as you try to hook and reel in your prize. The thrill of the sport is mixed with the serenity of beautiful, peaceful surroundings. Walking with the Lord has many similarities. Often the walk is quiet and undisturbed. But there is always that underlying anticipation that God may do something amazing or wonderful at any moment. After the thrill passes, life once again settles into a comfortable peacefulness—just my Savior and me enjoying the beautiful surroundings. When fishing I'm not put off by the periods of quiet; it's part of the sport. In my journey with the Lord I don't need to be anxious when nothing big is going on. Just because I can't see what's living beneath the water doesn't mean it isn't there. And quiet times don't mean God isn't living and moving in my life. I just need to keep my eyes on the line; one never knows when a fish might bite. Do you struggle when life is quiet and uneventful?

"The Lord is my shepherd,
I shall lack nothing.
He makes me lie down
in green pastures,
He leads me beside quiet waters,
He restores my soul."
Psalm 23:1 & 2

"I've found a Friend, oh, such a friend! So kind and true and tender,
So wise a Counselor and Guide, so mighty a Defender!
From Him who loves me now so well what pow'r my soul can sever?
Shall life or death, shall earth or hell? No! I am His forever."

Go fishing.

We just purchased a new young bull. Whenever a new cow, steer, heifer, or bull is introduced into the herd, a certain ritual occurs. The oldest cow or bull will bully the new member making sure its dominance is clear. The pecking order plays out as the one next in rank establishes its position and so on down through the herd. Over time the young animal will mature and rise in rank and position eventually becoming the leader, bringing new life into the herd. In order for our herd to be strong and healthy we bring in new genes to promote growth and diversity. Churches have this same need of diversity within their bodies and there is usually an unspoken pecking order. Older believers are often recognized for their knowledge and wisdom from years of learning through the school of hard knocks. Young, strong leaders are sought out and encouraged in their walk, mentored by the elders so they will mature and take their place of leadership. This passing of leadership from old to young needs to be unending to keep the church body healthy and vibrant. We should not be threatened by new blood coming into our church body. With encouragement they will find their place to serve and the church will be better for it. Are you a mentor or a mentee in your church?

"Don't let anyone look down
on you because you are young,
but set an example
for the believers in speech,
in life, in love, in faith,
and in purity . . .
Be diligent in these matters;
give yourself wholly to them,
so that everyone
may see your progress."
1 Timothy 4:12 & 15

"Oh, help me, dear Lord, to be ready
The task that Thou givest to do,
Not shrinking from labor or duty,
Devoted and faithful and true."

Recall someone who mentored you in your Christian walk
and thank God for them.

June 26

Read Hebrews chapter 12

"Endure hardship as discipline; God is treating you as sons.
For what son is not disciplined by his father?"
Hebrews 12:7

"Help me find my way, Lord, Help me find my way;
May I through each valley In Thy footsteps stay;
If 'twere but my choosing, I'd soon go astray;
Lest I faint or stumble, Help me find my way."

When my children were little they often needed help getting out of situations they got into. As their parent I was constantly giving them counsel, but sometimes they disregarded my instructions and had to try it their own way before they believed me. As they grew older I expected them to make better choices and let them suffer the consequences of poor ones when it would not harm them. God often deals with us in the same way. There is much He wants to teach us and He gives us the Bible as our instruction manual. But many times we have to try it our own way before we believe Him. Like children we call out to Him for help when we get in trouble hoping He'll rescue us.

Experience is the best teacher in life and living through our choices, feeling the pain, and consciously deciding we won't do that again is all part of the maturing process. He usually allows us to work our way out of these painful predicaments without interference knowing we need to learn the lesson so we're less likely to do it again. I always felt bad when my kids were suffering and I believe God doesn't like to see His children hurting either. But sometimes a little hurt now will prevent a lot more hurt in the future. Think of a time when you were in a painful situation and had to work your way through it. What did you learn from it?

Reflect back on lessons you have learned through the hard times.

> *"Tell me the story of Jesus,*
> *Write on my heart every word;*
> *Tell me the story most precious,*
> *Sweetest that ever was heard."*

Children learn by doing. When my kids were little I taught them to make their beds and fold laundry. At first the end product was not much better than the beginning but in time they were able to accomplish their tasks well. My granddaughters love to cook and their mother lets them work beside her in the kitchen. I'm sure it slows her down to have so many hands in the process, but they already show great potential at being good cooks one day. We learn by doing. Head knowledge is important but until we apply what we've learned it cannot be fully understood. We can read about God's love but not comprehend it. We can study books on meditation but never enter into a reflective time with God. We can know there's a Holy Spirit, but not understand until we experience Him ourselves. Our personal relationship with God starts just like a child learning something new. At first it's awkward and impersonal. But the more time we spend with Him the easier it gets to commune together. It's a learned process that grows deeper and richer the more we do it. If you're new at spending quiet time with God or working through a devotional or the Bible, don't give up because it's difficult or unfulfilling. Keep at it and eventually

you'll find yourself anticipating the time with Him having developed a very intimate and personal relationship. Remember you're His child and He wants you to sit at His feet and learn from Him. Are you comfortable being alone with God?

> *"Listen, my sons, to a Father's instruction;*
> *pay attention and gain understanding.*
> *I give you sound learning, so do not forsake*
> *my teaching. When I was a boy in my Father's*
> *house, still tender, and an only child*
> *of my mother, He taught me and said,*
> *'Lay hold of my words with all your heart;*
> *keep my commands and you will live.'"*
> Proverbs 4:1-4

Spend some time at the feet of your Master.

June 28
Read Psalm 9

On a recent plane trip I sat next to a man who was a fairly new Christian. Once he found out I knew the Lord he just bubbled with excitement about God. He shared how he couldn't get enough of church and wanted to be there day in and day out, just worshiping God and learning more about Him. His passion to share the saving Gospel message was foremost on his mind and he took classes and practiced how to share the Good News. He explained how every free minute he got he walked his neighborhood praying for, and with, those who lived around him. For over an hour it seemed he couldn't stop himself. The joy of the Lord was running like water out of him and splashing on me as I listened. As I contemplated his enthusiasm and love for the Lord I found myself questioning my own testimony. I love God deeply and want to see everyone come to know Him as I do. But my faith isn't flowing like a waterfall and splashing on all those around. No, I'm more like a quiet pool, deep and full of life, but from the surface it can appear that there isn't much going on. I think it's ok to be a

deep pool of faith, but I also think I need to make sure I have an outlet where water is spilling out of me and onto others. We can't all be waterfalls, but we need to make sure we're not the Dead Sea either. Have you ever met someone who loved the Lord so much they just bubbled over?

"I will praise you, O Lord, with all my heart; I will tell of all your wonders.
I will be glad and rejoice in you; I will sing praise to your name, O Most High."
Psalm 9:1–2

> *"We have heard the joyful sound: Jesus saves! Jesus saves!*
> *Spread the tidings all around: Jesus saves! Jesus saves!*
> *Bear the news to every land, Climb the mountains, cross the waves;*
> *Onward! 'tis our Lord's command; Jesus saves! Jesus saves!"*

Take some time this week and prayer-walk around your neighborhood.

When I mow the lawn I feed the grass clippings to our cows. When I start the mower they come running to the fence, eagerly awaiting their treat. It's comical watching them push and shove to be first in line. As soon as I dump a load of clippings they start eating and enjoying the delicate freshly-cut grass. The minute I dump another load, they run to the new pile. They run from pile to pile trying to be first and get the most. The clippings they leave behind are just as good as the ones they run to but telling a cow that is impossible. We humans often do the same thing. The old saying "the grass looks greener on the other side" is true for some people. We are satisfied until we look across the fence at what somebody else has and decide we have to have it. The reality is that what we leave behind is often just as good as what we chase after. We end up never feeling satisfied and leave worthwhile things behind in our haste. Before we chase after something new we need to evaluate our need and ask God what He wants us to have. We might already have all we need to be completely filled and satisfied in our life. Do you chase after what you don't have thinking it will make you happier?

"That every man may eat and drink,
and find satisfaction in all his toil—this is the gift of God."
Ecclesiastes 3:13

"Peace, peace, wonderful peace!
Flowing so deep in my soul;
Peace, peace, sweet peace,
How it maketh the sad heart whole."

Don't compare yourself with others
but be thankful for what God has given you.

"Crown Him, we'll crown Him,
Crown the blessed Savior Lord of all;
We'll crown Him, yes, crown Him,
Crown the blessed Savior Lord of all."

Most of us have heard the story of someone helping a butterfly emerge from the cocoon and how this well-intended gesture ended up destroying the butterfly. It is in the process of breaking out of the cocoon that the butterfly gains the strength to live. I like to think we resemble a caterpillar, wrapped up in a cocoon of earth, struggling to free ourselves from the bondage of the world and become the beautiful creation God has intended for us. Often we try to avoid difficult circumstances and challenges, looking for an easier way out. But God allows difficulties to come into our lives to shape and strengthen us. When we resist this process we become less than He has planned, stunted in our growth, and unable to soar on the wings He wishes to give us. Others can interfere in this process by trying to help us find relief from our pain, but often it is we who resist the process and run from every challenge we encounter. Nothing happens by random chance, but all things are allowed by God to pass from His hand into our lives for very specific purposes. God is the Creator and Ruler of all life, even ours, and we need to allow Him to accomplish His good and perfect will in our life. We will not be completely transformed until we reach the end of our days on earth and enter into life eternal. Do you embrace or run from challenges that come to you?

"The Lord has established
His throne in heaven,
and His kingdom
rules over all."
Psalm 103:19

Visit a butterfly exhibit and notice how intricate and different each one is.

> *"Safe in the arms of Jesus, Safe on His gentle breast;*
> *There by His love o'er shaded, Sweetly my soul shall rest."*

As a mother I tried to protect my children from harm when they were little. Don't touch that, don't go there, don't do that, move away from there, don't put that in your mouth, slow down; the list could go on and on. Sometimes my children would listen and respond immediately. Other times they would continue, all the while looking at me to see what I would do. Then there were the times they blatantly ignored me and went ahead with whatever they had set their mind upon. Many times they got hurt, physically or emotionally, when they chose to ignore my warnings. Hopefully, they were learning with each disobedient choice and growing in the process. God has given us the Bible and the Holy Spirit to guide, protect, and direct us in life. Usually it's just a quick awareness that God is speaking and I can choose how I will respond. Sometimes I behave childishly and continue down the path I am on, ignoring God. When I don't turn from my actions I always have consequences to deal with, some of them very unpleasant and painful. Hopefully I'm learning from my mistakes, growing in my walk with Him. Have you ever ignored the prodding of the Holy Spirit and gone your own way?

> *"I will instruct you and teach you in the way you should go;*
> *I will counsel you and watch over you."*
> Psalm 32:8

Reflect back on the last thing you know the Holy Spirit told you,
and recall how you responded.

July 2
Read Romans chapter 3

I have a drawer in my house that is filled with keys. They all fit a lock at sometime in my life. Now they are all jumbled together and I don't know which ones I need and which ones should be discarded. I'm hesitant to throw any away, for fear that sometime it might be the one I need. The Bible says there is just one key that gets us into heaven. That key is to ask Jesus into our heart, accept Him as our Lord and Savior, confess our sins and seek forgiveness. This opens the door to the pearly gates allowing us to spend eternity in heaven. There are some people who think there are other keys that work, but they've been misled. The only way to heaven is through the saving grace of Jesus Christ, not by works or anything else we may do. If you've been collecting a drawer full of keys, for heaven's sake it's time to clean house. There is only one way into heaven and a whole drawer full of keys will never open the door. Do you hold the key to heaven?

"This righteousness from God comes through faith in Jesus Christ to all who believe. There is no difference, for all have sinned and fall short of the glory of God, and are justified freely by His grace through the redemption that came by Christ Jesus."
Romans 3:22–24

"By the grace of God I am saved today,
I will walk by faith in the narrow way;
I will trust His grace to preserve my soul,
I will rest secure while the billows roll."

Give someone you know the key to eternal life.

"Live as free men, but do not use your freedom as a cover-up for evil;
live as servants of God. Show proper respect to everyone:
Love the brotherhood of believers, fear God, honor the king."
1 Peter 2:16 & 17

"Freedom from all the carnal affections,
Freedom from envy, hatred and strife;
Freedom from vain and worldly ambitions,
Freedom from all that saddened my life."

When our country was founded our forefathers wrote the Constitution of the United States to preserve our rights as a free nation. They based these principles on the Bible, using Christian beliefs as their cornerstone. Through time and neglect, these same principles have been corrupted and applied inappropriately. Freedom of speech, freedom to worship as we believe, and other principles have become so distorted that they no longer serve the purpose for which they were designed. Christians can use the free gift of salvation as a blank check to conduct their lives contrary to Biblical teachings. While we are no longer slaves to certain laws and regulations, we are told to live controlled lives, not in excess. Things which are good, such as food, can be carried to extremes and become harmful and unhealthy. We need to eat to live, but often we eat more than we need and, as a result, are not healthy. Living in excess, or abusing the very freedoms God has given us, can reduce our ability to serve and honor Him. Do you have any areas in your life you need to get under control?

Make a decision to listen to your body and only eat until you are full.

"These commandments that I give you today are to be upon your hearts.
Impress them on your children. Talk about them when you sit at home and
when you walk along the road, when you lie down and when you get up.
Tie them as symbols on your hands and bind them on your foreheads.
Write them on the doorframes of your houses and on your gates."
Deuteronomy 6:6–9

> *"He has sounded forth the trumpet that shall never call retreat;*
> *He is sifting out the hearts of men before His judgment seat;*
> *Oh, be swift, my soul, to answer Him; be jubilant, my feet!*
> *Our God is marching on."*

Seeing the American flag evokes deep emotions within me. I know that our freedom came at a great cost and many paid with their lives so I could live in a free country. I keep a flag on my front porch through the summer. It reminds me to pray for those serving in the military, protecting our freedom. Without the sacrifice of those who have gone before us our world would be greatly different. It is important to tell the story of our rich history to our children and grandchildren. They need to understand the cost of freedom and be grateful to those who fought for our country and for those who protect it now. Just like we share our heritage, we also need to share the story of Jesus' life on earth. He paid the ultimate price for us by giving His life so we could have eternal life, freeing us from the bondage of sin and death. Without His sacrifice, we would still be slaves to sin. The salvation story needs to be passed from one generation to another so they understand the great sacrifice given for them. Do you tell the story of Jesus to the young people in your life?

Call someone who is serving in the military and thank them.

My son and daughter-in-law have chosen to live close to us so their children can develop a close relationship with their grandparents. As their grandparents we must respect the parents' authority when they discipline one of the children and not interfere. If we were to console the child or make light of what they had done wrong, it would undermine the parents' efforts and the child would not learn from their mistake. God also disciplines us since we are His children. Often when someone is experiencing pain or a hardship we reach out to console and help them. Sometimes we may even relieve the situation by taking care of it for them. In reality we may be interfering in God's work. He may be disciplining them for poor choices they have made and wants them to experience discomfort so they can learn from it. He may be challenging them to grow, knowing their life could be so much more if they learned a valuable lesson. Interfering in the work of grace God is doing in another may hinder their spiritual growth. Let's seek God before we respond to cries of help and partner with Him to avoid interfering in what He has planned for someone's life. We should point them to the source of all hope, God, as we walk with them through a difficult time. Do you jump in to rescue someone in trouble or do you wait upon God's direction before you respond?

"My son, do not despise
the Lord's discipline
and do not resent His rebuke,
because the Lord disciplines
those He loves, as a father
the son He delights in."
Proverbs 3:11 & 12

"As you journey day by day with Jesus,
You will meet with problems hard to face;
If you're stuck, just ask your Friend to help you,
He will give you problem-solving grace."

Share some time with a special young one in your life.

July 6
Read Isaiah chapter 35

> "*Hallelujah! shout the chorus,*
> *Onward, upward is our song;*
> *Crowns of vict'ry lie before us,*
> *Boldly march against the wrong.*"

An airplane cannot take off if it is just sitting still. No matter how strong the wind blows, unless the plane moves down the runway, the wind will never pick it up and put it into flight. I think the same principle applies to life's challenges and opportunities. We can pray all we want and say we have faith, but if we want to take off and soar we must head into the difficulty we face, catch the wind, and rise above it. Every challenge is an opportunity to let God take us to new heights, but we have to be ready and willing to move. We can't stay hunkered down in fear and expect Him to drag us onto the runway. No, He wants our faith to be strong enough that we run out to meet Him. It's our steps of faith that unleash the power of God, and before we know it we're soaring above our problems. Don't be afraid to climb to new heights, just buckle yourself in and get ready for the ride of a lifetime. Are you afraid to taxi out to the runway of life?

"*Strengthen the feeble hands, steady the knees that give way;*
say to those with fearful hearts, 'Be strong, do not fear; your God will come,
He will come with vengeance; with divine retribution He will come to save you.'"
Isaiah 35:3 & 4

Spend an evening watching how effortlessly the birds fly
and envision yourself soaring on God's strength.

> *"Though hosts of sin should about us camp,*
> *We'll shout and sing the victor's song;*
> *For Christ, our Savior, within us dwells,*
> *To save and keep us from the wrong."*

Purple Loosestrife is a noxious weed that takes over wetlands and marshes. It spreads quickly with a single plant producing over 2.5 million tiny seeds per year. If left alone it eventually eliminates all native plant growth and dries the water flow. It was introduced from England because of its beauty. It can grow up to eight feet tall and its long purple stems are a masterpiece for those unaware of its destructiveness. The first year we moved to our new land the draw where our stream ran was filled with this weed and I remember thinking how beautiful it was. I later learned how destructive it is and we have taken steps to eliminate it. Sin often comes into our life in the same manner. It's almost always attractive at first, disguised as something beautiful and inviting. If it were ugly and dangerous-looking it would be easy to detect and run from. But we're usually drawn to it at first. It's only after it starts to take over that we realize it will cause death and destruction, if not eliminated. Because it is so hard to distinguish bad from good in its infancy we need to rely on God for wisdom and discernment before we let anything new take root in our life. Have you ever started something in innocence only to realize later it was not a good thing?

"But each one is tempted when, by his own evil desire he is dragged away and enticed.
Then, after desire has conceived, it gives birth to sin;
and sin, when it is full-grown, gives birth to death."
James 1:14 & 15

Research the noxious weeds in your community.

July 8
Read 1 Corinthians chapter 9

*I*f we want to become good at something we are going to have to train for it. When my children were young, they participated in sports and they had to practice off the field, so they would get to play during a game. How well they did in sports was directly related to how hard they worked at it. Practicing was never as much fun as playing the game, but necessary if they wanted to improve and be a valuable player on the team. Being a servant for the Lord and one of His Kingdom workers requires us to train, just like an athlete. We're going to have to make it a priority in our life, sacrifice and give up some of the other things we like to do, if we want to play in the big league for God. Being a part of the Lord's team will require us to personally know the coach—God, to know the rules in the handbook—the Bible, and to be fit for the challenge, which will take dedication and commitment. We have to be willing to go into strict training, laying aside everything that is a distraction, and keep our focus on the prize at all times. Not everyone will get to play in the big game, only those who have been willing to make it a priority and sacrifice for it. Do you have the desire to be part of the Lord's Kingdom team and are you preparing for it?

*"Everyone who competes in the games
goes into strict training.
They do it to get a crown
that will not last;
but we do it to get a crown
that will last forever."*
1 Corinthians 9:25

*"Crown Him the Lord of life! Who triumphed o'er the grave,
Who rose victorious to the strife for those He came to save.
His glories now we sing, who died, and rose on high,
Who died eternal life to bring, and lives that death may die."*

Commit to practicing a new skill on a regular basis.

*"Joyful, joyful, we adore Thee, God of glory, Lord of love;
Hearts unfold like flow'rs before Thee, op'ning to the sun above.
Melt the clouds of sin and sadness; drive the dark of doubt away;
Giver of immortal gladness, fill us with the light of day!"*

I stayed home one day burdened and heavy laden. I needed to sit before the Lord and see if I could figure out what was wrong. As I studied and prayed I felt the Lord show me I had lost my joy, which made everything seem huge and difficult. As I closed my eyes I could almost hear Him say, "Lois, come outside and frolic with me. Smell the flowers I have grown for you. Hear the birds I've filled with music. Run with me in the wind; just let it all go." I was even given the image of running into His arms and Him twirling me around while laughter filled the air. I did go outside that afternoon. I laid in the grass and felt the warmth of the sun. I smelled the flowers and listened to the birds. And then I started to run, wind blowing through my hair, and laughter bubbled up inside me. I found myself twirling around and around and laughing. The darkness I had felt was gone replaced with an afternoon of frolicking with my Lord and Savior. In Nehemiah 8:10 we are told "the joy of the Lord is our strength". Life can overwhelm us when it is absent. I've never forgotten that afternoon and the child-like delight I felt. Have you ever let go and frolicked with God as if you truly were His child?

*"I tell you the truth, anyone who will not receive the kingdom of God
like a little child will never enter it."*
Luke 18:17

Go outside and frolic with God today.

July 10
Read 1 Thessalonians chapter 5

We live on a farm and have farm cats, which means they run free, catch mice for dinner and don't come in the house. When the kittens are born it's important to catch and keep them in the garage so they get used to us or they'll be wild when they become adult cats. Keeping them in the garage is only part of it, we also have to hold them, cuddle them and stroke them so they get used to our touch. The more attention we give them as kittens, the tamer they will be once they live outside. If we neglect developing a relationship with them, when they become cats they will stray. Babies need attention too if they are to grow up into healthy, adjusted adults. Infants and children who are neglected have difficulty forming relationships when they grow older. The human touch is extremely important in their development, and when absent during childhood causes life-long problems. God created us as relational beings who have an inherent desire to be loved and to love. We were not made to live isolated and alone with no other human contact. Let's reach out to one another, extending our hand in love and friendship, for that's how God made us. Do you know someone who seems to be going astray? Can you extend your hand in friendship to them?

"Therefore encourage one another and build each other up,
just as in fact you are doing."
1 Thessalonians 5:11

"Rescue the perishing, care for the dying,
Snatch them in pity from sin and the grave;
Weep o'er the erring one, lift up the fallen,
Tell them of Jesus, the mighty to save."

If you have a pet give them a special hug thanking them for all they teach us.

The old saying, "sweep it under the rug," is a good visual for what happens when we hide or ignore a problem or conflict we feel. The more we sweep under the rug the bigger the bulge grows and eventually somebody trips, falls and gets hurt. I don't think anyone likes confrontation but letting things fester inside us can literally infect our whole body, physically and emotionally. Twice in my life, people became upset over something I said or did and didn't come to me. Instead they swept it under the rug hiding the wrong they felt. The initial hurt could have been easily corrected but as their emotions grew so did the problem. Although I could sense things weren't right, when I asked them they would respond everything was fine. Both times, when it finally boiled over, their emotions had escalated to a point where nothing could repair the damage and the relationship was lost. Because confronting is hard we either tend to talk to everyone but the person we're upset with or we don't tell anyone. The issue consumes our thoughts until it grows beyond reason. While sitting down to talk face to face may be uncomfortable it might salvage the relationship. I believe whenever something is bothering us and it's not going away, we need to "shine the light on it" so the enemy loses his ability to work in the dark. In other words, get it out in the open so it can be addressed before it grows out of control. Satan likes to cause factions and divisions and when something's hidden, it gives him control. Is there anything in your life relating to someone else you need to shine the light on?

"Hatred stirs up dissension, but love covers over all wrongs."
Proverbs 10:12

Contact or send a note to someone who could use an encouraging word.

July 12
Read Isaiah chapter 50

"But now, all you who light fires and provide yourselves with flaming torches,
go, walk in the light of your fires and of the torches you have set ablaze.
This is what you shall receive from my hand; You will lie down in torment."
Isaiah 50:11

"Have Thine own way, Lord!
Have Thine own way! Search me and try me, Master, today!
Whiter than snow, Lord, wash me just now,
As in Thy presence humbly I bow."

If we pick a rosebud before it blooms and try to force the petals open we will ruin the rose. It will not bloom and all the beauty that lies waiting to unfold will be destroyed. The same thing happens when we run from a difficult time in our life before God has opened the door. When we find ourselves in a dark time our natural tendency is to escape into the light. But God often puts us in a dark place to mold and grow us into a thing of beauty. Depending on the lesson being taught we can be left there for a while and begin to feel abandoned. I have learned it is extremely important not to circumvent the training by lighting my own candle. I have done this in the past and it has always brought disaster on me. Because the lesson was unlearned, I would soon be forced back into the darkness to try again. I now pray during those difficult times that I will learn whatever He is teaching me and to wait for Him. This was not an easy lesson. It took many times of facing the same trial before I realized that I was not embracing the situation, but enduring it, and thus not learning from it. I now thank God for what I will learn and pray for Him to create something beautiful out of my life. Have you ever tried to escape a difficulty and found yourself back there again because the lesson was unlearned?

Think of a difficult time and what you learned going through it.

I met a friend for lunch and could see there was something different about her. Her face glowed, her skin was vibrant, everything about her seemed full of life. It didn't take long to confirm my suspicions—she was in love. I was overjoyed that this widow had found a new love after the years of illness and hardship before her husband passed on. After sharing excitedly about him I could see she was also trying to share other things. But he was on her mind and heart and it was hard to talk of anything else. Have you ever met someone so in love with Jesus that it shows on their face, in their posture, and in everything about them? They seem to include His name in almost every sentence. They are so aware of His presence it's almost impossible to talk of anything else. I want my love relationship with God to get to that level. I want to glow with His love; I want my complexion and demeanor to reflect Him. I want to be filled with an excitement and joy for life that only He can give me. I want people to see the difference in me and know I'm in love—a love affair with God so He's all I can think and talk about. Are you in love with God?

"Jesus replied: 'Love the Lord your God with all your heart and with all your soul and with all your mind.' This is the first and greatest commandment."
Matthew 22:37 & 38

"Oh, how I love Jesus,
Oh, how I love Jesus,
Oh, how I love Jesus,
Because He first loved me!"

Write a love letter to God.

> *"There's a land that is fairer than day,*
> *And by faith we can see it afar;*
> *For the Father waits over the way*
> *To prepare us a dwelling place there."*

Whenever something major is happening in my life I find myself imagining what it will be like once it is accomplished. When we built our home we moved into a small camp trailer to live for twelve months until it was completed. It was parked on our land so each day I would go to the new home and imagine how it would look and what it would be like to live there. I can remember so clearly sitting on the staircase looking down into the living and dining area, daydreaming about that day. As I started this book, I listed all 366 days by month and started writing randomly through the year, marking off each day as I completed it. I remember as I completed the first 31 days seeing the other 335 unmarked days and wondering how it would feel when I had finished the last few. I'm almost there now and it's quite surreal as I realize this part of the journey is almost complete. Trying to imagine what living with God in eternity will be like falls into the same category. We are given small glimpses of what heaven will be like, but we can't really capture it with our earthly imaginations. Trying to picture living in my new home or experiencing the emotions of a completed book pale next to living the experience. Most of us have our own perception of heaven but only when we pass from this life to our eternal life will we really know what it is. Have you given any thought to what heaven might be like?

> *"There are also heavenly bodies and there are earthly bodies;*
> *but the splendor of the heavenly bodies is one kind, and the splendor of*
> *the earthly bodies is another . . . And just as we have borne the likeness*
> *of the earthly man, so shall we bear the likeness of the man from heaven."*
> *1 Corinthians 15:40 & 49*

Jesus has prepared a place for you in heaven. Are you ready?

"The sun will no more be your light by day,
nor will the brightness of the moon shine on you,
for the Lord will be your everlasting light,
and your God will be your glory."
Isaiah 60:19

"He abides, He abides; Hallelujah, He abides with me!
I'm rejoicing night and day—As I walk the narrow way,
For the Comforter abides with me."

The sunlight seems more dramatic and eye-catching when it is filtered through something. The contrasting shadows add depth and dimension, catching our eye and taking our breath away. Our lives can be like that also. We would lack character if we didn't have the shadows and darker moments to contrast with the light and easy times. God did not create us to be one-dimensional. We are multi-faceted and complex, a mixture of sunshine and shade. I'm drawn to people who aren't afraid to talk about the many facets of their lives. I find I don't relate as well to those who portray themselves as being without struggles, uncertainty or challenges in life. Sharing honestly with another is like inviting them to go on a walk through a beautiful forest. The path, though woven with sunlight and shadows, refreshes and renews us we share how Jesus has carried us. When was the last time you were transparent with someone you could trust about your struggles and your joys?

Invite someone you trust for a cup of tea and share some good conversation.

July 16

Read 1 Corinthians chapter 6

"Everything is permissible for me—but not everything is beneficial. Everything is permissible for me—but I will not be mastered by anything. Food for the stomach and the stomach for food—but God will destroy them both. The body is not meant for sexual immorality, but for the Lord and the Lord for the body."
1 Corinthians 6:12 & 13

"Moment by moment I'm kept in His love;
Moment by moment I've life from above;
Looking to Jesus till glory doth shine;
Moment by moment, O Lord, I am Thine."

God gave us five senses for enjoyment of His creation. Imagine how dull and drab our world would be if we could not see, hear, taste, feel or smell. Just losing one of these drastically changes our perception. Today's culture exploits personal pleasure and satisfaction and people do almost anything to stimulate their senses. Most sins involve indulging in some sensual act that entices us. Once we have whet our appetite for something pleasurable we find ourselves drawn to it more and more. Over-indulgence results from trying to find satisfaction and happiness in something that gives temporary enjoyment, but is incapable of providing lasting fulfillment. We have to make choices about how much and how often we indulge in sensual pleasures. Overeating, substance abuse, visual stimulation, sexually-explicit conversations and touching for pleasure are all ways we stimulate our senses and can draw us into sin. Satan takes what God created for good and entices us to use it for our destruction. Lasting satisfaction and fulfillment can only be found in God. Each of us needs to choose eternal values over temporary satisfaction and not abuse what God has given us. Are you exploiting one of your senses by over-indulging in some way?

Go for a walk and engage all your senses as you enjoy God's creation.

PS tracking systems are quickly replacing the need for maps as more and more people are using these handy devices to guide them where they want to go. Just put in your starting and destination addresses and it will verbally guide you there. It tells you which lane to be in, when you're going to turn, when you need to take an exit or get on a new road. If you get lost or make a wrong turn, it redirects you back to the right track. We need direction in our lives also and God has given us a heavenly tracking system if we'll just use it. The Holy Spirit and the Word of God, our Bible, will give us direction for anywhere we want to go in life. But just like a GPS tracking system, if you don't know where you want to go or put in an incorrect address you'll spend your time wandering aimlessly, lost and confused. If we want to live Christian lives and spend eternity with Jesus Christ, we need to pay attention to what the Bible and Holy Spirit are telling us and go the straight and narrow way. How much do you rely on the Bible to guide you through life?

"How can a young man keep his way pure?
By living according to your word."
Psalm 119:9

"I have decided to follow Jesus;
I have decided to follow Jesus;
I have decided to follow Jesus;
No turning back, no turning back."

Follow a path in your neighborhood and see where it leads you.

We cannot earn our salvation; it is a gift from God. Ephesians 2:8 states, "for it is by grace you have been saved, through faith—and this not from yourselves, it is the gift of God—not by works, so that no one can boast." But we are also told to work out our salvation, so what does that mean? When I exercise I work out to get in shape. It takes commitment and regular attendance to see any progress. I have to keep pushing myself, challenging my body beyond its comfort level. The progress is up to me and the results are directly proportional to my effort. Accepting Christ as our Savior is the start of our Christian journey, not the end. We are told to work out our salvation like we would an exercise program. We must be committed, study regularly and stretch ourselves beyond our comfort zone. If we don't work out our faith it will be weak, powerless and stunted. The faith God can use is strong, vibrant and healthy. Working out our salvation will not come easily or naturally. But as we consider standing before our Lord and Savior one day it should motivate us to reach our full potential. Accepting the gift means spending the rest of our lives on the exercise mat using the Bible as our work-out manual. How are you progressing at "working out" your salvation?

"Therefore, my dear friends, as you have always obeyed—not only in my presence, but now much more in my absence— continue to work out your salvation with fear and trembling, for it is God who works in you to will and to act according to His good purpose."
Philippians 2:12 & 13

"By the grace of God I will live for Him, will trust His power to keep from sin; I will never doubt, but resist the foe, I will grow in grace as I onward go."

Establish a daily work-out routine that will grow your faith.

"Jesus calls us o'er the tumult
Of our life's wild, restless, sea;
Day by day His sweet voice soundeth,
Saying, "Christian, follow Me!"

There are stories throughout the Bible of people who answered immediately when God called. In Genesis 17 we read that Abraham responded the same day God gave him specific instructions. In Matthew 4 we read that Jesus called to Peter and Andrew while they were fishing to follow Him, and they immediately left their nets and went. As I reflect on these stories a couple of points come to mind. First, they had to believe in God and know Him personally to recognize His call. Without a daily relationship with God we are apt to miss the opportunity when it comes. If our quiet times with Him are not consistent it will be too late to do what he wanted done on Tuesday when we don't check in with Him until Friday. Secondly, because they didn't hesitate, God was able to use them mightily in His work. Delayed obedience is better than disobedience but not as good as instant obedience. When God calls us to be about His work His timing is perfect. We need to know and trust Him enough that we don't question why or how, but respond believing that if He has called He will also make a way. How do you respond when you feel Him nudging your heart?

"They were casting a net into the lake, for they were fishermen.
'Come, follow me,' Jesus said, 'and I will make you fishers of men.'
At once they left their nets and followed Him."
Matthew 4:18–20

Commit to a daily quiet time with God.

July 20
Read Romans chapter 1

*T*he trees in the Redwood Forest are huge. I remember going there as a young child and Dad driving our car through one of the trunks. A friend recently shared with me an interesting and eye-opening fact about the redwood trees. Their roots do not go deep into the ground as one might think. No, their roots spread outward, intertwining with the neighboring trees' roots. It is because of this intertwining of roots that they are able to grow so tall and not fall over. Like the trees, we are so much stronger when we are joined together with other believers. We can reach across all sorts of divides and difficulties and help each other withstand life's storms as they rage around us. God is a relational God and He did not create us to live alone. He created us to have a relationship with Him and, from that, learn to have relationships with each other. Do you have a support system around you that helps you stand in the stormy times?

"I long to see you so that I may impart to you some spiritual gift to make you strong — that is, that you and I may be mutually encouraged by each other's faith."
Romans 1:11 & 12

"Help somebody today,
Somebody along life's way;
Let sorrow be ended, the friendless befriended,
Oh, help somebody today!"

Call someone who is struggling
and offer them a word of encouragement today.

> "We have heard the joyful sound: Jesus saves! Jesus saves!
> Spread the tidings all around: Jesus saves! Jesus saves!
> Bear the news to every land, climb the mountains, cross the waves;
> Onward! 'tis our Lord's command; Jesus saves! Jesus saves!"

Those who have experienced forgiveness, healing and Christ's love are called to tell others who have not heard or do not understand. When the grandkids are out irrigating with us, we don't jump across the ditch and leave them behind because they don't know how to cross. We reach out and help them to the other side. Once we have experienced Christ's amazing love and healing grace we need to watch for those still looking for the way. Ours is not to judge or criticize their present status, but to instruct them as we have been instructed by others. The love and forgiveness you received was freely given not earned. Do the same for others, giving freely and abundantly. The well you draw from will not run dry. We should not live satisfied that we have crossed over to the promise of eternal life. Our hearts should be burdened for those left behind. Jesus wants all to hear the saving message and He needs us to stand with our hands reaching out. They may not see or take our offered hand of hope; the decision is not in our control. But each of us must do what we can to reach those who've yet to hear. Does your heart break for the unsaved?

"I tell you the truth, whoever hears my word and believes Him who sent Me has eternal life and will not be condemned; he has crossed over from death to life."
John 5:24

Think of someone who doesn't know Christ
and pray for an opportunity to share with them.

"Woe to you, teachers of the law and Pharisees, you hypocrites!
You give a tenth of your spices—mint, dill and cumin. But you have neglected
the more important matters of the law—justice, mercy and faithfulness.
You should have practiced the latter, without neglecting the former."
Matthew 23:23

"Give of your best to the Master; naught else is worthy His love;
He gave Himself for your ransom, gave up His glory above.
Laid down His life without murmur, you from sin's ruin to save;
Give Him your heart's adoration; give Him the best that you have."

Gifts given for the wrong reasons can be insulting and hurtful. I'll never forget receiving a bouquet of flowers from my former husband while I suspected his involvement in another relationship outside our marriage. It felt more like a slap in the face as he tried to appease me with them and I threw the flowers away, hurt by a display of affection that was false. Jesus spoke harshly to the Pharisees who made an outward show by giving of their tithe but withheld their affection and love from Him. He chastised them saying they should practice the latter without neglecting the former. God is not interested in a gift given from obligation rather than love. The size of the gift is not as important as the condition of the heart. We can give out of our abundance and yet not give from our heart. When we give out of our poverty it becomes a decision of the heart more than the head. A handful of flowers picked by a child and given to mommy out of love has much more value than a beautiful, expensive bouquet sent to appease a relationship that's far from the heart. God knows if our gift is motivated by guilt, pride or love. He knows whether we have sacrificed to give out of our poverty or have handed Him some leftovers from our abundance. A gift given begrudgingly to God does not please Him and in fact causes Him pain. Let us search our hearts and discern what motivates us to give. Is it out of obligation or love?

Don't just give of your leftovers but give what you value and let God bless you.

Have you ever been so thirsty that even the thought of a drink of water made your mouth salivate? I have, especially when I'm working outside in the heat or going on a long walk. I find myself anticipating how good the water will taste; how it will feel going down my throat; how it will quench my intense thirst. When I finally get a drink, it is every bit as good as I imagined it would be. I drink until I have replenished my parched body. We are told to drink often and much to keep our body hydrated and to wash away impurities within us. As I mature in my Christian walk I have recognized that same thirst deep within my soul. The desire to retreat with God and replenish my dry spirit with His living water begins to consume my thoughts. I think about how good it is going to feel and find myself hurrying to complete my task so I can get away with Him. When I do, I love to linger in the richness of His presence, letting Him quench my inner thirst and replenish my dry and depleted spirit. We need to drink deeply from the well of living water to keep us spiritually healthy and cleansed of all impurities in our soul. Do you desire to drink from the well of living water?

"As the deer pants for streams of water,
So my soul pants for you, O God.
My soul thirsts for God, for the living God."
Psalm 42:1 & 2

"My soul today is thirsting for living streams divine,
To sweep from highest heaven to this poor heart of mine;
I stand upon the promise, in Jesus's name I plead;
Oh, send the gracious current to satisfy my need."

Prepare your favorite refreshing drink and take a moment with God.

> *"Fairest Lord Jesus, Ruler of all nature,*
> *O Thou of God and man the Son,*
> *Thee will I cherish, Thee will I honor,*
> *Thou, my soul's glory, joy and crown."*

Caring for a farm involves more than just taking care of the land. We also have to care for our equipment. Before my husband goes to cut or bale hay he spends considerable time checking the piece of equipment he will use, greasing it and making sure everything is in top condition. If anything is loose or bent he fixes it before starting. If he doesn't invest the time up front it won't be long before the equipment wears out or malfunctions and puts a halt to the harvest. We need to give the same attention to ourselves before we go to work every day. Time spent seeing if anything is broken or bent will keep us from falling apart during the day. Prayer and reading God's Word is similar to giving ourselves a good grease job. Once we are lubricated with the Holy Spirit we'll be able to work without undue friction or stress. We might feel we don't have time in our morning to check on things and fill up. But if we continually start our day without these morning lube jobs we'll eventually break and the work we were so intent on comes to a halt. If you've been making unpleasant noises and putting out sub-standard work you've probably been neglecting your prep time. Time with God each morning is the best way to stay in tip-top shape and out of the repair shop. Are you preparing yourself before you head into your day?

"Blessed are all who fear the Lord, who walk in His ways. You will eat the fruit of your labor; blessings and prosperity will be yours."
Psalm 128:1 & 2

Fill up with God so He can spill out on others through you.

We have a few cows whose curved horns form an enclosed "C" on the sides of their faces. One of these cows had gotten a 40-foot length of irrigation pipe stuck through the horn and was dragging it around the field. We think she had been eating around the pipe, and it slipped through the horn. It slid forward until the end, with the sprinkler head lodged against her face. I noticed her dilemma, but when I tried to approach her she backed away, dragging the pipe. My husband, whom the cows trust, was able to walk up to her and pull the pipe through the horn, setting her free. We can also get into a situation that traps us. We resemble the cow, dragging a huge impediment around with us because under our own power we're unable to get free of it. Others may try to help us, but if we don't know or trust them we might retreat in fear and make our problem worse. God is trustworthy and we need to run to Him with all our burdens and predicaments. He can help free us from unwanted baggage and bring us into the fullness of life He promised. Are you stuck in an impossible situation hauling unnecessary baggage around, and have you called out to God to free you?

"Humble yourselves, therefore, under God's mighty hand, that He may lift you up in due time. Cast all your anxiety on Him because He cares for you."
1 Peter 5:6 & 7

"Would you be free from the burden of sin?
There's pow'r in the blood, pow'r in the blood;
Would you o'er evil a victory win?
There's wonderful pow'r in the blood."

Carry something around today to remind yourself how it feels
to be burdened with unnecessary baggage.

July 26
Read John chapter 15

> "What a friend we have in Jesus, all our sins and griefs to bear!
> What a privilege to carry everything to God in prayer!
> Oh, what peace we often forfeit, Oh, what needless pain we bear,
> All because we do not carry everything to God in prayer!"

I have had a lot of close acquaintances in my life but few are close and personal friends. Being a friend to someone requires an investment of time. If I want the friendship to grow I have to make them a priority, communicating with them regularly and finding time for them. I have met many people who might have become close friends to me but I did not invest the time and energy required. I have to be selective in how many people I choose to develop a deep friendship with or I will end up neglecting some friends due to lack of time and over-commitment. Jesus has called us His friend. He desires us to enter into a close and personal relationship with Him. He will be there whenever we call. It is up to us to make the decision if He is going to become a personal friend of ours. If this is what we want we have to commit to regular time and communication with Him. We have to make Him a priority for our relationship to grow. Being Jesus' friend is available to all of us—the choice is ours. Would you say Jesus is a close and personal friend of yours?

> "I no longer call you servants, because a servant does not know
> His master's business. Instead, I have called you friends, for everything
> that I learned from my Father I have made known to you."
> John 15:15

Call a friend and tell them how much you appreciate their gift of friendship.

> *"And He walks with me, and He talks with me,*
> *And He tells me I am His own;*
> *And the joy we share as we tarry there,*
> *None other has ever known."*

My husband and I had the privilege of spending a week in a remote and private ranch located in the wilderness area of Idaho. I didn't know what to expect yet looked forward to having some down time with my husband and God. It turned out to be one of the most wonderful weeks of my life. The peacefulness and tranquility of God's beauty and His wildlife were refreshing. A blessing I hadn't expected was being freed from making decisions. For five days there were no choices: what to eat—meals were prepared for you; where to go—anywhere your feet took you; outside communication—limited except for emergencies; what to wear—one small bag for everything. Nothing interfered with our days because there was no one else around. For the first time in my life I got a taste of the simple life and I liked it. Making decisions, little or big, can be draining. Our days are filled with what to wear, what to eat, where to go, who needs to talk to us, who we need to talk to—the list is endless. Simplicity is hard to find in modern America. Occasionally we need to make the decision to leave the rush of life

and go to some place restful and removed from all commotion. There in the quietness we can reflect on the true meaning of life and get back to the basics—loving God and being family. Everything else just clutters up our minds. Have you ever retreated to a remote place for some down time?

> *"The Lord your God is with you,*
> *He is mighty to save.*
> *He will take great delight in you,*
> *He will quiet you with His love,*
> *He will rejoice over you with singing."*
> *Zephaniah 3:17*

Plan a retreat with just you and God.

July 28
Read Psalm 145

"Come, Thou Fount of every blessing, Tune my heart to sing Thy grace;
Streams of mercy, never ceasing, Call for songs of loudest praise.
Teach me some melodious sonnet, Sung by flaming tongues above;
Praise the mount! I'm fixed upon it, Mount of Thy redeeming love."

When we take our grandchildren camping, they love to go exploring by themselves. They find it so exciting to head down a forest path and see where it leads. They always have to ask permission and then off they go but an adult is right behind them. We would never let them venture out on their own—we follow to make sure they don't need our help or get lost. We want them to gain confidence and not be afraid to go new places and see new things, but we also want to make sure they are safe. They know we're right behind them and this gives them the courage to go down a new path to see where it leads. It's so fun to have them call to us, telling us what they're seeing and sharing their journey with us. God wants us to explore His world and all the beautiful things He has prepared for us. He doesn't want us to cower, never leaving the known for fear of the unknown, yet we don't go alone either. He's always with us, never letting us out of His sight, but encourages us to run ahead and see what delight He has just around the corner. He wants us to call to Him, sharing all we experience, including Him in our journey. It brings me joy to share my grandchildren's journey and God is delighted when we share our journey with Him. He created all things for our enjoyment and He likes to hear our giggles of delight as we explore His world. How long has it been since you've gone exploring with child-like eyes?

"Great is the Lord
and most worthy of praise;
His greatness no one can fathom.
One generation will commend
your works to another;
they will tell of your mighty acts.
They will speak of the glorious
splendor of your majesty,
and I will meditate
on your wonderful works."
Psalm 145:3–5

Go for a walk and include God in your journey.

We all fight temptation and sin in our life. What entices me may be different from what you feel drawn to. Pornography, an unhealthy sexual appetite, over-indulging, gossiping, lying, deception, stealing, manipulating others, controlling attitudes, pride, addictions, substance abuse, a critical spirit—these are just a few of the sins we can be drawn into. We need to know our weaknesses because Satan attacks where we are most vulnerable. Once you've identified your weak areas find a plan of attack for resisting them. We cannot allow ourselves to be caught off guard in areas where we struggle to say no. Find an accountability partner you can talk to when you're facing temptation. Devise an escape plan and use it whenever you feel drawn to commit sin. Go to the Lord the instant your mind entertains a sinful thought, confess it and ask for strength to resist the temptation. Memorize Scriptures relative to your weakness reciting them as your sword of defense. Don't be caught unaware and unprepared. In our strength we may fail but in His strength we can be victorious. What sins are you drawn to and struggle to resist?

"For we do not have a high priest who is unable to sympathize with our weaknesses, but we have one who has been tempted in every way, just as we are— yet was without sin."
Hebrews 4:15

"There's power in the blood to save from sin,
To bring the peace of God where guilt hath been;
A new and happy life will then begin,
There's power in the blood of Jesus."

Find an accountability partner to help you in an area of weakness.

Have you ever had someone say to you or found yourself saying, "I wish I could do more, but I will pray for you"? Or have you said you would pray for someone and then forgotten to? Why does it seem that prayer is a second-rate answer, not the most important thing we can do? Often prayer is a last-ditch effort after we've fervently tried to fix things on our own and failed. And even those prayers may ask God to bless what we've been trying to do rather than placing it in His hands. The Bible tells us to pray unceasingly and to pray with a believing heart. Prayer should be the first thing we do. How we pray is also important. We shouldn't tell God what to do but seek His will for our life. When we pray we must be willing to leave it with Him, waiting for His answer and prepare our hearts to receive it. We may offer a prayer about something but are in such a hurry to solve it that we run right past God's answer as we set out to fix things. It's hard to leave it with Him when I feel an urgency about a problem, but that's what faith is about—trusting God. Now, when I say I will pray for someone, I ask if I can pray while they are with me. And after I have prayed, I ask them what else I can do to help. In a difficult time do you pray or act first?

"And pray in the Spirit on all occasions with all kinds of prayers and requests.
With this in mind, be alert and always keep on praying for all the saints."
Ephesians 6:18

"Sweet hour of prayer! Sweet hour of prayer! That calls me from a world of care,
And bids me at my Father's throne make all my wants and wishes known.
In seasons of distress and grief, my soul has often found relief,
And oft escaped the tempter's snare, by thy return, sweet hour of prayer!"

Decide that if you say you will pray for someone, you will do it.

> "The vict'ry is mine, the vict'ry is mine;
> I never shall fear, while Jesus is near;
> He's with me alway, by night and by day;
> His comforting Word, my bosom doth cheer."

*D*rifting down river is much easier than trying to go upstream against the current. Most of the world is drifting downstream surrounded by others and enjoying the ride. What they don't realize is that underneath the seemingly calm water is danger. Strong, swift currents are pulling them in directions they'll not be able to escape from and perilous cliffs await them if they don't turn around. Their destiny is death yet they float along oblivious to what lies ahead. Those who want to follow Christ find themselves straining at the oars, fighting the current as they row upstream. It's difficult and lonely, and they can't let their paddles down for even a moment, or they'll find themselves gliding backward, pulled by the undertow. That's why the Bible says few will get to Heaven—it's not the easy choice. Most of God's commandments go against the current—love your enemies, give with no expectation of getting anything in return, be a servant to others, put others' needs before your own, die to self—things that don't come easily. But the one thing we have going for us is the passenger who rides in our boat. Jesus has promised to be with us always and when we are weak He'll be our strength. So when life seems difficult, just remember there's a pair of scarred hands holding onto the oars with you,

helping you each stroke of the way. As long as you keep Jesus in your boat you'll make the journey. Have you ever felt like you were rowing against the current and hardly getting anywhere?

"The flood would have engulfed us, the torrent would have swept over us, the raging waters would have swept us away."
Psalm 124:4 & 5

Think of something you are struggling with
and imagine Jesus is beside you helping you.

When we were teaching one of our granddaughters how to ride a bike, she became afraid after a bad spill and wanted to quit. We kept trying to encourage her to try again, but each time we would let her go, she would cry out loud, "I can't, I can't, I'm going to fall." And, without any self-confidence she always did fall, reinforcing her belief that it was impossible. I decided to reverse the tactic and reminded her of the story about the little blue train that repeated, "I think I can, I think I can" all the way up the hill until it reached the boys and girls. I suggested she repeat it over and over as she tried it again and I would say it with her. She agreed and off she wobbled as we started to chant, "I think I can, I think I can." It wasn't long before I couldn't keep up with her as she sailed around the road, smiling broadly at her achievement. Too often we talk ourselves out of something, repeating negative thoughts in our mind. We need to remind ourselves that Jesus is running beside us whispering, "I know you can, I know you can" each step along our path. Have you given up on a challenge you faced recently?

"Forgetting what is behind and straining toward what is ahead, I press on toward the goal to win the prize for which God has called me heavenward in Christ Jesus."
Philippians 3:13 & 14

"Oh, when the saints go marching in, Oh, when the saints go marching in; Lord, I want to be in that number, When the saints go marching in."

For those impossible tasks try repeating, "I can do all things through Christ who gives me strength." —Philippians 4:13

Words are powerful to either build up or tear down. The Bible often speaks about what we say, how we say it and when we say it. It is one of the areas I have struggled with all my life. I'm not short on words and always seem to have an opinion on things. I don't retreat in a battle. I like to defend my cause and state my case, even if it costs me dearly. I have learned from past mistakes that words can be as destructive as a fire. Just a little statement can be the spark that creates a huge explosion that quickly becomes a forest fire, destroying everything in its path. And often, once the damage is done, it takes days, weeks, months, or even years to rebuild a trusting relationship. Sometimes a careless word escalates into a raging fire so rapidly I don't even understand how it started. Often I have wished I could erase it from the hearer's mind, but that's not possible and I have to live with the consequences. It's very

important to think before speaking and "take captive every thought to make it obedient to Christ," 2 Corinthians 10:5. I want my words to be divinely directed to build up, not destroy, those who are listening. Have you ever felt regret over something you said and wished you could erase it?

"Likewise the tongue is a small part of the body, but it makes great boasts.
Consider what a great forest is set on fire by a small spark.
The tongue also is a fire, a world of evil among the parts of the body.
It corrupts the whole person, sets the whole course of his life on fire,
and is itself set on fire by hell."
James 3:5 & 6

"I am weak, but Thou art strong;
Jesus, keep me from all wrong;
I'll be satisfied as long
As I walk, let me walk close to Thee."

Focus on thinking before you speak today and see if it makes a difference.

> *"Oh, love of God, how rich and pure!*
> *How measureless and strong!*
> *It shall forevermore endure—*
> *The saints' and angels' song."*

Dredging for gold and silver was common in the early 1900's in central Idaho. Large machines powered by river water scoured the land's surface in search of precious metals that lay hidden. Huge tracts of land still bear the devastating scars of this era. God designed each of us with precious buried treasure, mostly lying undiscovered inside us. In order for our greater value to be discovered we must be willing to be opened and exposed through trials of many kinds. God is the One who will break us open and tear apart those earthly things we cling to. He knows what gifts lie undiscovered and covered over by earthly adornments. These trials can often seem as destructive as a mining dredge leaving nothing unturned in its path. Yet we have the assurance that God is at the helm of our lives and knows exactly how deeply He must go to refine us for His glory. Too often we are focused on escaping our trial, instead of learning from it. We will then be of no more value than the

rock left behind as the dredge worked its way down the river basin. Embrace life's challenges and allow God to expose your inner beauty. He won't leave you scarred and worthless in the wake of the trial. Rather you will come forth as gold, refined and genuine, which will result in great glory to God.

> *"In this you greatly rejoice, though now for a little while you may have had*
> *to suffer grief in all kinds of trials. These have come so that your faith—of greater*
> *worth than gold, which perishes even though refined by fire—may be proved genuine*
> *and may result in praise, glory and honor when Jesus Christ is revealed."*
> *1 Peter 1:6 & 7*

Reflect back on a painful time in your life
and the wonderful treasure you discovered as a result.

"Blessed is the man who perseveres under trial, because when he has stood the test, he will receive the crown of life that God has promised to those who love Him."
James 1:12

I can and preserve fruits and vegetables for my family. Some things are processed in an open water bath but many vegetables are processed in a pressure cooker. Jars are prepared, placed in the cooker, the lid tightened and the pressure raised. The heat is adjusted to hold the desired pressure for an allotted amount of time, and then turned off so the pressure will drop slowly until the lid can be opened. Pressure canning is an exact process and doing it correctly is important. Processing at too high of a pressure might cause an explosion, while processing at too low of a pressure won't preserve the product. If the lid is opened before the pressure has dropped, valuable liquid will boil from the jars and they will not seal, leading to spoilage. God often

allows challenges in our life in order to produce new growth and fruit. This period of growth may resemble time in a pressure cooker. It can get intense as things heat up and, if uncontrolled, the pressure can cause us to explode. But if we walk away from the situation too early the lesson may be unlearned and the fruit He was preparing for our life might become spoiled and useless. We need God to watch our gauges because harvesting and preserving the fruit in our life is an exact and intense process that needs to be left in His hands for maximum results. Have you ever felt under so much pressure you thought you might explode?

"And it holds, my anchor holds:
Blow your wildest, then, O gale,
On my bark so small and frail;
By His grace I shall not fail,
For my anchor holds, my anchor holds."

Reflect on some new fruit you gained as a result of a challenging time.

A successful marriage is a lot of work. I've had two husbands and found both equally challenging despite the fact they were polar opposites. Often my frustration comes from unmet expectations. I set myself up for disappointment because my husband usually doesn't have a clue what I'm expecting him to do. When I focus on what I want and how I feel, it's all about me. I'm sure to feel let down at some point. A successful marriage can't be all about me and yet what I do makes a huge difference. It can't be about what I want, it has to be about what I can do. It can't be about how I feel, it has to be about how I respond. It can't be about my expectations being met, it has to be about setting myself aside and focusing on meeting my husband's needs. Having a happy marriage will not come easily because I'm a complex person. We all are. But I have learned that I cannot expect him to change. I have to see what I can change and leave the rest up to God. That doesn't mean I won't communicate how I feel to my husband. But after I've expressed myself I have to take control of the only thing God's given me control of—myself. With the help of God and the love and forgiveness of my husband, I can become more of the godly wife He wants me to be. Do you allow your expectations of others to disappoint you?

"A wife of noble character who can find?
She is worth far more than rubies.
Her husband has full confidence in her
and lacks nothing of value.
She brings him good, not harm,
all the days of her life."
Proverbs 31:10—12

"There is beauty all around, when there's love at home;
There is joy in every sound, when there's love at home;
Peace and plenty here abide, smiling sweet on every side,
Time doth softly, sweetly glide, when there's love at home."

List the attributes of a godly wife found in Proverbs 31.

*"Come, poor sinner, yield to Jesus,
At His throne of mercy bow;
Oh, the Spirit bids you welcome,
Come, and He will save you now."*

Occasionally I have a pretty weed bloom in my yard. Often, the bright flower is attractive against the deep green and I find myself ignoring it and not uprooting it immediately, thinking what harm can it do—I'll dig it out once it's done blooming. Then it seems almost overnight the flower's wispy seeds are blowing everywhere. This single plant has now invaded my yard and I have the potential of an out-of-control weed problem. Sin can creep up on us like that too. It is not always unattractive when it first sprouts and we may think it's not causing any real harm and ignore it. What might start as some tiny little thing can quickly grow and spread until it infects our thoughts and behavior. Before we know it we have a big sin problem in our life. No matter how innocent and harmless something may seem, if God has warned us about it we need to acknowledge it as sin, confess it and uproot it from our lives before it has a chance to spread. Do you have anything you need to uproot in your life?

*"Test everything.
Hold on to the good.
Avoid every kind of evil."*
1 Thessalonians 5:21 & 22

Go on a walk and notice how many weeds are spreading seeds.

August 7
Read 2 Corinthians chapter 1

"Church of the Living God, so peaceful is thy rest,
For God has placed thy members all as pleaseth Him the best;
No envy breaks thy peace; the Father gave His Son
To cleanse thee from each vain desire, and mold thee all in one."

I find God's creation fascinating. I marvel at how He made such variety and uniqueness in all things. The intricacies and coloring remind me of what an amazing God we serve. Many creatures resemble their surroundings as a defense mechanism against predators. They blend with their environment and it's hard to even see them. The chameleon even has the ability to change its color to resemble its environment. Christians are supposed to have their own unique markings and mannerisms that make them stand out, not blend with the rest of the world. We have been told to be in the world but not of the world. But I have found that many Christians find this command difficult. Sometimes we try so hard to be different that we appear aloof and uninviting. Other Christians have more of the chameleon's characteristic and seem to change depending upon whom they are around. God wants us to resemble Christ. He wants our differences to be inviting to others, not repulsive. We shouldn't have a better-than-thou attitude or be judgmental of others. And we can't live as a hypocrite and confuse people because we keep changing our behavior. Maybe if we focus on the characteristic God said is most important—love—we will stand out in a good sort of way. Do you think others see the markings of Christ in you?

"Our conscience testifies
that we have conducted ourselves
in the world,
and specially in our
relations with you, in the holiness
and sincerity that are from God.
We have done so not
according to worldly wisdom
but according to God's grace."
2 Corinthians 1:12

What Christian traits do you see in yourself?

> *"How firm a foundation, ye saints of the Lord,*
> *Is laid for your faith in His excellent word!*
> *What more can He say than to you He hath said—*
> *To you who for refuge to Jesus have fled?"*

Life for many of us, me included, has been pretty good here in the United States. I've lived a blessed life and have had an abundance of things and comforts. Even my poorest times cannot compare to many third world countries and the extreme poverty many endure. Sometimes I think I've been just like the seagull, sitting beside the beautiful ocean and thinking this is as good as it gets, but is it? Perhaps I've settled for good when God wants me to have something better—His best. It's not easy to motivate ourselves to change when we're comfortable and life is easy. In fact it's hard not to get complacent and lazy. Recently our economy has entered a recession and our good life is being shaken up a little. Many have lost their jobs, homes, and complete life's savings—almost without warning, and no one has been left untouched. The "good life" as we've been living it is on shaky ground now and it might be exactly what is needed to get us back on our knees and looking up. The things of this world are not as secure as they once seemed, and our false sense of security is fleeting. God is our only real hope. He is our firm foundation, both now in the present and for our future. Maybe all the good things we've been enjoying have robbed us of the best thing we could have—a deep and personal relationship with God. Perhaps what's going on is really the best thing that could happen—if it takes us back to God. How has the recession affected you personally?

> *"Wealth and honor come from you;*
> *You are the ruler of all things.*
> *In your hands are strength and power*
> *to exalt and give strength to all."*
> *1 Chronicles 29:12*

Encourage someone who is going through a difficult time
in their life because of the economy.

August 9
Read Proverbs chapter 15

I was cleaning around the shed in my yard and reached inside a piece of pipe to drag it away. Immediately I was attacked by yellow jackets who must have been nesting inside. I got stung several times before I could wave them away. Luckily, I'm not allergic to stings but they are irritating and usually hurt. Insects sting when they feel threatened, whether they are or not. We can inflict wounds on one another with stinging remarks that often insinuate something hurtful and rude. These stinging comments are difficult to receive and more difficult to refute. Often, when I'm the recipient, I'm caught off guard, and I strike back in defense. The result resembles a hornet's nest with hurtful comments being flung without regard, hurting and stinging those in the way. When a hornet or bee stings me I back away and try to keep my distance or destroy their nest so they'll have to go elsewhere. People who make a habit of stinging with their comments drive others away. Let's try to keep our stingers in place and bite our tongues when we want to strike out. Have you been stung by something somebody said?

"A gentle answer turns away wrath, but a harsh word stirs up anger.
The tongue that brings healing is a tree of life, but a deceitful tongue crushes the spirit.
The heart of the righteous weighs its answers, but the mouth of the wicked gushes evil."
Proverbs 15:1,4 &28

"Sweetly echo the Gospel call, wonderful words of life;
Offer pardon and peace to all, wonderful words of life;
Jesus, only Savior, sanctify us forever.
Beautiful words, wonderful words, wonderful words of life;
Beautiful words, wonderful words, wonderful words of life."

Pause and think before responding to stinging remarks.

> *"I must tell Jesus all of my trials, I cannot bear these burdens alone;*
> *In my distress He kindly will help me, He ever loves and cares for His own.*
> *I must tell Jesus! I must tell Jesus! I cannot bear my burdens alone;*
> *I must tell Jesus! I must tell Jesus! Jesus can help me, Jesus alone."*

Criticism is usually difficult to receive, yet constructive criticism can be used for improvement. Not all criticism is warranted, however, and is often given without discernment or forethought. I find that while I cannot stop hearing it, I do have a choice in what I do with it. I try to ask the Lord to give me discernment to know what to receive and what needs to flow off like water. When handling a long-stemmed rose, if I grab it too quickly or tightly, the thorny stem will probably prick me. But if I avoid it altogether, I will miss the beautiful fragrance of the flower. I need to deal with criticism in the same way taking it gently and, with God's help, discern if I can learn from it. Words of criticism aren't easy to receive, and usually come disguised as thorns at first, but with thoughtful contemplation they can prove to have the beauty of a rose. When someone's criticism wounded you, did you take it to the Lord to see if it was valid or not?

"Do not let any unwholesome talk come out of your mouths, but only what is helpful for building others up according to their needs, that it may benefit those who listen."
Ephesians 4:29

Ask God to help guard your words so they are constructive not destructive.

August 11
Read Nehemiah chapter 1

One of the difficult and uncomfortable things I had to learn as Executive Director of a ministry was how to ask for things or money from people who had the means or ability to help. It would be nice if every need of the ministry could be placed before the Lord in prayer and He would do the rest. But it doesn't work that way. He wants us to be bold and courageous and not just ask Him, but ask those on earth who can provide the answer. In today's passage we see how Nehemiah, a cupbearer to the king, needed to ask for help to accomplish what God had put on his heart. He first prayed to God for wisdom and success, then risked his job and asked the King. He didn't ask for just one thing, but for everything needed for success—permission, protection, and provision. All three were large requests but he found favor with the king and they were granted. Often we are unable to accomplish God's work because we are afraid to ask for help. God may not bless a private request made to Him that we are afraid to publicly make known to others. The next time you are convinced God has called you to do something for which you need money or authority, pray. Then in boldness place your requests before those who can make it happen. Don't give up if at first you are told no. God will direct you to the person whose heart He has prepared to fill the need. Do you have difficultly asking others to help you accomplish something God has put on your heart?

"O Lord, let your ear be attentive to the prayer of this your servant and to the prayer of your servants who delight in revering your name. Give your servant success today by granting him favor in the presence of this man."
Nehemiah 1:11

"Have we learned the secret of the Christian's pow'r?
Victory, victory, all the way along;
List'ning and obeying, trusting every hour,
Victory all along through Jesus."

If you've been putting off asking someone to help you in ministry, perhaps now is the time.

Often I feel very inadequate as the Executive Director of a large ministry. I especially feel this way when starting new ministries in unchartered territory. I know everything we have achieved has been from the Lord and we can do nothing without His blessing and yet, occasionally, I feel the burden of the work. When I let my mind become consumed with all the things that need to happen, the provision we need, and the multitude of challenges I easily can feel overwhelmed. Today was one of these days! Then God brought to mind the intricacies of the bumblebee, the vastness of the starry heavens, the majestic mountains, the delicacy of the flower, the miracle of human life, and it almost made me laugh. This God who created everything is the same God I call upon to help me with my challenges. How small they must seem to Him! If I were to list every need and concern I could think of it would be simplicity in my Father's hands. He reminded me not to look around, but to fix my gaze heavenward and remember that He controls everything and will help me. Nothing is impossible for Him. Are you feeling burdened and overwhelmed? Look up and see God smiling down at you.

"I lift up my eyes to the hills—
where does my help come from?
My help comes from the Lord,
the Maker of heaven and earth."
Psalm 121:1

"'Let not your heart be troubled,' His tender word I hear,
And resting on His goodness, I lose my doubts and fears;
Though by the path He leadeth, but one step I may see;
His eye is on the sparrow, and I know He watches me;
His eye is on the sparrow, and I know He watches me."

Reflect on God's creation and offer a prayer of thanksgiving.

Why is it that God often sends people to the desert for an extended stay? Abraham, Moses, the Israelites, John the Baptist and even Jesus spent time in the desert. Having lived in or near deserts all my life I can relate to the sparsely covered landscape and the focus on the basics: food, water, and protection. Distractions common in life: people, things, noise and activity are reduced or non-existent in the desert. So does God send us to the desert to remove these distractions so we'll hear Him better? Perhaps there we'll turn to God because there's no one else around. Being sent to the desert does not always mean a literal desert. We can experience a desert when we become seriously ill, lose our job, lose our spouse or close friend, fall hostage to depression, or the harshness of life makes us feel cast aside, abandoned, alone and fighting just to survive. Obviously God found great value in placing His people in the desert. It seemed to be where He prepared them for His work. Maybe when we find ourselves in a desert we should embrace it as a training ground for something in our future. Think back to a desert time in your life—did it teach you something?

"They will neither hunger nor thirst, nor will the desert heat or the sun beat upon them.
He who has compassion on them will guide them and lead them beside springs of water."
Isaiah 49:10

"In your pathway have you found some cruel thorns?
Jesus bore them on His brow, and He knows;
Does the world look down upon you with its frown?
All the world forsook your Lord, and He knows."

Can you find beauty in the desert?

When I first met my future husband one of the things that intrigued me about him was his inner peace and joy. As I got to know him better, I began to realize that he possessed the fruit of the Spirit in abundance. He is a quiet man whom one doesn't get to know through words. I witnessed a deep walk with God in his everyday life through his actions and behavior. I was getting to know a man who communed deeply with his Lord. For a good share of my life the fruit of the Spirit had seemed elusive to me. I wanted to see evidence of it in my life. I was trying to cultivate it not understanding that only God could manifest the fruit as my relationship with Him grew. The fruit of the Spirit is just that—it is the fruit that comes from the Holy Spirit living within us. We are incapable of growing the fruit on our own. As we die to self and submit to God the fruit will start to bear witness for others to see. As my relationship with God has deepened I have begun to see evidence of the fruit in my own life and I give God all the glory. Is your life bearing fruit, evidence of the Holy Spirit living within you?

"But the fruit of the Spirit is love, joy, peace, patience, kindness, goodness, faithfulness, gentleness and self-control. Against such things there is no law."
Galatians 5:22 & 23

"We are dwelling in the Spirit, by our Father's blest design;
Through His grace we're made partakers of His nature, pure, divine.
By His faith alone I'm living, for with Christ to sin I died;
I will bear abundant fruitage, that His name be glorified."

Tell someone who bears evidence of the fruit of the Spirit
that you see God in them.

August 15
Read Psalm 16

One day as I was hiking a mountain trail, I came upon a huge rock wall, that soared high above me. It was so majestic I had to stop and consider God's magnificent creation. It was then I noticed the small scrubby tree growing out of a tiny crack in the surface. It seemed to make a statement that it could grow in spite of its surroundings. We may be able to relate to that scraggly tree, jutting out from the rock. Our lives get difficult and everything around us seems hard and unmovable. And yet we have found a crack and we're trying to grow a life out of it. We may not be able to choose where we find ourselves planted, but we do have a choice. We can choose to persevere and grow, in spite of our surroundings, sending down deep roots in the spot God has opened for us. If we do this, we will be a testament to others to reach down deep inside and grow also, even when they find themselves clinging to a rock wall. Do you know someone who is struggling to grow where they've been planted?

*"Lord, you have assigned me
my portion and my cup;
You have made my lot secure.
The boundary lines have fallen
For me in pleasant places;
Surely I have a
delightful inheritance."
Psalm 16:5 & 6*

*"All the way my Savior leads me, cheers each winding path I tread,
Gives me grace for every trial, feeds me with the living Bread.
Though my weary steps may falter and my soul a thirst may be,
Gushing from the Rock before me, Lo! A spring of joy I see;
Gushing from the Rock before me, Lo! A spring of joy I see."*

Call and encourage someone who is struggling in their life right now.

"Have Thine own way, Lord! Have Thine own way!
Hold o'er my being absolute sway!
Fill with Thy Spirit till all shall see
Christ only, always, living in me."

I am so much more a Martha than a Mary personality. In fact I get irritated by the Marys in my life who relax while I wear myself out for them. I've struggled with Jesus saying Mary chose the better way. I mean, if we were all Marys who would feed everyone, get the guest rooms ready and clean the bathroom? It seems like Martha has a pretty important role in the whole guest thing. So I've spent plenty of time with the Lord on this Scripture asking Him to help me understand what He meant. I think I've figured out part of it. It wasn't what Martha was doing that was so bad. It was the condition of her heart that needed examining. She was critical of what Mary was doing and complained to Jesus. Her service was tainted because her heart wasn't pure. I don't think Jesus looks down on us Marthas, but He uses this story to remind us to check ourselves. Sometimes we get so caught up in serving that we ignore who we're serving. We wear ourselves out, feel used and unappreciated and never really enjoy it. God honors work done with the right attitude. He doesn't expect me to be like Mary. But He does want my relationship with Him to be more important than my work. Are you a Martha or a Mary personality type?

"'Martha, Martha,' the Lord answered, 'you are worried and upset about many things,
but only one thing is needed. Mary has chosen what is better,
and it will not be taken away from her.'"
Luke 10:41 & 42

If you're a task-oriented person try to relax
and enjoy some down time with God.

I purchased a new refrigerator and it ran very quietly when they first delivered it, but after a few weeks it started making a humming sound when the motor ran. I waited a few months before requesting the store to send someone to see if it was working correctly. The repair man came and tightened a loose fan that was vibrating and it's been running better ever since. It was good I called when I did because the limited warranty on all repairs was expiring that month. I'm glad God, our Maker, hasn't put a limited warranty on us. No matter what happens, or how worn out we become, we have a life-time guarantee. If we go back to our Creator, we're still covered and He'll work with us to get us back up and running. Sometimes I start to feel old and antique, like I'm breaking down and worthless. I just need to place a call heavenward and the Holy Spirit will come knocking at my door to help fix whatever's wrong. Do you feel like you're rattling apart and you'd better place a call to your Maker for a check-up?

"See, I will make you into a threshing sledge, new and sharp, with many teeth."
Isaiah 41:15

"Just when I need Him, Jesus is near,
Just when I falter, just when I fear;
Ready to help me, ready to cheer,
Just when I need Him most."

Give yourself an afternoon retreat and refresh yourself in the Lord.

*"They were broken off because of unbelief, and you stand by faith.
Do not be arrogant, but be afraid.
For if God did not spare the natural branches, He will not spare you either."*
Romans 11:20 & 21

*"I want to live above the world,
Though Satan's darts at me are hurled;
For faith has caught the joyful sound,
The song of saints on higher ground."*

One of my rose bushes produces wild shoots. These branches grow rapidly from the base of the plant but never flower. At first they appear like all the other rose stems and even look like they are producing a bud at the top. But the rosebud never appears and in time I can identify them and take action. They quickly become large and out of control and I have to cut them at the base of the plant to control further growth. They sap energy and spoil the beauty of the plant in the flowerless, out-of-control way they grow. Sometimes, something can take root in our life that is equally unproductive and out of control. We may not notice it at first because it resembles other good things we are doing. But then it seems to grow more rapidly, take a lot of energy and not bear fruit even though it looked promising. We soon find other fruitful efforts are pushed to the side as this wild shoot tries to take over. Just cutting back is not the answer. We need to identify the root of the problem and do some radical pruning, eliminating it completely if we want to control it. Often this deep cutting will be painful and sometimes criticized by others. But if left to grow this wild shoot will take over and our life will become fruitless. Is there something in your life sapping strength from other fruitful ventures?

Go for a walk through a rose garden.

y grandchildren love to go exploring with Grandpa. One of our campsites has a steep rocky trail that leads to an abandoned cave overlooking the valley. They love to climb to it, feeling on top of the world as they look down on the valley below. It would be dangerous to send them on this trail alone and Grandpa is always there to lend a hand as they make the steep climb. But it would also be unfortunate if they did not trust Grandpa and refused to go out of fear. There is much in this world that God would like us to explore and experience and He calls us to go with Him down new paths. Often we hold back out of fear of the unknown, not trusting that He will help us along the way. Other times we set out on a new venture and forget to include Him, soon finding ourselves in dangerous territory and needing His assistance. We need a close and personal relationship with our Heavenly Father so we will know when He wants to take us on a new venture, or when He is warning us the trail is too steep and difficult and we should not go. There is so much in this world that God wants to share with us. Do you trust Him enough to go when He calls?

"I guide you in the way of
wisdom and lead you
along straight paths.
When you walk,
your steps will not be hampered;
when you run, you will not stumble.
Hold on to instruction,
do not let it go; guard it well,
for it is your life."
Proverbs 4:11—13

"Jesus knows all about our struggles,
He will guide till the day is done;
There's not a friend like the lowly Jesus,
No, not one! No, not one!"

Plan a hike to some place you've not explored before.

My husband and I grew up in different cultures and we don't always see things from the same perspective. When I first married him I really struggled with this because I did not understand where he was coming from much of the time. But, through the years, I have come to respect and greatly value the gift of seeing life through his eyes also. My husband's perspective, coupled with mine, allows me to have a more rounded viewpoint on matters and helps me be less critical and more understanding of others. I am drawn to people who think like me because it takes less effort to agree on things if we both see from the same vantage point. But I am finding that, without my husband's opinion, I have a much narrower view of things. So, now I often seek out his opinion knowing that he might shed light on the subject from a different direction, and I'll be better for it. Do you have someone in your life who sees things differently from you, and do you purposely seek out their opinions?

"There are different kinds of gifts, but the same Spirit. There are different kinds of service, but the same Lord. There are different kinds of working, but the same God works all of them in all men. Now to each one the manifestation of the Spirit is given for the common good....All these are the work of one and the same Spirit, and He gives them to each man, just as he determines."
1 Corinthians 12:4-7 & 11

"I need Thee every hour, most gracious Lord;
No tender voice like Thine can peace afford.
I need Thee, oh, I need Thee; Every hour I need Thee;
Oh, bless me now, my Savior, I come to Thee."

Become familiar with another culture besides your own
and see if it changes your perspective on life.

> *"So be careful, dear ones, what kind of seeds you sow,*
> *Lest some day there will be sad regrets and misery;*
> *Be careful, I say, what kind of seed you sow today,*
> *Lest some day you will weep when you reap what you sow."*

What we sow is what we reap. If I want to grow a corn crop I won't plant bean seeds. If I want to raise peas I won't plant radishes. The seeds I plant are what I can expect to take root. If we want a life of joy and peace let us sow joy and peace. If we want to receive grace and forgiveness from others we need to sow grace and forgiveness for others. If we want to see our desires blessed and take root, let's sow seeds of encouragement and hope in the lives of others. A critical heart will always find things to criticize. Eyes that look to see what people do wrong will never see what they do right. Ears that are open to gossip will always hear lies about others. Change has to happen inside us before we see change in our world. Our life is a reflection of how we live, think and act. My mother says that what we look for is what we will find. We can either see the good in people or their faults—we all have both. How we treat others is how they're going to treat us. It's all a matter of what we're planting and what we hope to harvest. What are you sowing in your life?

> *"Do not be deceived: God cannot be mocked. A man reaps what he sows.*
> *The one who sows to please his sinful nature, from that nature will reap destruction;*
> *the one who sows to please the Spirit, from the Spirit will reap eternal life.*
> *Let us not become weary in doing good, for at the proper time we will reap*
> *a harvest if we do not give up."*
> Galatians 6:7–9

Would you say you're a negative or positive person most of the time?

> "All to Jesus I surrender;
> Lord, I give myself to Thee;
> Fill me with Thy love and power;
> Let Thy blessing fall on me."

My parents say I was not an easy child to raise and stubborn as a goat. They tell stories of my strong-willed "me do it" attitude at a very early age and I am embarrassed. God, in all fairness, gave me an equally strong-willed daughter who challenged me in her early years. This daughter recently called to tell me she did not believe the stories I told about her until she saw her two-year old daughter behaving the same way. It seems this strong-willed trait is making its way generationally through our family. Books are written on raising a child who is difficult and strong-willed without breaking their spirit. It requires a lot of love and discipline to get through those years. Many adults have a "me do it" attitude when it comes to submitting to God. He gives us free will to make our own choices but offers firm guidelines for what is best for us. Often, even when we do submit to Him, we're like the child who finally sat down after being threatened by his mother and said, "I may be sitting on the outside but I'm standing on the inside." God knows when we reluctantly give in to Him. He knows when we really haven't submitted control of our life to Him—we may appear obedient on the outside, but we're rebelling on the inside. God doesn't want to break our spirit but to mold us into whom He has created us to be. Perhaps it's time to quit being a difficult child and completely surrender to His authority. After all, He does know best— He is our Heavenly Father. Do you struggle surrendering everything to God?

*"As obedient children,
do not conform
to the evil desires
you had when you
lived in ignorance."*
1 Peter 1:14

Ask God to give you a spirit of submission to Him.

"Lead me gently home, Father,
Lead me gently home, Father,
Lest I fall upon the wayside,
Lead me gently home."

We had a black lab named Mickey who we inherited when my husband's brother passed away. The dog was very gentle and loving and we quickly grew attached to him. He adapted quickly to his new home and never wandered off. One morning when my husband went out to do the chores Mickey was gone. We were surprised and expected him to return within the day. But days grew into weeks and Mickey did not return. My husband was especially close to Mickey, and from the day of his disappearance went out each day calling and looking for him. He posted signs all around the valley and visited the animal shelter several times a week in hopes he had been found. But Mickey never returned home and we don't know what happened to him. Even though it's been over a year I find myself still looking for him and I know my husband does also. The Bible tells us that God pursues us in the same way when we become lost. He will leave everything and search for us persistently, calling out our name, desiring us to come back to Him. As I watched my husband's unrelenting search for Mickey I felt it must be similar to God's pursuit of us. He loves us and seeks us out when we go astray. Have you ever wandered off and felt the Lord pursuing you, wanting you to return to Him?

"Suppose one of you has a hundred sheep and loses one of them. Does he not leave the ninety-nine in the open country and go after the lost sheep until he finds it?. . . I tell you that in the same way there is more rejoicing in heaven over one sinner who repents than over ninety-nine righteous persons who do not need to repent."
Luke 15:4 & 7

If you have a pet give it a special love rub
and thank God for the companionship they give.

"O God, our help in ages past,
Our hope for years to come,
Be Thou our guard while troubles last,
And our eternal home."

At different times Satan has asked God for permission to test one of His devoted followers. Job is an example. In Job Chapter 1, Satan and God have a conversation about Job. Satan claims Job is only faithful to God because he has been blessed and if he loses his possessions he will turn on God. So God tells him to go ahead and take his things but not to touch Job. The story continues and we see Job fall to his knees to worship God after he has lost everything. Satan goes back to God and asks permission to take his health. God grants his request, but tells him he cannot take Job's life. The trials are great and though Job often despairs for his life he never rejects God. Job wins the fight and God blesses him abundantly the rest of his life. One would think that God would shield His most faithful followers from Satan's attacks instead of exposing them. But God knows that as their faith grows so does their ability to endure great trials and persecution. Instead of needing more protection they are fit and ready for the battle, having been trained by the Master Himself. So God allows them to go into the ring, knowing the battle will be hard and He'll have to watch from the corner. But He also knows He will have a winner when the final punch is thrown. Perhaps the next time life really beats you up it might be that God knew you were ready for the challenge. You need to look and see Who is in your corner and know you've been chosen because you're a winner. Are you one of God's prized fighters and would He let you go into the ring for Him?

"His wife said to him,
'Are you still holding
on to your integrity?
Curse God and die!'
He replied, 'You are talking
like a foolish woman.
Shall we accept good from
God, and not trouble!'"
Job 2:9 & 10

Think of a way to praise God in your challenges.

August 25
Read 2 Thessalonians chapter 1

 have always been drawn to tree-lined lanes. I remember as a child traveling and seeing such a lane and wishing we could drive down it. It enticed me and I would daydream that at the end of it was a special inviting and peaceful place. I have never outgrown my attraction to these inviting lanes and hope one day to create my own. I think our lives can bear witness in much the same way. Have you ever met someone who seemed to draw you in with just their presence and mannerisms? There was something so warm and inviting about them that you wanted to know them better. It's like driving down the lane to see what is there and who resides at the end of it. I have often found their attraction is the deep inner peace they have found in the Lord. This peace envelops their entire being, embracing others just like the trees embrace the driveway. I want to cultivate this inner peace so my presence will invite, not repel, others. I have a saying posted in my dining room that says, "Live so that those who know you and don't know Him will want to know Him because they know you." I want to be a living testimony to my God and Savior and live my life so it entices others to want to know Jesus. What does your life witness say about your Lord?

"We pray this so that the name of our Lord Jesus may be glorified in you, and you in Him, according to the grace of our God and the Lord Jesus Christ."
2 Thessalonians 1:12

*"The way of the cross leads home,
The way of the cross leads home;
It is sweet to know, as I onward go,
The way of the cross leads home."*

Take a drive in the country and enjoy the natural beauty.

> *"What a fellowship, what a joy divine, leaning on the everlasting arms;*
> *What a blessedness, what a peace is mine, leaning on the everlasting arms.*
> *Leaning, leaning, safe and secure from all alarms;*
> *Leaning, leaning, leaning on the everlasting arms."*

I had just settled in for some quality down-time on the hammock when a pesky bird starting squawking nearby. Pretty soon all I could hear was that bird and I grew more irritated by the minute. There were a lot of other birds singing, but my mind had locked onto that one irritating squawk and all other sounds seemed muted. It's interesting that people's comments often have the same effect. If someone compliments me I'm quick to push it aside out of embarrassment, almost deflecting it from my mind. But if someone says a negative or critical comment I seem to allow it to enter my mind blocking everything else out as it takes over, just like that pesky bird. I don't think I'm the only one who struggles with receiving compliments or criticism. God has instructed us to care more about what He thinks than what others think. The best way for me to do this is to take all things I hear to Him to see if they have merit. The compliment may have been heaven-sent to encourage me, and I need to hear it and thank Him. The criticism may also have been sent to correct my way or it may not have come from God at all. I need to ask Him to reveal what He wants me to hear and dismiss all else from my mind instead of letting it consume my thoughts. Once I quit focusing on the squawking bird I was able to relax and find peace. Don't let the opinions of others dominate your mind. Go to God and let Him direct your thoughts and you'll find peace in your life.

"He guides the humble in what is right and teaches them His way."
Psalm 25:9

Remember a compliment you've received recently and thank God for it.

August 27
Read 1 Samuel chapter 8

Have you ever played a game of tug-a-war? A rope is held by two teams with a center line clearly defined. The object is for one side to pull the other side across the center line to win. You want the strongest and biggest people on your side if you want to win a game of tug-a-war. I think we sometimes play tug-a-war with God. We want something and we're trying to get Him to see it our way. In I Samuel Chapter 8 the Israelites want Samuel to appoint a king to rule them. Samuel consults God who says it isn't a good idea, and Samuel conveys this message to the elders. They ignore the warning and continue to ask for a king. The Lord gives in and tells Samuel to appoint one, knowing this is a disastrous win for the Israelites. They should have listened to God who said that when they cry out for relief from the king He will ignore them. God always has our best interests at heart. When you find yourself on the opposing team from Him, you're on the wrong side. The only way you can win is if God lets you win and that usually means consequences that won't be pleasant. Next time you find yourself whining, complaining and recruiting others to petition God for something that is not in accordance with His will, stop and think about what you're doing. You just might want to cross the center line and get on the other team—His team—and become a winner. Do you ever plead with God to give you what you want?

"But the people refused to listen to Samuel. 'No!' they said.
'We want a king over us. Then we will be like all the other nations,
with a king to lead us and to go out before us and fight our battles.'"
1 Samuel 8:19 & 20

"I'll follow, I'll follow,
I'll follow Jesus all the way;
I'll follow, I'll follow,
To the home of everlasting day."

Thank God for knowing what is best for you.

"Have you been to Jesus for the cleansing pow'r?
Are you washed in the blood of the Lamb?
Are you fully trusting in His grace this hour?
Are you washed in the blood of the Lamb?"

Southern Idaho is a high plains desert and it is not uncommon to go without rain from the end of May until September. Our summers are usually hot and dry and things become covered with layers of dusty dirt by fall. Sometimes we might receive a spattering of rain, teasing us with a few drops here or there, but in reality it only serves to enhance the dirty atmosphere, leaving speckles in the dirt. In due time though, a thunder storm will come through and the heavens will open up and drop buckets of deep, cleansing rain upon us. The parched earth drinks deeply from the rich, refreshing rainfall and everything glimmers when the sun finally chases the storm away, leaving new life in its wake. We are told to drink deeply from the fountain of living water, to quench our thirst and fill to overflowing. This requires spending quality time with God; going into His word for more than a few minutes, and residing in His presence for longer than a brief thought. I don't want my testimony to just muddy up my witness to those around me by

splattering a few drops of water here and there. If I've replenished myself deeply and am filled to overflowing, my life will spill out on those around me, refreshing and encouraging new growth in them also. Is your life witness a spattering of rain drops or a deep and life-giving rain shower?

"If a man is thirsty, let him come to me and drink. Whoever believes in me,
as the Scripture has said, streams of living water will flow from within him."
John 7:37 & 38

Spend some quality time with God and replenish your spiritual thirst.

August 29
Read 1 Corinthians chapter 10

> "Than to be the king of a vast domain,
> Or be held in sin's dread sway;
> I'd rather have Jesus than anything
> This world affords today."

My grandchildren love to collect rocks and I find them left in odd places. Sometimes, when they're bored, I'll send them out with buckets and suggest they collect some pretty rocks. Usually they're back in a couple of minutes with a pail of rocks, being more concerned with getting them as quickly as they can than with being selective and picking really special ones. When my five and six-year old grandkids did this recently I had them pick out only those that meant something to them. I suggested they wash them and look for special things about each one before deciding which ones to keep. They returned a while later with a much diminished pail of rocks. We then looked at each rock and they talked about what made it special. We often bring God our pail of rocks, wanting Him to bless them. We put everything we find in our pail and run back to Him hoping He'll make them into something special. Perhaps He wants us to spend more time being selective in what we keep in our life by making sure it has value and is worth our time and investment. God wants the best for us and He's created a wonderful world full of beautiful things. If we're too quick to fill our pail with the ordinary we won't have time for those extraordinary things He wants to share with us. Are you selective in what you're putting in your life "bucket"?

"Everything is permissible—
but not everything is beneficial.
Everything is permissible—
but not everything is constructive."
1 Corinthians 10:23

Look at your life's collections and ask God
if some of it should be tossed aside.

God designed our bodies to run most efficiently when we feed them consistently. Most of us enjoy eating, and skipping meals is usually not planned. In fact I think very few of us purposely choose not to eat at least once a day. Taking a bite out of God's Word every day is just as important to our spiritual health. We need to feed our minds with spiritual instruction daily to be emotionally, mentally and spiritually growing. Yet many of us don't read the Bible regularly. We're hit and miss with our quiet times and then wonder why we struggle with Christian growth. If we only ate random meals we would find ourselves running out of strength, weak and eventually breaking down. The same thing happens when we aren't taking in spiritual nourishment regularly. We struggle, lack strength and find ourselves emotionally exhausted. It's time to make our spiritual feedings as regular as our meal times. If you only ate as often as you read the Bible would you be hungry?

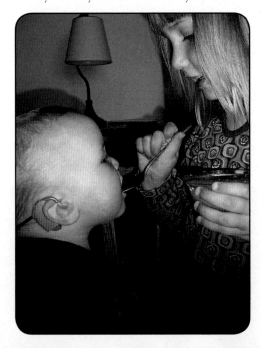

*"My son, pay attention
to what I say; listen closely
to my words. Do not let them out
of your sight, keep them within
your heart; for they are life
to those who find them
and health to a man's
whole body."*
Proverbs 4:20–22

*"Beautiful words, wonderful words,
Wonderful words of life;
Beautiful words, wonderful words,
Wonderful words of life."*

Set aside time to read the Bible daily.

"I have found a friend in Jesus, He's everything to me,
He's the fairest of ten thousand to my soul;
The Lily of the Valley, in Him alone I see
All I need to cleanse and make me fully whole.
In sorrow He's my comfort, in trouble He's my stay;
He tells me every care on Him to roll."

One day I sat and watched a bumblebee as he pollinated one of my flowers. He didn't just fly quickly to the stamen of the flower and buzz away. He went deep into the petals, immersing himself until every ounce of his being was covered in pollen. He became so coated it was hard to see where he ended and the stamen began. After he was finished with that blossom, his pollen-covered body flew to the next flower and he started all over again, spreading pollen from one flower to the next. That's how God wants us to read the Bible. He doesn't want us to quickly read a verse and go about our day. He wants us to get deep into His Word and stay there until we are saturated with Scripture. He wants His Word to cover us so completely that it becomes hard to tell where we end and He begins. Then as we go about our day we will pollinate Christ's love to everyone we meet. Imagine what a beautiful bouquet the world would become if we all became busy bees for Christ, instead of busy bodies. How deep do you get into God's Word? Deep enough you come out covered in Scripture and rubbing off on others?

"But the man who looks intently into the perfect law that gives freedom, and continues to do this, not forgetting what he has heard, but doing it— he will be blessed in what he does."
James 1:25

Watch the bees working in the flowers.

The Oregon coastline has some beautiful lighthouses and on a recent trip we toured a couple of them. I was amazed to learn that the wattage of their single bulb was not that great. What makes the light visible for up to twenty-one miles, are lenses and prisms placed together perfectly to reflect the light. The light from one bulb bounces off the glass prism, making it shine brightly and for long distances. We are told that we need to have Christ's light shining out from within us. Perhaps the more willing we are to be broken by Him and remolded, the more our life will brilliantly reflect His light. Each single life can be a "lighthouse" for Christ, shining brightly from their corner of the world. Is your life reflecting Christ's love to others, beckoning them to the safety of His arms?

"Your eye is the lamp of your body. When your eyes are good, your whole body also is full of light. But when they are bad, your body also is full of darkness. See to it, then, that the light within you is not darkness."
Luke 11:34 & 35

"Send the light, the blessed Gospel light;
Let it shine from shore to shore!
Send the light, the blessed Gospel light;
Let it shine forevermore!"

Think of someone who has brightened your life lately
and call to thank them.

September 2

Read Psalm 51

> *"Deeper, deeper! though it cost hard trials,*
> *Deeper let me go!*
> *Rooted in the holy love of Jesus,*
> *Let me fruitful grow."*

I recently attended a retreat titled "Leading From the Heart" which focused on delving deep into the core of our heart. The speaker gave a great analogy of the heart using an onion and its peel. An onion is made up of many layers that have to be removed if we want to get to the onion's heart. When peeling an onion, the strong smell may bring tears to our eyes and some onions are more overpowering than others. If we want to get to the center of our heart, we must peel back the layers of stuff we've allowed to surround our heart, just like we peel an onion. This may be a painful, tearful process taking several weeks, months, or even years, depending upon how long we've let things build up and how many layers we have to work through. But if we want a deep relationship with God, we're going to have to do the process—there's no other way to the center of our heart. Do you have some layers that need peeling back around your heart?

"Create in me a pure heart, O God, and renew a steadfast spirit within me."
Psalm 51:10

Next time you peel an onion
remember that God wants to get inside your heart too.

When Jesus returned to His hometown of Nazareth He knew the people would not see Him as a prophet but rather as Joseph's son. They were amazed by what He said yet questioned His authority. When Jesus confronted their lack of faith it infuriated them and they crowded around him trying to push Him off a cliff. He did not become distracted and try to defend Himself or convince them of His Heavenly authority. He did not fear for His life. He kept His eyes on God and continued on His way walking past them as if they didn't exist. He had singleness of vision and nothing was going to sway or frighten Him from the work He had come to do. Do we let our critics distract us from the work we've been given? Do we waste time and energy trying to convince them of the call we have received? Are we fearful when openly opposed by others and begin to doubt ourselves? Let us learn from Jesus and narrow our vision until we only see God and what He has laid on our heart. Let us walk right past the barriers and opposition as if they didn't exist. Have you let others distract you from what you've felt led to do?

"But He walked right through the crowd and went on His way."
Luke 4:30

"When I survey the wondrous cross
On which the Prince of glory died,
My richest gain I count but loss,
And pour contempt on all my pride."

Reflect on what might be distracting you from your calling.

> "I can hear my Savior calling,
> I can hear my Savior calling,
> I can hear my Savior calling,
> 'Take thy cross and follow, follow Me.'"

When I accepted a position with the ministry of Love INC the only thing I knew for sure was that I was answering a call from the Lord. I had never been a volunteer, had never worked for a non-profit and had never worked with people in need before. Six years earlier God had planted a seed of desire to work in a ministry and I knew it meant I was going to grow some new fruit in my life. For those six years I prayed, studied, and investigated many different opportunities seeking the place where God was calling me. Waiting for Him to place me seemed like an eternity, but looking back I understand there was a lot of cultivating and weeding going on to prepare me for this new venture. When I heard about Love INC I felt a nudge in my soul and eventually entered the foreign field of local mission work. God has proven faithful and guided my every step since that day. Over time I realized that much of my life's journey had been in preparation for this opportunity. God had been teaching me through the ups and downs of my life so He could use them to His good and for His glory. God has a plan for each of us. We have not been randomly created but have a purpose and role to play in His Kingdom work. Have you heard the call of the Lord and are you serving Him today?

> "I know, O Lord, that a man's life is not his own;
> it is not for man to direct his steps."
> Jeremiah 10:23

List what you are passionate about
and ask God how it can be used for His glory.

id you play the game "Simon Says" when you were little? A line would form at a starting point and the lead person, "Simon," would give instructions. As long as the instructions included "Simon Says" you were to do what "Simon" said. But if the leader gave instructions without saying "Simon Says" you were to ignore the direction and stay put. If you moved when you shouldn't you had to go back to the beginning and start all over. The first one to reach "Simon" won. Following Jesus is similar to this children's game. We are to stay close beside Him moving when He says to and staying put otherwise. It requires that we be very focused on Him because the enemy is also trying to give us directions. Satan hopes we will get confused and follow his instructions, which lead us astray and away from Jesus. We can also get impatient and move when Jesus hasn't told us, not wanting to be still

any longer. In order to distinguish between Jesus, Satan, and our own impatience we must listen very closely and make sure it is Jesus directing us. If we're not paying attention we can move when we shouldn't and have to start over again. Do you find it difficult to hear Jesus' voice?

"Show me your ways, O Lord,
teach me your paths; guide me
in your truth and teach me,
for you are God my Savior,
and my hope is in you all day long."
Psalm 25:4 & 5

"He leadeth me, He leadeth me,
By His own hand He leadeth me;
His faithful foll'wer I would be,
For by His hand He leadeth me."

What was the last clear direction you received from the Lord?

September 6
Read 2 Thessalonians chapter 2

My grandchildren love to spend hours outside on the tree swings in the summer. At first they were too little to make the swing go and had to be pushed. As they grew, they mastered the art of pumping and can swing by themselves. They still enjoy being pushed because it takes less effort. Whenever someone comes into the yard they call out for a push. When I work really hard on a project, and don't stop, I can get a lot done. But if I stop and include God in my plans through prayer, it's like He's pushing the swing and I can go higher and faster than on my own. God has gifted us with talents and abilities and we can do a lot, but we can accomplish so much more if we allow God to push. Next time you have a big project, imagine yourself sitting on a swing seat pumping with all your might. Then imagine calling to God to give you a push and picture the burst of new energy you feel. You'll find yourself flying to new heights and enjoying the ride. Do you need God to give you a push for something?

"May our Lord Jesus Christ Himself and God our Father, who loved us and by His grace gave us eternal encouragement and good hope, encourage your hearts and strengthen you in every good deed and word."
2 Thessalonians 2:16 & 17

"There's power in the blood of Jesus,
There's power in the blood of Jesus;
To save the soul today, Wash every sin away,
There's power in the blood of Jesus."

Find a swing and go for a ride.

There was a time in my life when I was too sick to work, take care of my children or even take care of myself. It was a difficult period. After months of struggling to regain my strength my health was restored. God taught me much during that season. I remember lying in bed promising Him that if I became healthy and strong again I would always be grateful for my ability to work. Much satisfaction comes from accomplishing something and even more when we get paid to do it. I've never forgotten that time in my life and have daily thanked the Lord for my job. When I am faced with an unpleasant task I remind myself that at least I have the opportunity and health to do it. I thank Him for allowing me to be productive. I thank Him because I have a job and earn wages from my efforts. I thank Him for the strength to do the work before me. I thank Him for the satisfaction I feel after a hard day's work. Work is a gift from God and we should "work at it with all our heart, as working for the Lord, not for man," Colossians 3:23. If you have a job, are you grateful for the work God has given you?

"Make it your ambition to lead a quiet life, to mind your own business and to work with your hands, just as we told you, so that your daily life may win the respect of outsiders and so that you will not be dependent on anybody."
1 Thessalonians 4:11 & 12

"Oh, the glory of Calv'ry's love story,
Oh, the glory that's in my soul;
Hallelujah, I'll never get over
Praising God for saving me while ages roll."

Thank God for the strength to do your job.

Stoplights certainly help control the flow of traffic. They just have to quit working for us to see how quickly traffic backs up. As Christians, I think we sometimes wish following Jesus was that clearly defined. Wouldn't it be easier if we only went when He gave us the green light and we knew exactly when to stop and how long, when we saw the red one. And of course, we would slow down if He was flashing us the yellow light. But our Christian walk isn't clearly marked with colored indicators. In fact, if you are like me, it's been very seldom I absolutely knew when I should go, stop, or be extra careful. But when I think about it, if all the directions became clearly marked, my need to stay close to Him and in His Word would cease to be important. I could just rev up my engine and head into life, almost without thought, hardly noticing the lights changing as I sped along. God doesn't hide the way, but He knows that there's a lot to be taught in the trip, not just getting to the destination, so He needs my focus the whole time. He has promised to take me one step at a time, and I guess that's all the assurance I need to head out. If we're tuned into Him, He'll show us the green, red, and yellow lights when it's time. And in those confusing in-between times, He wants our attention to be on Him anyway, so it doesn't really matter if we can't see the next traffic light up ahead. Are you hesitant to even begin the journey if you can't see down the road?

*"I will instruct you
and teach you in the way
you should go;
I will counsel you
and watch over you."*
Psalm 32:8

*"Following Jesus, following Jesus,
Gently He leads me in the heavenly way;
Watching and praying, trusting, obeying,
He will restrain me from going astray."*

When you're driving to work, take time to
have some quality conversation with Jesus.

J'm not an athlete, in fact I'm downright uncoordinated. I remember hating it when teams were picked in grade school. I knew I wasn't going to be the first choice and was often the last one picked. When I wasn't the last one selected I felt sorry for the one who was. It's one of those growing up memories you wish you could forget. All of us want to belong. We don't want to be the last one chosen, or the one not included when everyone is planning something. But Jesus seemed to have a different selection process than my old school mates. When He picked the twelve disciples He picked those who had been overlooked by the rabbis. Often the ones He chose to eat and stay with were not the "chosen people" but the outcasts. He wasn't impressed with outward abilities or status. He looked deeper and saw people who needed His love and forgiveness and within whom He saw potential. He has also chosen you and me! That's right, we've been picked to be on His team. There are requirements to play on the Lord's team and we have to decide if we're going to meet them. But He's chosen us so now it's our decision. Whose team are you playing on?

"Listen, my dear brothers: Has not God chosen those who are poor in the eyes of the world to be rich in faith and to inherit the kingdom He promised those who love Him?"
James 2:5

"On that bright and cloudless morning when the dead in Christ shall rise,
And the glory of His resurrection share;
When His chosen ones shall gather to their home beyond the skies,
And the roll is called up yonder, I'll be there."

Invite someone for dinner who may not often receive an invitation.

September 10
Read 2 Timothy chapter 2

You've probably heard the old saying, "one bad apple will ruin the whole batch." If you've ever bought a sack or bushel of apples and had one rot in the bottom, you know that the saying is true. One apple, gone bad, will cause all the other ones to also rot if it is not discovered and removed. I think the same thing can happen in a workplace, church group or any group of people who get together regularly. If there is one person who complains, finds fault, gossips about others, or just plain has a rotten attitude, it can affect the attitude of everyone in the group. I believe that when a person is behaving in this manner the one in charge should approach them, in love, about changing their behavior. Once the concerns have been shared, and if there is no change in attitude, further action may be needed to save the group. It is not worth risking the loss of the whole group, just because one of them has a rotten attitude. Have you ever been part of a group which had a "bad apple" in it? Did you notice how it affected others in the group?

"Avoid godless chatter, because those who indulge in it will become more and more ungodly. Their teaching will spread like gangrene."
2 Timothy 2:16–17

"I want to be like Jesus,
I want to heed His Word,
To tell the sweet, old story
To those who've never heard."

Put an apple on your desk or counter to remind yourself not to gossip.

254

We raise Hereford cattle. They produce good meat but how meat is cured and butchered makes a difference in its tenderness and flavor. Meat cut the wrong way can be tough and difficult to cook. Some cuts of meat need to be tenderized by pounding or marinating in a blend of spices and seasonings. A good cut of meat cooked right is hard to beat. One of the characteristics I desire in myself is a tender and soft spirit. I tend to speak my mind quickly and bluntly and know I can sound tough or insensitive if I'm not careful. I need to marinate in God's Word and allow the Holy Spirit to soften my demeanor. Occasionally God needs to pound me to work out something that is making my personality tough and hard for others to chew. Only God knows how deep to cut my heart to get out the gristle and hardness that keeps my spirit insensitive. I want to be tender and my words soothing to those who hear them, not tough and hard to digest. Do you need a little tenderizing by the Holy Spirit to be more palatable to others?

"A gentle answer turns away wrath, but a harsh word stirs up anger."
Proverbs 15:1

"O Jesus, Lord and Savior, I give myself to Thee,
For Thou, in Thy atonement, didst give Thyself for me;
I own no other Master, my heart shall be Thy throne;
My life I give, henceforth to live, O Christ, for Thee alone."

Speak gentle words of encouragement to someone today.

September 12
Read 2 Corinthians chapter 3

hildren love to write on sidewalks with chalk. It's a harmless, fun activity that spawns many a budding artist. Because chalk isn't permanent, it doesn't matter how good the artist is—it's only there for a short time anyway. I have many happy memories spending hours with a piece of chalk using the concrete as my blank canvas. Paul spoke to the Corinthians about their life bearing witness for Christ. A letter not written by ink, but by the Spirit of the living God, written not on stone, but on human hearts. When my children were growing up I taught them that their lives would be a witness to those around them. They would either be a witness for Christ or a witness against Him, by how they lived. They needed to understand their actions and words would leave a permanent mark on those around them. It wasn't like playing with chalk where you could create a different image every day. If they called themselves children of God they needed to leave His mark wherever they went. We are God's letter to the unbelieving world. Let's make sure our witness honors Christ. Do others know you are Christian by your walk?

*"You yourselves are our letter, written on our hearts, known and read by everybody.
You show that you are a letter from Christ, the result of our ministry,
written not with ink but with the Spirit of the living God,
not on tablets of stone but on tablets of human hearts."*
2 Corinthians 3:2 & 3

*"I love to tell the story, more wonderful it seems
Than all the golden fancies of all our golden dreams;
I love to tell the story, it did so much for me,
And that is just the reason I tell it now to thee."*

Practice sharing your faith testimony so you're a ready witness for Christ.

Have you ever been betrayed by someone you thought was your friend? I have always found the wounds inflicted by those I called friend much more painful and deep than the wounds from those I expected to attack me. While any attack is hurtful getting blindsided by someone you trust can seem almost unbearable. I wonder if the present-day Church doesn't often wound Jesus more than His enemies. What does Jesus feel when He sees the people who carry His name bickering about the color of the carpet, whether there should be multiple musical instruments up front, what kind of worship songs should be sung and so on. Jesus died for us. He laid down His life and endured incredible and unthinkable pain for us and now we split over church decorations and service styles! Faith is personal and we are often passionate about what we believe and feel. But have we allowed our passion to be used as a weapon to hurt those around us? If Jesus came to visit, would you see sadness in His eyes because of something you have said or done in the name of religion? We need take a look at ourselves—are we a good friend to Christ or have we become so caught up in the little stuff that we've hurt our best friend?

*"The entire law is summed up
in a single command:
'Love your neighbor
as yourself.'
If you keep on biting
and devouring each other,
watch out or you will
be destroyed by each other."
Galatians 5:14 &15*

*"Have we trials and temptations? Is there trouble anywhere?
We should never be discouraged—Take it to the Lord in prayer.
Can we find a friend so faithful, Who will all our sorrows share?
Jesus knows our every weakness; Take it to the Lord in prayer."*

Send a note of encouragement to someone at your church.

September 14
Read Psalm 3

*I*n the spring and fall, I like to open our doors and windows at night and let in the cool refreshing air. The nighttime breeze washes through our home removing the stagnant air and bringing a sweet fresh fragrance for the new day. When it's too hot or cold and I can't leave the doors open the air becomes almost oppressive as if a weight were pressing me down. Spending time with Jesus at the end of my day is like opening the door of my heart. As I talk about my day I let out everything that would weigh me down. As the stagnant, depressing thoughts leave my mind I can be refreshed in the Lord through the night. His presence is like the cool night air washing over me and preparing me for another day. So before you go to bed tonight fling wide open the door of your heart and let out everything that filled your day, both good and bad. We get stale, stagnant and oppressed if we try to keep it all inside. Give your day to Jesus and prepare yourself to welcome the fresh morning dew of a new day. Do you share your day with Jesus before you go to sleep?

"I lie down and sleep; I wake again, because the Lord sustains me."
Psalm 3:5

"The Lord's my Shepherd, I'll not want;
He makes me down to lie
In pastures green; He leadeth me
The quiet waters by."

Open the doors of your home and your heart tonight and be refreshed.

*"All things bright and beautiful,
All creatures great and small,
All things wise and wonderful:
The Lord God made them all."*

God's creation is so amazing and diverse. I love the colorful display autumn brings as it starts to glide into the winter months. The brilliant oranges, yellows, and reds tease the different hues of green almost as if to say, "aren't you changing too, my dear?" And I imagine the green laughs back as it answers, "in time my love, in time." There is no conflict in nature. Each color earns its own respect and place on earth. It's no wonder that the same God who created this vibrant display is also the God who created diversity amongst humans. Yet we seem to struggle with our differences, wrestling for rank and honor. But a leaf is a leaf, whether it is red, yellow, or brown, and God created all humans equal no matter how He chose to color them. It's time to look at each other as God intended us to, all beautiful and unique, without privilege or status. We are His children creating a kaleidoscope of color as we blend our lives together in perfect harmony. What are you doing to embrace the diversity and uniqueness in others?

*"It is I who made the earth and created mankind upon it.
My own hands stretched out the heavens; I marshaled their starry hosts."*
Isaiah 45:12

Reflect on the diversity in your life
and thank God for all the variation you find around you.

September 16
Read John chapter 14

*J*esus did many miracles during the last three years of His life. He healed the sick, restored sight to the blind and hearing to the deaf and made the lame walk again. He drove out demons and brought people back to life. He shriveled up trees with a single command and walked on water. After He left earth His disciples continued to do miraculous things. In Acts 9:40 we read that Peter restored Tabitha to life after she had died. So why do we see so few miracles today? I haven't met anyone who has raised someone from the dead, walked on water, or shriveled trees with just a command. Jesus said that we will do even greater things than He did because He is sitting with His Father and will intercede for us. For me, it's not that I lack faith in God. I believe everything that is written in the Bible and I believe that God can do anything He wants. My problem is believing in myself. While I know God can do it, I lack faith that He would choose to work through me. I don't see myself as God sees me and this misperception gets in my way. It's not enough to just believe God can do it, I have to also believe that I can do it through His strength. Have you witnessed or done any miracles lately in Jesus' name?

"I tell you the truth,
anyone who has faith in me
will do what I have been doing.
He will do even greater things
than these, because I am
going to the Father.
And I will do whatever you ask
in my name, so that the Son may
bring glory to the Father.
You may ask me for anything
in my name, and I will do it."
John 14:12–14

"Praise the Lord, praise the Lord, let the earth hear His voice!
Praise the Lord, praise the Lord, let the people rejoice!
Oh, come to the Father, through Jesus the Son,
And give Him the glory, great things He hath done."

Do something today that will bring God glory.

"Then in fellowship sweet we will sit at His feet,
Or we'll walk by His side in the way;
What He says we will do, where He sends we will go;
Never fear, only trust and obey."

rusting others is difficult for me. Trust was broken in my first marriage and I have struggled with it ever since. Even when I try to be trustworthy there are times when I fall short and let others down. Other times I will have my trust betrayed by someone and feel disappointment. If it is difficult to trust people whom we can see and know, how much more difficult is it to trust God whom we cannot see and whose ways we cannot understand? Do you believe God is Who He says He is? Do you believe He can do all that He says He will do? Have you placed your trust in Him and are you living out your faith by walking in that trust? God is trustworthy and He has proven it throughout history. We need to read the Bible and recall the countless stories of His faithfulness through the ages. What He has said He has done and is doing. Who He says He is, is unchanging and steadfast. His promises are there for each one of us to take hold of and believe in. Are you able to trust God and take Him at His Word?

"Trust in the Lord with all your heart and lean not on your own understanding;
in all your ways acknowledge Him, and He will make your paths straight."
Proverbs 3:5 & 6

Look up passages in the Bible on trust and memorize a favorite one.

September 18
Read Luke chapter 6

> *"Jesus wants me to be loving,*
> *And kind to all I see;*
> *Showing how pleasant and happy,*
> *His little one can be."*

When my husband is grumpy I tend to get grumpy also. It's challenging not to respond in like manner when someone is gruff with me. God has told us to treat others as we want to be treated, not as we are being treated. I find this command difficult to honor. Sometimes the clients we are trying to help at Love INC are difficult and rude. They can be demanding and demeaning if we cannot give them exactly what they want, when they want it. It's tempting to just end the conversation and hang up the phone. While we don't want our volunteers to be in the firing line it is important for staff to reach out to the clients in spite of their negative attitudes. Often if our offered help is not the quick fix they want they refuse it and hang up on us. But throughout the conversation we try to be Christ's hands and feet speaking gentle words of care regardless of their words coming back at us. Early in the ministry we started sending prayer notes to everyone who called. This allowed us to speak kind words even if they cut the conversation short in anger. It's not easy to love those who are prickly but God can give us the strength to do that which we cannot do on our own. Do you let other's actions dictate your response? How do you respond to someone who is grumpy to you?

> *"Do to others as you would have them do to you."*
> *Luke 6:31*

The next time someone is grumpy at you give a soft answer.

One of my grandsons shows extraordinary athletic ability at the young age of two. His father has noticed his skill in catching and throwing the ball and plays with him to help develop this natural ability. He has a good chance of growing into a fine athlete one day if he continues to practice and perfect this God-given talent. We are all uniquely created with different gifts and abilities. I often hear people say they don't believe they have anything special to offer in His service. But I believe everyone has something of value to offer in this life. They may not have identified their talents or have been unwilling to develop them into all they can become, but they are uniquely gifted in some way. Our Heavenly Father, who knit us together in our mother's womb, knows each of us personally. We need to ask Him to help us identify our talents and work hard to develop these unique abilities so we can become all He has planned for us. Do you know what you are naturally good at and have you worked to develop it to its full potential?

"We have different gifts, according to the grace given us."
Romans 12:6

"Give of your best to the Master; Give Him first place in your heart; Give Him first place in your service; Consecrate every part. Give, and to you will be given; God His beloved Son gave; Gratefully seeking to serve Him, Give Him the best that you have."

Think of what you enjoy doing—this may be a God-given talent.

September 20
Read Ecclesiastes chapter 7

*F*all is a beautiful season. I love the changing and vibrant colors, the warm days, and cool nights. Not every fall has the same vibrancy though. Sometimes the colors seem flat and lackluster and sometimes the leaves go from green to dead and just fall off the trees. The difference, I hear, comes from a combination of warm days and cool nights. It's the contrast, without extremes, that makes for the most beautiful fall time. If the days get too cold too quickly, or the nights stay too warm for too long, the leaves will not be nearly as colorful and vibrant. We are told to be passionate about Christ, creating vibrancy that will attract others to Him. God has created us uniquely in His image, but if we live our life in extremes without self-control we can lose our witness to others. Our passion for living needs to be tempered with common sense, and the everyday needs to be sprinkled with the unpredictable. Everything about creation speaks of variety. Finding balance and self-control in life is important in creating a beautiful blend of colors to display His glory. What kind of statement does your life make to those around you?

"Do not be over righteous,
neither be over wise—
why destroy yourself?
Do not be over wicked,
and do not be a fool—
why die before your time?
It is good to grasp the one
and not let go of the other.
The man who fears God
will avoid all extremes."
Ecclesiastes 7:16–18

"Brighten the corner where you are!
Brighten the corner where you are!
Someone far from harbor you may guide across the bar;
Brighten the corner where you are!"

Ask someone you trust if they think you need to let something go in your life that seems to be throwing it out of balance.

"*All to Jesus I surrender;
All to Him I freely give;
I will ever love and trust Him,
In His presence daily live.*"

My husband's work took him to the island of Guam for an extended period of time. I found myself burdened with the responsibility of the kids, my job, the house, our farm, and the cattle. It seemed I was working all the time and getting more tired with each passing day. My conversations with my husband were often filled with complaints from me and prayers that God would bring him home. One night, after another complaint-filled conversation, my husband said I had better be careful what I prayed for. With frustration I asked him what he meant and he replied God just might give me what I prayed for and I might not like the answer. He could lose his job; he could become seriously ill or some other disaster could force him home. Although I didn't like his answer, I knew he was right. I changed my prayers, asking for strength for each day, protection for all of us and gratitude that he had a job and I had good health. When the Israelites were wandering in the desert the Lord provided them with daily manna for their food. But they grew tired of it and began grumbling for meat. They longed for the old days in Egypt and complained about how much they had sacrificed in the desert! God heard their prayers and answered by sending them quail. They gathered as much as they could but God was angry with them for complaining and sent a plague that killed some of them. The answer was more than they had bargained for. I'm careful what I pray for now; God just might give me what I want and I might not like it. Have you ever received something you really wanted only to find it wasn't a good thing?

"*The rabble with them began to crave other food, and again the Israelites started wailing and said, 'If only we had meat to eat! We remember the fish we ate in Egypt at no cost—also the cucumbers, melons, leeks, onions and garlic. But now we have lost our appetite; we never see anything but this manna!'*"
Numbers 11:4-6

Try to find something good in every situation and thank God for it.

> "Love lifted me!
> Love lifted me!
> When nothing else could help,
> Love lifted me!"

Little children seem to fall a lot and often get bruised and scraped as a result. They cry and come running to mommy to make it all better. It's amazing that even when they have gotten a pretty good scrape a little love and a band aid seem to go a long way in making things better. It's not long before their tears have dried and they're scooting off mom's lap to go back at it again. Adults get bruised and scraped from living life too. It's not usually a physical injury that makes us hurt but a comment, unjust act or criticism inflicted by others. We need to respond more like a child and call out to God running to Him for comfort when we've fallen. He's not going to ignore us any more than a mother ignores her hurt child. He wants us to bring all our concerns and worries to Him so He can put His arms around us and comfort us. A little time in His presence will go a long way in putting us back together again. It won't be long before we're scooting off His lap to get back at it, feeling restored and loved by His presence. Do you run to your Heavenly Father when you've fallen?

"Shout for joy, O heavens; rejoice, O earth; burst into song, O mountains!
For the Lord comforts His people and will have compassion on His afflicted ones."
Isaiah 49:13

Visualize climbing into your Heavenly Father's lap for a hug.

I love to go to the Oregon coast and try to visit it at least twice a year. I look forward to doing nothing but spending time by the water with God. There is something about the roar of the ocean, the vastness of the open seas and the miles of sandy beaches that draw me into His presence in a very special way. In Isaiah chapter 40 we are given a powerful visual description of our God—how He set the boundaries of the water and measures them in the palm of His hand; how He can hold all the dust of the earth in a bucket. When I look across the ocean I am reminded that I can't even begin to under-stand God and all that He has done and will do. But the message that touches me deepest when I'm walking on the beach is that He has told me His thoughts of me outnumber the grains of sand. It's beyond my ability to comprehend; He loves me that much! And His words aren't just written for me, they're written for each one of us. Hopefully you also have a place that

reminds you of how omnipotent God is and reassures you of the depth of His love for you. I need these spiritual retreats to fill me and encourage me that I am His and I have value. Do you have a place where you feel especially close to God?

"How precious to me are your thoughts, O God! How vast is the sum of them!
Were I to count them, they would outnumber the grains of sand."
Psalm 139:17 & 18

> *"O Love that wilt not let me go,*
> *I rest my weary soul in thee;*
> *I give thee back the life I owe,*
> *That in thine ocean depths its flow*
> *May richer, fuller be."*

Get a small jar of sand and keep it by your nightstand
to remind you of His love.

September 24
Read James chapter 4

> *"Perfect submission, perfect delight,*
> *Visions of rapture now burst on my sight;*
> *Angels, descending, bring from above*
> *Echoes of mercy, whispers of love."*

We live in a culture where being independent is sought after. We raise our children in hopes they will live independently one day. We want them to have their own life, families, dreams, jobs and ambitions. We try to give them the skills they need to live on their own. When people become elderly we do everything we can to help them remain independent as long as possible. Assisted living facilities have sprung up all over the country providing limited assistance for those who want to live on their own. Being dependent on others is not something we usually strive for. I'm extremely independent and have been since I was a young child. "Me do it" were my very first words and I've always been prone to do it on my own. When I became a Christian and learned that I had to die to self and live for Christ it went against my natural instincts. The Bible instructs us to be obedient and submissive to God's leadership. We should not to strive to do it on our own but seek His help in every detail of our life. It isn't the natural thing to do—but then God's ways are not our ways. We can't understand His reasoning but we can make the choice to follow Him. Submission to God is difficult but the rewards are great. When we allow Him to be Master of our life all of our weaknesses become strengths in His hands. When we relinquish needing to be in control it frees us to be used mightily by Him. So even though it goes against my nature I desire to be obedient and submissive to God—throwing the "me do it" attitude out the window. Are you dependent upon God?

"Submit yourselves,
then, to God.
Resist the devil,
and he will flee from you."
James 4:7

Give God control of your life and see how blessed you'll be.

There are many aspects of a finished diamond that are dependent on the diamond's cut. A skilled craftsman studies the rough exterior and determines the ideal place to cut to allow light to pass through the diamond and produce maximum brilliance. He knows that when cut into a particular shape and polished it will reveal its beauty. However, in the hands of a novice a diamond can be so damaged that it loses value or even becomes worthless. Our lives are like diamonds in the rough. In the wrong hands the potential that lies inside us can be ruined by devastating cuts and comments. God sees deep inside us and knows the potential jewels waiting to be extracted. We need to place ourselves in His hands and allow Him to make the perfect cuts. He knows how to bring out our best qualities and shape us to reflect His light with maximum brilliance, reflecting His glory. It's time to trust God and allow Him to make something beautiful of our ordinary lives. Is your life a brilliant reflection of God's glory?

> *"It shone with the glory of God, and its brilliance was*
> *like that of a very precious jewel, like a jasper, clear as crystal."*
> Revelation 21:11

> *"God omniscient, God all-wise,*
> *With Thy ever-searching eyes,*
> *Look within me, view my heart;*
> *Keep me pure in every part."*

Study a diamond and see how it reflects and refracts the light.

> "What can wash away my sin?
> Nothing but the blood of Jesus;
> What can make me whole again?
> Nothing but the blood of Jesus."

Camping has always been one of my favorite things to do. I love the mountains, campfires and lazing around doing whatever I like. But one thing I don't enjoy is giving up my daily shower. Sponge baths are taken regularly but they are a poor replacement for standing under a full stream of water and feeling it wash all the dirt away, cleansing me completely. I look forward to getting in the shower when I get home and don't really feel refreshed until I do. Often our time alone with God resembles a sponge bath—better than nothing but not what we need to really get refreshed. It can be sporadic and piecemeal, a few minutes here or there, but nothing deep and enriching. These stolen minutes, similar to a sponge bath, will wash away the dirt close to the surface but can't get into those hard to reach areas like a flowing shower can. Getting away for a couple of hours with nothing but our Bible, a good book and God is similar to taking a nice hot shower. When we bathe our souls completely in the Holy Spirit He will wash away the impurities of life deep inside us and leave us restored and refreshed. Have you bathed in the Holy Spirit or do you only find time for a sponge bath?

> "Let us draw near to God with a sincere heart in full assurance of faith,
> having our hearts sprinkled to cleanse us from a guilty conscience
> and having our bodies washed with pure water."
> Hebrews 10:22

Plan a mini-retreat with Christ.

"Jesus! the Name that charms our fears,
Blessed be the Name of the Lord!'
'Tis music in the sinner's ears,
Blessed be the Name of the Lord!"

When it was time for the Israelites to enter the land of Canaan God told Moses to send twelve men to explore and report what they saw. In forty days they returned and all agreed the land was fertile and flowed with milk and honey. But ten of them were afraid of the giants they saw and spread a bad report to all the camp, scaring everyone. Two of them, Caleb and Joshua, who also had explored the land, saw something different—a fertile land promised by God. Most of the Israelites still did not trust God even though this was the land He had promised them years ago. They allowed the fear of a few to destroy the hope of many. In the end, only Caleb and Joshua were allowed entry into the land. What do you see when you look around you? Do you only see the giants or do you see the Lord? Do you let others scare you from the blessings God wishes to give you? Each of us has the responsibility to develop a knowing and trusting relationship with Him. We cannot allow others to dictate our future. In order to receive all that God has promised we must focus on Him and trust His lead. The world is filled with people whose fear of the giants scare others away from God's blessings—don't let them. What do you see, God or the giants?

"The land we passed through
and explored is exceedingly good.
If the Lord is pleased with us,
He will lead us into that land,
a land flowing
with milk and honey,
and will give it to us."
Numbers 14:7 & 8

Reach out and take hold of a blessing promised by God.

September 28

Read Colossians chapter 1

*"I walked one day along a country road, And there a stranger journeyed, too,
Bent low beneath the burden of His load: It was a cross, a cross I knew.
'Take up thy cross and follow Me,' I hear the blessed Savior call;
How can I make a lesser sacrifice, When Jesus gave His all?"*

One weekend, I was headed to do a church presentation and saw a road-sign that said the name of the little town I was going to, so I turned onto it. I was out in the country and it wasn't long before that road ended and I had to make a decision to take a left or a right, neither one having any signage of the place I was going. So I made a choice and soon had to make another turn, and on and on it went. I finally found myself back at the main road and ended up taking the long way there, making it just in time for the service. I wonder if at times our Christian witness isn't similar to my road trip. We may start out strongly, pointing others to Christ, but once we start them on their way, we leave them to meander through unfamiliar territory, trying to find their own way. They will face many road crossings in their faith journey, and without good directions from someone who's traveled the road before, may take several wrong turns along the way. I need to make sure my witness is clear and doesn't just point new believers in a direction and then leave them wandering around by themselves. I need to offer good directions, including the Bible, other fellow believers, a church home, and my personal testimony, to help them in their journey. I don't want my witness to lead them astray and stranded, forlorn on their journey to Christ. Have you ever felt misled in your spiritual journey?

*"We proclaim Him, admonishing and teaching everyone with all wisdom,
so that we may present everyone perfect in Christ."*
Colossians 1:28

Go for a drive in the country and enjoy the fall scenery.

outhwestern Idaho is a high plains desert. The soil is rich, the growing season ideal but until the early 1900's the ground was unproductive due to the lack of water. Sage brush littered the landscape and the potential of the ground lay unrealized. Early settlers knew there was great potential in the earth. Money and time were invested in drilling wells and building canals. Without water the land would remain untouched and barren. But once an extensive water system was in place the area became known for its varied and magnificent crops. Today Idaho raises a rich variety of crops and seeds, all because effort was taken to water the land. God has created us with diverse and amazing potential. But without the living water of Jesus Christ and the refreshment of the Holy Spirit we remain as unproductive as desert land. Our full potential can never be realized until we come to know the Lord. Only He can bring the living water that transforms us to the fullness of life He has promised. Are you drinking the living water of Jesus Christ from the well of eternal life?

"Everyone who drinks this water will be thirsty again, but whoever drinks the water
I give him will never thirst. Indeed, the water I give him will become in him
a spring of water welling up to eternal life."
John 4:13

"Hallelujah! Thine the glory.
Hallelujah! Amen.
Hallelujah! Thine the glory.
Revive us again."

Plant two seeds. Water one and not the other and see the difference.

> "Tell me the story of Jesus,
> Write on my heart every word;
> Tell me the story most precious,
> Sweetest that ever was heard."

Stained glass windows are beautiful but they also served a very important purpose for the early church. The windows arranged in chronological order depicted the story of Jesus' life. In those days people did not have the written Word of God so they went to church, and under the guidance of their priest, could read the story of Jesus from the windows. Today most people can get a Bible if they want one and going to church to read the windows is not practiced. Even though the written Word is much more available today many people either don't own a Bible or have never opened the one they have. You've probably heard the cliché that Christians are the only Bible many people will read. I believe it is a true statement. If we attend church or publicly profess to be a Christian, people may watch us to see what it means. I think we often give them mixed signals. Many people attend church and participate in religious activities for one day of the week. But the rest of the week their behavior and choice of activities contradict what they profess to believe. Our lives need to reflect Christ so those watching us will be drawn to Him, and not be confused and frustrated by mixed messages. Love INC's first core value is "we are Christian in all we think, say, and do." But are we? When people read your life what story do you tell?

"Live such good lives among the pagans that, though they accuse you of doing wrong, they may see your good deeds and glorify God on the day He visits us."
1 Peter 2:12

Try to be a Christian in all you think, say, and do.

*I*n the late fall, when the brilliance of the fall colors has started to fade I need to prepare my flower beds for winter. It's at this time that most of my bushes and roses will be pruned back, removing the summer growth. Almost two thirds of the plant lay around the base after I have finished as I rake up the debris and dead leaves, leaving naked, scarred stems sticking up from the soil. It would seem that pruning something this deeply would stunt or even kill the plant. But, in reality, if I don't prune in the fall, the growth is stunted, wild, and out of control in the spring. The health of the plant is directly related to the pruning it has endured. It may be uncomfortable, but we need to allow God to take His pruning shears and cut us back as He sees fit. Pruning isn't just cutting back the dead stuff, sometimes it's cutting into

actively growing areas, leaving us raw and exposed when it's finished. But God knows what He is doing, and if we want to be strong, vibrant, and fruitful Christians, we have to submit to His shears on a regular basis. Has God recently pruned something in your life and how did it make you feel?

"I am the true vine and my Father is the gardener.
He cuts off every branch in me that bears no fruit,
while every branch that does bear fruit He trims
clean so that it will be even more fruitful."
John 15:1 & 2

"Take my life and let it be
Consecrated, Lord, to Thee;
Take my hands and let them move
At the impulse of Thy love."

Take a few minutes and thank God for something in you
which had new life after a painful pruning.

October 2

Read Mark chapter 4

Charlie, our new golden lab puppy, was so cute and loveable, but a lot of work! For the first year of his life he often left a trail of destruction in his path. One day I looked out the window of my house to see Charlie shaking an empty bag in the front yard. He was delighted with his new-found toy and his body wiggled from head to foot with glee. As I went to see what the bag was, I discovered to my dismay that a once full bag of pasture grass seed had been spread in mounds across my Kentucky Bluegrass. I was horrified because I knew that if the seed sprouted it would overcome the Bluegrass. I literally vacuumed the yard with a shop vacuum, mowed and raked it several times and then sprayed it with herbicide multiple times. I still didn't get all the seed and large clumps of pasture seed have sprouted since, forcing me to apply more herbicide to kill it. Charlie, in his innocence, had no idea he was planting destructive seeds everywhere. We too can be naïve at times and plant seeds of worry, distress, gossip, discouragement and other sins, that may affect other people's spiritual growth. We need to act wisely, not foolishly, and be careful what we say—that seed just might take root and grow. Have you ever had someone say something negative to you that started to take root and grow in your own life?

"Other seed fell among thorns, which grew up and choked the plants, so that they did not bear grain."
Mark 4:7

"Sowing in the morning, sowing seeds of kindness,
Sowing in the noontide and the dewy eve;
Waiting for the harvest, and the time of reaping,
We shall come rejoicing, bringing in the sheaves."

Plant a positive thought today by giving someone a sincere compliment.

nce toddlers start to talk it seems they are never quiet, or at least that's how my children were. One of my sons in particular was either telling or asking me something non-stop. He talked so much when I was driving that if he didn't think he had my full attention he would ask me to turn off the radio so I could hear him better. Occasionally, I would have to tell him he couldn't talk for a while just so I could regain my senses. I loved their early years of development, but some of my most special moments with my toddlers were when they would fall asleep in my arms. I loved to hold them, stroke their soft, innocent faces and whisper sweet nothings in their ears. Those precious times are still near to my heart and fresh in my memories. I wonder if sometimes God feels the same way about us? I wonder if we chatter His ears off with our unending questions and comments—why God, when God, how God, are you there God? I like to imagine that some of His favorite times with me are when I rest in His presence, the questions cease and He whispers sweet nothings in my ear. Perhaps we should curl up with God and take a few more naps—I'm sure He wouldn't mind. Have you spent time with the Lord in silence lately?

*"Be still, and know
that I am God;
I will be exalted
among the nations,
I will be exalted
in the earth."*
Psalm 46:10

*"Oh, the pure delight of a single hour
That before Thy throne I spend,
When I kneel in prayer, and with Thee, my God
I commune as friend with friend!"*

Take a break, put your feet up and be still before God for a while.

> *"Turn your eyes upon Jesus,*
> *Look full in His wonderful face,*
> *And the things of earth will grow strangely dim,*
> *In the light of His glory and grace."*

I recently met a man who shared a trial he was facing. He had been a Christian for twelve years and felt great joy and satisfaction in his walk with the Lord. One day in particular had been a real spiritual high; the presence of the Lord felt close and personal. Later that same day his whole world fell apart. He was unfairly accused of a wrong he had not committed. He was fired from his job and monies owed him were withheld. He had never experienced such injustice and all efforts to clarify and rectify the wrong were ignored. He plummeted into a deep low, experiencing nightmares when he slept and joyless days as he tried to make sense of it. As I listened I thought of past times in my life when a gross unfairness had shaken my world. I too had struggled to get through it and wondered why it had happened. As I matured I realized that God allows those times in our lives to grow us spiritually. He wants us to know the joy that comes in spite of our circumstances, not through our circumstances. We learn this lesson by experiencing trials and tribulations we don't deserve. At some point every Christian will face a trial that is unfair and undeserved. Take heart and know that you are not alone, for the One who has allowed it to pass to you is also walking it with you. Have you ever been treated unfairly?

> *"Dear friends, do not be surprised at the painful trial you are suffering,*
> *as though something strange were happening to you. But rejoice that you participate*
> *in the sufferings of Christ, so that you may be overjoyed when His glory is revealed."*
> *1 Peter 4:12 & 13*

Reflect on a difficult time in your life and journal
what you learned through it.

"I'm redeemed, I love to tell it
To the world of sinners lost;
In the Savior's cleansing fountain
I was saved at boundless cost."

Is there something in your past you are ashamed of that hinders you from serving God today? We are all sinners and in need of grace. Everyone has had times in their life when they did not honor God with their choices and actions. We tend to categorize sin listing the really bad sins, such as murder, adultery and abuse at the top of the list. Pride, gossip and self-centeredness are placed at the bottom of the list. But the Bible doesn't prioritize sin from greatest to least—sin is sin and we have all sinned and are in need of God's forgiveness and grace. From early childhood I have always recognized God as my Savior, but it has not kept me from making some really poor choices. I bear the consequences of those choices the rest of my life. Satan tries to convince us that our past mistakes make us a poor choice for Kingdom work. But God can use our failures to His glory if we allow Him. He is the potter and when we become marred He has the ability to reshape us into a different pot that He can use. We are never so far gone that God cannot restore us to a thing of beauty and service. But if we resist Him and refuse to be remade, clinging to our present shape in spite of its sinful condition, He has said He will smash our pot to pieces, beyond repair, and cast it to the side (Jeremiah 19:11). Don't let Satan convince you you're beyond restoring and don't be resistant to God when He wants to reshape you into a useful vessel. Do your past sins hold you back from all God wants for you?

"But the pot he was shaping
from the clay was marred
in his hands;
so the potter formed it
into another pot, shaping it
as seemed best to him."
Jeremiah 18:4

Examine yourself and see if you need to be restored for His glory.

October 6
Read Psalm 32

I love to camp and used to go a lot as a child and young adult. There have been a few times in the late summer when an unexpected storm dumped snow on us. It always caught us totally off guard and unprepared. The previous day had been beautiful and full of sunshine, with no indication of an impending snow storm. The snow was inconvenient, but it never lasted long and warm weather returned within a day or two. Life can dump on us like an unexpected snow storm. Things can be going smoothly and everything seems sunny and beautiful. Then, without warning a storm will rage against us, leaving us shaken and befuddled. We are unprepared and ill-equipped for the challenge and struggle to get through it. I have learned one thing from these storms—we don't have to go through them alone. God is always there to show us something beautiful. We just have to turn our eyes away from the circumstances and onto Him. His peace will warm us and bring the sunshine back into our lives. Have you ever been caught off guard and felt dumped on by something unexpected?

"You are my hiding place; You will protect me from trouble and
surround me with songs of deliverance."
Psalm 32:7

Think of something beautiful that came in an unexpected way.

> *"At the cross, at the cross where I first saw the light,*
> *And the burden of my heart rolled away,*
> *It was there by faith I received my sight,*
> *And now I am happy all the day!"*

Does your happiness correlate with your abundance or lack of things? Have you ever thought that if you could live in a bigger house, had a reliable car, or find your soul mate and get married, you would be happy? When I was younger I struggled with being happy. I felt that my unhappiness was a result of what I didn't have. But twice in my life I have lost most of my personal possessions and have learned that happiness is not connected to things. The first time my husband and I lost our farm, vehicles and home. We headed back to our hometown to start all over again with three little children and no money or work. God was sufficient and we found a cheap place to live, a loaned vehicle and work for both of us within a week. The second time was during my divorce. In order to divide things fairly and allow me to keep the house for the kids, I gave up most of the furniture. While it was humbling to borrow a kitchen table, live without a TV and put our books on cinder block shelves, God provided for our needs and we got through it. During each of those times I found the things I lost of little significance. Relationships were all that mattered. I've lived abundantly and without and I can honestly say that things don't make the difference—God and people do. Is your happiness based on your possessions?

"I know what it is to be in need,
and I know what it is
to have plenty.
I have learned the secret
of being content in any
and every situation,
whether well fed or hungry,
whether living in plenty
or in want."
Philippians 4:12

Simplify your life by giving away some of your possessions.

October 8
Read Matthew chapter 11

I recently ate at a buffet and the array of food seemed endless. I tried to be selective and only take what I would eat, but still ended up with an over-flowing plate and more than I needed. I found myself wanting to eat it all, consequently eating too much, and then still wishing I could go back for one more trip down the dessert aisle. Afterwards I felt guilty for my self-indulgence, knowing I would pay for it with an upset stomach now and added pounds in the future. Sometimes my to-do list in life resembles a buffet plate. It's over-flowing with things demanding my time. While I try to set boundaries, I find myself unable to say no to the things I would like to do or feel obligated to do. As I struggle to manage it all, guilt sets in as some things start to slide, and I feel anxious over getting it all done. Soon I feel weighted down and physically exhausted from the schedule. Overeating at a buffet, no matter how good the food is, is not good for my health. And trying to do too much, no matter how worthy the tasks, is equally harmful not only to my health, but my mental and spiritual well-being also. We all need to learn how to walk through the buffet line of life and know what we can and cannot do, and leave the rest for someone else. Have you over-obligated yourself and are you struggling with the load?

"Come to me, all you who are weary and burdened, and I will give you rest. Take my yoke upon you and learn from me, for I am gentle and humble in heart and you will find rest for your souls. For my yoke is easy and my burden is light."
Matthew 11:28-30

List your current obligations and ask the Lord if you are over-committed.

The "Bucket List" is a movie about two old, terminally-ill strangers who wrote down things they wanted to do before they died and then set out together to do them. My husband and I discussed what would be on our "bucket list" if we had one. I get so busy living that I often don't take time to smell the roses. There is much I want to do someday, when I have time. I wonder if that magic day will ever arrive. I think we need to make a "bucket list" of things we want to say or do for the special people in our lives. We shouldn't put off telling our family how much we love them and the things we appreciate about them. We need to take time with our children and grand-children to read stories and play with them. We need to take a walk with that special someone in our life and share the attributes we love about them. We don't know when our last day on earth is, we only know that everyone has a last day. Let's not put off those things we need to do or say to those special people around us. Make your "bucket list" and do at least one thing a day until you've written every encouraging note, said, "I love you" to each person you care about and have taken time to smell the roses with the people important to you. Is there someone you need to express your love or thankfulness to?

"Moreover, no man knows when his hour will come."
Ecclesiastes 9:12

"In the sweet by and by,
We shall meet on that beautiful shore;
In the sweet by and by,
We shall meet on that beautiful shore."

Write a note expressing your thoughts to someone close to you.

chipmunk should be afraid to sit and eat out of a human's hands, but as you can see from the picture below, this one had moved past his fear. He probably lived in a tourist area and had learned that humans had good things to eat; things he couldn't necessarily find in his natural habitat. I imagine at first he was timid and probably scurried away in fear each time the human moved. But as he tasted the morsels thrown at him, he became braver, until he finally ended up in the palm of the hand, enjoying the delicacies and ignoring the danger that could occur. Satan often uses the same tactics to get us eating out of his hands. He entices us with something we really like and our interest is piqued. He throws us a few more morsels and we find them enjoyable and come a little closer. We ignore the dangerous territory we are entering and eventually start to feel at home. After a while, we no longer recognize what we are doing as sin and before we know it, we're eating out of his hand. We are told to turn and run from sin the minute we are enticed by it. If we let it tease our senses it becomes harder and harder to resist. So the next time something sinful entices you, flee as if your life depended on it, because it does. Have you ever been enticed by something you knew you shouldn't do? How did you respond?

"But you, . . . flee from all this, and pursue righteousness,
godliness, faith, love, endurance and gentleness."
1 Timothy 6:11

"Have we learned the secret of the Christian's pow'r?
Victory, victory, all the way along;
List'ning and obeying, trusting every hour,
Victory all along through Jesus."

Memorize I Corinthians 10, verses 12–13, for times when you feel tempted.

*O*K, I admit it. I'm an over-achiever and find satisfaction in completing tasks. I like to work and rate success by how much I have done. Yet I never feel I've done enough. My life often resembles a machine intent upon producing and completing the end product. God's rating system is different. It's good to be a worker but He is more focused on the person than the accomplishment. The end result is more about what God was able to do in me, than getting a job done. How successful I am depends upon how obedient I am. God is not interested in all my activity; He is looking at the attitude of my heart and what motivates me. While I'm focused on production He's focused on transformation. While I'm trying to be a strong warrior for Him He's asking me to be submissive to Him. God doesn't find delight when I wear myself out. I don't have to prove my worth to Him; He wants my love. Often He has to wait until I come to Him exhausted and empty, frustrated that my work did not bring me the satisfaction I desired. And then He puts His arm around me, pulls me into His lap and asks me to rest in Him. He assures me I don't have to earn His love; He could not value me more. He gently reminds me that it's not about what I can do but what He can do through me that counts. What do you base your worth on—your accomplishments or who you are in Christ?

*"In repentance and rest
is your salvation,
in quietness and trust
is your strength."*
Isaiah 30:15

*"When you have done your best, let Jesus do the rest,
He knows what's good for you;
Still trusting, look above and rest upon His love,
And see what He will do."*

Take some time and rest in the Lord.

October 12
Read Colossians chapter 2

My daughter called to tell me they had bought a new pair of shoes for their three-year old son and he was so excited. All he could talk about was how he could run faster and jump higher than ever before. He ran and jumped until he was exhausted so they laid him down for a nap, shoes off beside his bed. Later they went into his room to check on him and there he lay, new shoes on, sound asleep, not wanting to part with them for even a moment. Even though new shoes don't necessarily make a difference he probably was faster because he believed he was. In our relational program at Love INC one of the most amazing transformations I see is when clients make a mental shift in their perception of themselves. They usually come in beat up and discouraged, believing they can do nothing right. When they realize they have the ability to make good choices and decisions, even though very little may have changed in their situation, they behave differently and it changes everything. We live up to our own expectations and rarely beyond them. One of the greatest gifts we can give someone is renewed belief in themselves. Their actions, decisions, and choices will change as they start to see themselves as someone with potential instead of as a failure. If you've been pretty hard on yourself lately maybe you need to get a new pair of "shoes"—it just might help set you on a new and better path. Do you need to see yourself through God's eyes possessing lots of potential and talents?

"My purpose is that they may be encouraged in heart and united in love, so that they may have the full riches of complete understanding."
Colossians 2:2

List your strengths and thank God for how He has gifted you.

Throughout the Bible we see how God used unlikely people and unusual methods to accomplish His will. We also see how many of His chosen ones argued with Him about being selected. In Judges Chapter 6 & 7 we see Gideon questioning God when chosen to save Israel. He reminded God he was from the weakest clan and the least in his own family. None of that seemed to matter to God and, to further complicate matters, God reduced his army from 32,000 men to 300. He had Gideon divide them into three groups of one hundred and armed them with trumpets and clay jars with torches inside. Then He told Gideon to go defeat the enemy. Can you imagine how Gideon must have felt going into battle knowing his army had been reduced to only a handful of men armed with clay jars? But God gave him the victory and was glorified. Do you feel inadequate for the task before you? Go ahead and talk it over with God. It won't be the first time He has been questioned over His choice. And after you've had your heart-to-heart talk don't be surprised if He further complicates things by taking away

resources that would help you be victorious. God is looking for our obedience, not our credentials. He delights in opportunities to show His strength through our weakness. If you feel weak and inadequate you're probably a good candidate for His next miracle. Have you ever questioned God about something that has happened to you?

"Dividing the three hundred men into three companies, he placed trumpets and empty jars in the hands of all of them, with torches inside."
Judges 7:16

> *"The vict'ry is mine, the vict'ry is mine;*
> *Through Jesus my Lord, obeying His word;*
> *He conquers the foe, wherever I go;*
> *I'm living with Him, in holy accord."*

Think of a time when God blessed you
to accomplish something beyond your abilities.

October 14
Read Colossians chapter 3

When I get ready in the morning I have a routine. I take a shower, take my vitamins, eat breakfast, brush my teeth, fix my hair, put on my makeup, get dressed and have my first cup of coffee. I wouldn't skip any of these steps if I was going to leave the house that morning. But another extremely important part of my morning includes my quiet time with God. Each day I get up early enough to allow time to clothe myself with the traits God has said are important—compassion, kindness, humility, gentleness and patience. When I don't find time to study His Word and pray I feel naked as I leave the house. I know I haven't clothed myself with His presence and power and I feel unprepared for the day. He has also given us one other instruction that we are to put on each day—love, which binds everything together in perfect unity. What does your morning routine look like? Does it include time with God to make sure you have "put on" everything He has instructed?

"Therefore, as God's chosen people, holy and dearly loved, clothe yourselves with compassion, kindness, humility, gentleness and patience . . . And over all these virtues put on love, which binds them all together in perfect unity."
Colossians 3:12 & 14

"What a wonderful change in my life has been wrought
Since Jesus came into my heart;
I have light in my soul for which long I have sought,
Since Jesus came into my heart."

Start your day right by taking time with God.

> *"Moment by moment I'm kept in His love;*
> *Moment by moment I've life from above;*
> *Looking to Jesus till glory doth shine;*
> *Moment by moment, O Lord, I am Thine."*

I love the four distinct seasons in Idaho and find I can relate them to the seasons in my own life. My seasons may not follow the calendar, but when I have an important event coming up, it feels like summer—active and alive. The event itself often resembles the fall—vibrant, eye-catching, and exciting. But after the event, it seems I enter into a time of dormancy. I find myself tired, lethargic, unable to focus on any one thing, anxious because I think I should be getting more done. After experiencing this several times, I have come to understand that I need the winter to restore and replenish myself and should not be anxiously looking around, wondering what is wrong. Spring has always come in due time, and I find new ideas budding in my mind and once again life seems fresh and inviting. It's not long before there is new growth and I enter into summer once again. What season are you in right now and are you embracing it or fighting against it?

> *"There is a time for everything, and a season for every activity under heaven."*
> *Ecclesiastes 3:1*

Thank God for something specific He is doing in this season of life right now.

October 16

Read Mark chapter 9

*P*eter is probably my favorite disciple because I can relate to his strengths and weaknesses. His passion for Christ moves me but he was also impulsive and often got in trouble. He was the one to jump out of the boat and start to walk on water toward Jesus. However, his boldness quickly changed to fear and he sank. When Jesus asked the disciples, "Who do you say I am?" Peter was quick to answer, "You are the Christ." But then he soon found himself being rebuked by Christ who said, "You do not have in mind the things of God, but the things of men." It seems Peter's walk was sprinkled with times when he was keenly attuned to Christ. Other times he spoke rashly from a need to take control and do something when things became unsettling. I have often felt similar emotions. Some days I feel strong in the Lord, anchored to the rock. Then there are times when I'm confused and unsure, stumbling around trying to find my way. I find it challenging to know how to lead with boldness and still walk in humility with Christ. It makes me wonder how often I unintentionally put my own agenda in front of God's. The more authority I am given, the less adequate I feel for the task. It keeps me on my knees and that's probably a good thing—it's harder to run from that position. I don't want to run away, but neither do I want to run ahead of my Lord. Are you more impulsive or timid in your walk with the Lord?

"Peter said to Jesus, 'Rabbi, it is good for us to be here. Let us put up three shelters—one for you, one for Moses and one for Elijah.' (He did not know what to say, they were so frightened.)"
Mark 9:5 & 6

*"My hope is built on nothing less
Than Jesus' blood and righteousness;
I dare not trust the sweetest frame,
But wholly lean on Jesus' name."*

Balancing authority and humility
is something only done through God's strength.

ope is so important in our lives. I remember when I first got divorced I felt like everything I had planned and worked for was gone. All my dreams were crushed and I felt hopeless. I felt my future was stolen and I could see nothing to look forward to, as I struggled through each day. It took a long time to heal and realize that even though that part of my life was changed there was still much to be hopeful about. Through the support of my family and friends during this difficult time I was able to cling to their hope that a brighter day was coming until I could see it for myself. We all need hope. Most of the clients who come to our New Hope Relational Program have lost hope that anything will change in their lives. They have given up believing life could be different as they struggle to get through each week. But as we encourage them in their potential and guide them in decisions, they start to cling to the hope we offer them. At first they cannot see how it is possible, but because we have hope, they begin to believe in their future and the tiny seeds of their

hope begin to grow again. God has promised a better life and we can look forward with hope to our future. Is there someone in your life that needs encouragement and restored hope? Can you play a part in their healing process?

*"And we rejoice in the hope of the glory of God. Not only so,
but we also rejoice in our sufferings, because we know that suffering produces perseverance,
perseverance, character; and character, hope. And hope does not disappoint us, because
God has poured out His love into our hearts by the Holy Spirit, whom He has given us."*
Romans 5:2–5

*"There are some rays of hope divine,
To cheer the darkest heart;
Around the cross they ever shine,
Where life anew may start."*

Put steps in place to help you realize your dreams.

October 18
Read Mark chapter 2

A paralytic lay on a mat, unable to go anywhere by himself. He heard Jesus was in town but was powerless to get to Him in his own strength. Yet he was surrounded by friends who must have cared for him because they carried him on his mat to Jesus. When they arrived the crowd was so large they still could not see Him. They could have turned around, telling the paralytic they had done all they could do. But no, they persevered and dug a hole in the roof lowering him down to Jesus, who saw their great faith and healed him. This story is a wonderful example of interceding for those who become too weak to carry the load on their own. Over the last few years several Love INC volunteers have experienced difficult bouts of cancer. It seemed at times they became too weak physically even to pray, though their spirits stayed strong. It was during those times we had the privilege of picking them up and carrying them to Jesus through intercessory prayer. What an honor to step in the gap and lift them to Jesus when the journey became too difficult. God responds to the prayers of His people and He works great miracles because of their faith. Let us not be slack in caring for our brothers and sisters in need. Who has God put on your heart to carry in prayer?

"When Jesus saw their faith, He said to the paralytic, 'Son, your sins are forgiven.'"
Mark 2:5

Send someone a note telling them you are praying for them.

"Faith of our fathers, living still,
In spite of dungeon, fire, and sword;
Oh, how our hearts beat high with joy
Whene'er we hear that glorious Word!"

The feeding of the five thousand is a well known and favorite Bible story. As I have meditated on the passage I have tried to imagine what my response would have been. If I had been the one with the few fish and loaves of bread, would I have given up what I had brought or would I have clung to it fearing I would also go hungry? If someone had offered what they had, no matter how small or trivial, would I have thanked God believing He could multiply it? Or would I have continued looking for something bigger and better to meet the need and overlooked the provision at hand? If I had been the one handed a basket and told to share it with others, would I have tried to rationalize and argue that there wasn't enough to go around, and been hesitant to participate in something that seemed sure to fail? These were all opportunities to demonstrate faith—faith to give up what I have so it can be multiplied; faith to receive with thanksgiving the seemingly inadequate provision; faith to be responsive and obedient to whatever God asks, no matter how impossible it looks. I'm not sure how I would have responded had I been there, but I know God wants my faith to grow until I will give it up, look up, and be obedient regardless of the enormity or impossibility of the task before me. How are you doing in your faith journey?

"The number of those who ate was about five thousand men, besides women and children."
Matthew 14:21

Think of a time when your faith was stretched by what seemed impossible.

October 20

Read Jeremiah chapter 18

Pumpkins are just pumpkins until someone carves a face on them. Then they are transformed into Jack-o-Lanterns and they take on the personality of the face etched into them. Some appear gleeful and friendly while others seem wicked and scary. It's fun to see the different personalities emerge from pumpkins but I think all too often the same thing can happen with us. God has created us in His image, but people can shape us by their own perception of us whether it's right or wrong. It seems the more other people believe this perception, the more we begin to think that's how we are and we start living up to this image. It's almost as if they have carved out a new face on us and it's what we have become. Are you letting God, or others, shape you?

"Like clay in the hand of the potter, so are you in my hand, declares the Lord."
Jeremiah 18:6

"Revive us again; fill each heart with Thy love;
May each soul be rekindled with fire from above.
Hallelujah! Thine the glory. Hallelujah! Amen.
Hallelujah! Thine the glory. Revive us again."

List several qualities you believe God has given you
and thank Him for making you unique.

When we got Charlie, our new golden labrador, I wasn't looking forward to training him but knew it had to be done. An untrained dog is difficult to enjoy. If they won't heel, they'll pull in every direction, chasing after anything that catches their eye. If they don't learn to sit they can never be controlled. If they don't learn to stay they can't be left unguarded. If they won't come when called they can never be let loose. If they don't learn to retrieve they can never be sent on a task. As we train Charlie, we will instruct him verbally and physically first using constant rewards. As he matures he will begin to respond to our verbal commands without expecting a reward. We anticipate many blessed years with Charlie because we're investing the time and training required to have a dog who is obedient and responsive. As Christians we need to be trained by our Master if we want to live life to the fullest. We have to recognize His commands and respond in obedience. We have to know how to sit and be still for long periods trusting in His timing. We can't try to lead Him around chasing after everything that catches our eye. And if we never learn to work for Him He won't be able to send us into the mission field. Are you willing to let the Master train you so you can live a full life and be a wonderful companion to Him?

"We have much to say about this, but it is hard to explain because you are slow to learn. In fact, though by this time you ought to be teachers, you need someone to teach you the elementary truths of God's word all over again. You need milk, not solid food!"
Hebrews 5:11–13

"My life, my love, I give to Thee,
Thou Lamb of God who died for me;
Oh, may I ever faithful be,
My Savior and my God!"

Start a new discipline that will help you mature as a Christian.

"Do not store up for yourselves treasures on earth, where moth and rust destroy, and where thieves break in and steal. But store up for yourselves treasures in heaven, where moth and rust do not destroy, and where thieves do not break in and steal. For where your treasure is, there your heart will be also."
Matthew 6:19–21

"I'd rather have Jesus than silver or gold;
I'd rather be His than have riches untold;
I'd rather have Jesus than houses or lands;
I'd rather be led by His nail-pierced hand."

Before I married my husband I had no experience with livestock. While I love having our Hereford cattle around I struggle with them when they break down the fences and get out. A few times they have damaged my yard, and each time it has caused me pain. Once I was out of town when the bull got out and broke several of my newly planted trees. My husband greeted me at the entrance to our drive way when I arrived home to share the bad news before I drove into the yard. Recently the cows got into our yard again. The bull found the orchard and broke off several of our new trees that were heavily laden with fruit. Again I felt loss and despair when something we had worked on and taken pride in was destroyed. Both times the damage was irreparable and we lost things we valued. As I've contemplated these incidents, I am reminded how fleeting earthly things are. Things we value and invest time and money in can be gone in a minute and we may never get them back. Only treasures stored in heaven last for eternity. We need to make sure our investments are storing up heavenly treasures as well as giving us earthly satisfaction. Have you ever lost something you treasured?

Make a list of what you cherish most—does it have eternal value?

*"Let us hold unswervingly to the hope we profess, for He who promised is faithful.
And let us consider how we may spur one another on toward love and good deeds.
Let us not give up meeting together, as some are in the habit of doing, but let us
encourage one another—and all the more as you see the Day approaching."*
Hebrews 10:23-25

*"Softly and tenderly Jesus is calling,
Calling for you and for me;
See, on the portals He's waiting and watching,
Watching for you and for me."*

My daughter doesn't live close by and when she makes plans to visit me, I find myself filled with excited anticipation for her arrival. I enjoy spending time together as we catch up on each other's lives. We often sit for hours sharing our joys, our sorrows, and our special needs for prayers. I feel loved and appreciated that she takes time from her busy schedule to plan these times with me. Occasionally, sickness or work prevents her from coming and I experience disappointment that we will miss this special time. I like to think that Jesus looks forward to my visits with Him in the same way. I imagine Him waiting in a chair by the window,

looking out in expectation for me to arrive. He desires for me to share my joys, sorrows and prayer requests with Him. He delights when I take time for Him and I believe He experiences sorrow when I ignore Him. When I find myself getting busy and struggling to take time for the Lord, I think of the visual image of Him sitting in the chair, looking out of the window and waiting for me to come. When I look at it from this perspective I usually stop what I'm doing and go meet Him there. Have you ever visualized Jesus waiting for you to come and share your day with Him?

Have an empty chair in the room when you pray, visualizing Jesus in it.

"Though your sins are like scarlet, they shall be as white as snow;
though they are red as crimson, they shall be like wool."
Isaiah 1:18

"Have you been to Jesus for the cleansing pow'r?
Are you washed in the blood of the Lamb?
Are you fully trusting in His grace this hour?
Are you washed in the blood of the Lamb?"

Have you ever gotten yourself into a real mess and known you're not going to be able to cover it up? My two-year old grandson took the cap off a five gallon bucket of white paint and proceeded to reach his arm through the hole and paint himself. He realized he shouldn't be doing this and tried to wipe it off, which of course just spread it even further. By the time his mother noticed, there was paint all over him and the floor. You can imagine what a mess it was to clean up. He had paint spots on his body for days. Sometimes we get into something we shouldn't and when we realize what we've done we try to cover it up, but it just keeps spreading further and further. The more we lie and try to disguise our involvement the more evident it becomes, until we're caught "white-handed" so to speak.

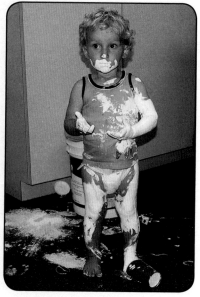

When we get to that point we can either go through the painful, drawn-out process of cleaning up or be stained for life. Cleaning up these big messes isn't quick or easy. Often those helping us get covered too, causing further damage to innocent parties. But letting it scar us for life isn't good either. God can help remove the stains and, in time, things will settle down. But often the impact on our life and those closest to us will be long-lasting. Only God can take a big mess and work it into something good. It means we'll have to confess, seek forgiveness and own up to it. He can't work if we're still trying to keep it hidden. Have you ever gotten into a really big mess and needed God to help clean it up?

Write down how God brought good out of something bad.

*"I've found a Friend, oh, such a friend! So kind and true and tender,
So wise a Counselor and Guide, So mighty a Defender!
From Him who loves me now so well. What pow'r my soul can sever?
Shall life or death, shall earth or hell? No! I am His forever."*

I have acquaintances with whom I struggle to communicate. I often find that what I say is misconstrued or criticized, so I choose my words very carefully. I get nervous when I need to communicate with them anticipating they won't hear what I'm trying to say. I may be misunderstood and have to explain what I was trying to say, or find myself becoming defensive at their response. Either way I avoid communicating with them and we both miss opportunities to share our lives. Some people say they are afraid to talk to God because they're not sure how to approach Him, but God is always approachable. There is no magic formula when praying to Him. He doesn't need any particular language or style. The attitude of our heart is more important than the eloquence of our words. He just wants us to talk to Him simply and honestly. He wants us to tell Him all our feelings, angry or happy. He already knows how we feel, so it's not going to surprise Him. Don't miss sharing every moment of your day with Him; He's never too busy to lend you His ear. Do you find it easy to talk to God?

*"In Him and through faith in Him
we may approach God with freedom and confidence."*
Ephesians 3:12

Spend some time telling God how you feel about your life right now.

October 26
Read John chapter 17

"Early let us seek Thy favor, early let us do Thy will;
Blessed Lord and only Savior, with Thy love our bosoms fill.
Blessed Jesus, blessed Jesus! Thou hast loved us, love us still.
Blessed Jesus, blessed Jesus! Thou hast loved us, love us still."

Doing ministry work "In the Name of Christ" carries a huge responsibility. Since accepting the position with Love INC, I have been keenly aware that discerning God's will and engaging in His work was my most important task. As each person calls our Clearinghouse for help I know we need to pray about what God wants us to do for that person. I believe each one is heaven sent to us by God. Discerning God's will takes a commitment to pray before responding. A client may have many obvious needs. We can get distracted meeting the obvious and miss what God wants us to do. This point was made especially clear to me one night in a dream shortly after I started working for Love INC. I was standing before my Lord and Savior and He said "Lois, you have done a lot of things in my name." Then there was a pause and I heard two possible statements. He said either, "Well done my good and faithful servant" or "I wasn't involved in any of those things you did." I know which answer I want to hear on Judgment Day and it affects how I oversee the ministry today. Have you spent time in prayer asking God what He wants you to do, or have you been so busy doing a good work you haven't had time to listen to Him?

"I have brought you glory on earth by completing the work you gave me to do."
John 17:4

Make a decision to pray before you work each day.

"But I know Whom I have believed,
And am persuaded that He is able
To keep that which I've committed
Unto Him against that day."

Is there something in your life that seems utterly impossible? Is there an opportunity that has you feeling completely out of your comfort zone, totally inadequate and unable to see where the provision will come from? If you find yourself in this kind of situation, praise God, you are probably about His work! God's work is never something we can accomplish on our own. His work always seems impossible and beyond us. When we only plan those things we can accomplish under our own power and through our own resources, we don't need Him. But when God calls us to His work the only thing we "do know" is that we "don't know." God has put the desire for a campus and community center on my heart—a place where the unified Church can come together to train and mentor those in need—a place where broken families can be healed, restored and transformed. When I first felt this call I wouldn't even speak it to others; it seemed so crazy. Now, several years later, I continue to believe that this impossible thing will be done by Him. I don't know how, when, where, or through what means, but I'm ok with that. My part is to believe and be

obedient as He shines His light on the next step. Is it scary? Do I face ridicule from others? Do I wonder if I'm over my head? Yes, I feel all these emotions, but I also have an excited anticipation about being involved in something much bigger than I am. Has God called you to be a part of something impossible? Have you said yes?

"I will go before you and will level the mountains; I will break down gates of bronze and cut through bars of iron. I will give you the treasures of darkness, riches stored in secret places. So that you may know that I am the Lord, the God of Israel, who calls you by name."
Isaiah 45:2&3

Make yourself available to God for something impossible.

October 28

Read Philippians chapter 4

I was a young teenager in the late sixties and remember how excited I would be to play a new record I had purchased. I always felt bad when the record got a scratch in it, causing it to repeat the same sound over and over again, unable to move on. I would have to move the needle past the scratch to hear the rest of the song. When I became an adult, I started to struggle with negative thoughts in my mind, playing them over and over again much like a scratch on a record. I found myself frustrated at my inability to control my mind and move beyond them. As I've matured in my Christian walk, I have found the best way for me to move past consuming thoughts and worry is to visualize myself giving it to God. I imagine placing it in His hands, usually in a box, and walking away leaving the box behind. Then each time the thought returns, I remind myself I don't have it anymore, I left it with God, and I thank Him for taking care of it. Replacing worry with an attitude of praise has been an important step in eliminating the scratches in my mind—allowing me to think beautiful thoughts that glorify God. Have you ever struggled with repetitive thoughts that you can't seem to control?

"Do not be anxious about anything, but in everything, by prayer and petition, with thanksgiving, present your requests to God. And the peace of God, which transcends all understanding, will guard your hearts and your minds in Christ Jesus."
Philippians 4:5–7

> *"Cast thy cares upon the Savior,*
> *He will bear them all for thee;*
> *And thy soul which now is burdened,*
> *Shall be kept forever free."*

When you find yourself starting to worry, give it to God, and leave it there.

*I*n a time of need do you find yourself wondering how you will make it? Are all your earthly provisions almost gone? Have you lost hope? In I Kings the story of Elijah and the widow gives me hope. He met her while she was gathering twigs to make a last meal for her and her son. She had nothing left but a little flour and oil, only enough for the two of them. Death was just around the corner. Elijah, after hearing her story, asked her to bring him a drink and make him a small cake of bread from what little she had. He said the Lord would supply flour and oil until He gave rain to the land if she did what he asked. I wonder what my response would have been? She had to give up what she had, her only earthly hope, and put her trust in a stranger who seemed to be promising the impossible. Would I have had the faith to do it? She did, and the Lord was true to His word. When times get tough we cling to what we have, but God wants us to release everything to Him trusting that He will provide. Has God asked you to let go and let Him provide? Let God unwrap your fingers from whatever you're clutching and reach your hand out to Him. He is trustworthy. You have little to lose and much to gain. What are you clinging to?

"She went away and did as Elijah had told her.
So there was food every day for Elijah and for the woman and her family. For the jar of flour was not used up and the jug of oil did not run dry, in keeping with the word of the Lord spoken by Elijah."
1 Kings 17:15 & 16

"*Trusting as the moments fly,*
Trusting as the days go by;
Trusting Him whate'er befall,
Trusting Jesus, that is all."

Hold everything loosely.

October 30
Read John chapter 3

I recently went to the Love INC National Convention. When you entered the hotel lobby, a large Love INC logo was displayed on the wall behind a waterfall. The projection came from a very small image of the logo reflected onto the wall making a bold statement for all to see. As one of the Executive Directors came up to offer prayer during a session, he commented on how it had reminded him that no matter how small and insignificant we may think our life is, when we let God shine His light through us, it can cause a bright and wonderful reflection of Christ for others to see. So often we think we have to do great things or be someone important to make a difference for Christ. But in reality the less people see us the more they will be able to see Christ in us, and that's what being a Christian is all about. So the next time you feel insignificant remember Christ doesn't need much to leave a lasting impression of Himself. Can you think of a time when something you did reflected Christ's glory?

"He must become greater; I must become less."
John 3:30

"There is a fountain filled with blood,
Drawn from Immanuel's veins,
And sinners plunged beneath that flood
Lose all their guilty stains."

Do a secret good deed for someone.

"I tell you that this man, rather than the other, went home justified before God. For everyone who exalts himself will be humbled, and he who humbles himself will be exalted."
Luke 18:14

> *"Just as I am, without one plea,*
> *But that Thy blood was shed for me,*
> *And that Thou bidst me come to Thee,*
> *O Lamb of God, I come, I come."*

My children loved to dress up on Halloween and pretend to be something different than they were. One son especially liked his Popeye costume and wanted to wear it year after year. I think he enjoyed hiding behind the mask thinking no one could guess who he was. As Christians we often don our masks before church pretending to have a perfect life with everything under control. We falsely believe that if we are a good Christian we will always be happy and never have struggles. We feel a need to hide the reality that getting to church itself was a struggle. We fought with the kids or our spouse on the way, we're exhausted and feel removed from Christ, discouraged and anything but joy-filled. We put on our

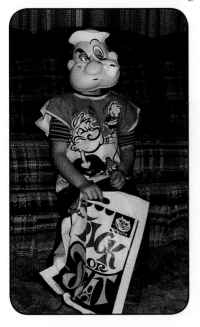

masks and march into the church resolved to make sure no one gets close enough to see we're unraveling on the inside. Church needs to be a safe place, a haven where we can be real about our journey. We can't tell everything to everyone, but we don't need to pretend we never struggle. The Bible tells us we will have trials on earth with discouragement and challenges. Let's get rid of our false pretenses and be genuinely honest with each other, admitting when we need prayer and quick to pray for others. Being a Christian doesn't mean we're perfect, but that we're forgiven and have the hope of better days ahead. Have you ever put on a false front when you walked through the church door, and kept your distance so no one would know you're struggling?

Ask for prayer from someone you trust when you are struggling.

November 1

Read 2 Corinthians chapter 2

> *"Grace, grace, God's grace,*
> *Grace that will pardon and cleanse within;*
> *Grace, grace, God's grace,*
> *Grace that is greater than all our sin!"*

Idaho has a lot of cattle ranches and dairies, many of them very large. In fact there are some areas where you know you are in cow country long before you see a feedlot or dairy. Let's just say you can follow your nose, it won't lead you astray. In the last few years we've had a large influx of people moving to Idaho to get out of the city. What they hadn't bargained for were the smells that come with living in the country. To an outsider the smell is dreadful, but to a rancher or dairyman, it is the sweet smell of their livelihood and it doesn't bother them at all. The aroma of a Christian is mentioned in the Bible. It says that to some it is the sweet fragrance of life and to others it is the stench of death. Our tendency may be to cover up the smell to those who think it stinks, but that's not what God wants us to do. We need to carry the aroma of Christ wherever we go and not worry about what other people might think of us, after all it is the smell of life everlasting to those who believe. Do you have the aroma of Christ pervading your life wherever you go?

> *"For we are to God the aroma of Christ among those who are being saved*
> *and those who are perishing. To the one we are the smell of death;*
> *to the other, the fragrance of life. And who is equal to such a task?"*
> *2 Corinthians 2:15 & 16*

Tell someone who reminds you of Christ how much you appreciate them.

> *"In Thy dear hands of love I lay,*
> *Fulfill Thy purposes in me;*
> *Teach me to say from day to day,*
> *Thy will be done in me."*

Southwestern Idaho experienced amazing growth for several years and land was bought and developed all over the valley. Then the recession hit and everything came to a screeching halt. Developments were left unfinished leaving the landscape eerie and unkempt. An unfinished golf course close to our home was soon taken over by rolling tumbleweeds with paved golf paths leading nowhere amidst the unfinished landscape. The future of this abandoned course looks bleak. Thankfully our lives are not like that in the Lord's eyes. We are a work in progress. God will never give up or abandon us. He's not going to run short on resources and leave us half finished. He's got a beautiful design in mind and as long as we are willing He'll keep on molding us into something special. It's reassuring to know that God's ability to finish what He has started doesn't depend upon our resources or the economy. He's got everything He needs to create an amazing masterpiece. Do you see yourself as a valuable work of art in God's eyes?

"Therefore, if anyone is in Christ, he is a new creation;
the old has gone, the new has come!"
2 Corinthians 5:17

Think of a special quality God has given you and thank Him for it.

November 3
Read Isaiah chapter 11

"Holy Spirit, keep us still,
Help us do the Father's will;
Give us grace and strength each day,
Keep us in the living way."

There are thousands of books and poems written about love. We can read and study extensively about what it is and how it feels. But no matter how much we study, nothing can prepare us for the emotions we feel when we fall in love for the first time. We move beyond anything we have learned or read to something we experience deeply within our being and it changes us forever. Learning about God is a similar experience. The Bible instructs us in everyday life and tells us how He desires us to live. There are also many scholars who have penned their thoughts to help us become more knowledgeable about God. But there is only so much that can be taught. At some point we have to move beyond what we learn and enter into the spiritual realm with Him. The Holy Spirit cannot be taught or explained—He must be experienced. When we start to understand God on a spiritual level we start to understand His heart. Devotion to God moves us into a more intimate relationship with Him. As our heart melts in surrender to His will, we become pliable in His hands and He is able to accomplish much more through us. Without the intervention of the Spirit we are unable to receive divine direction and revelation. Draw close to God and move out of religion and into a love relationship with Him. Have you experienced the Spirit of the Lord?

"The Spirit of the Lord will rest on him— the Spirit of wisdom and of understanding, the Spirit of counsel and of power, the Spirit of knowledge and of the fear of the Lord— and he will delight in the fear of the Lord."
Isaiah 11:2 & 3

Spend time in prayer asking God to fill you with His presence.

"J am Thine, O Lord, J have heard Thy voice,
And it told Thy love to me;
But J long to rise in the arms of faith
And be closer drawn to Thee."

My prayer life has changed since I started working for Love INC. Since my teens I've had my devotion and prayer time and once a day seemed sufficient. But in Love INC I was so far out of my comfort zone and expertise I realized that God and I were going to have to meet a lot more often. Little did I know my time with God was about to take a dramatic turn. I started to wake up around 3:00 struggling to go back to sleep. After several nights of sleeplessness I got up in frustration and stepped outside in the cool, brisk air. It was there, under the starlit skies, I encountered God in a new and powerful way. He had been calling to me night after night but it had taken me a while to realize He was waking me up. These late night visits became a fairly regular thing, and God and I started to communicate on a new and deeper level. There's something about the stillness of the night that seems to magnify His presence and I feel intimately loved and precious to Him. This God who created the heavens and the earth and placed each star in the sky, calls to me even in my sleep, so we can commune together. He loves you this much too and desires to spend time with you in a very special way. It may not be in the middle of the night but He is calling to you. Have you learned to recognize His voice and are you responding?

"He determines the number of the stars and calls them each by name. Great is our Lord and mighty in power; His understanding has no limit."
Psalm 147:4 & 5

Go outside tonight and gaze upon the Lord's wondrous display of stars.

> *"Through this world of toil and snares,*
> *If I falter, Lord, who cares?*
> *Who with me my burden shares?*
> *None but Thee, dear Lord, none but Thee."*

We were care providers for my husband's mother for the couple of years she lived with us. It was a blessed time in our life and God often spoke to me through circumstances that arose while caring for her. With each passing month she grew more unsteady on her feet and often fell. We tried to come to her aid quickly, but she would struggle to get up only to fall again before we could reach her. Much of her bruising and soreness came from her struggling and the second fall. We encouraged her to stay still and wait for us but to no avail. I remember feeling frustrated and unsure how to help her see the value in waiting rather than struggling on her own. Then God reminded me that I often behave in much the same manner in my own life. When life knocks me off my feet I'm quick to jump up and get busy again never pausing to reflect on what just happened. My inability to slow down has often complicated things and I find myself knocked down again, repeating the same mistake. In watching my mother-in-law struggle I realized that both of us needed to slow down and ask for help. I now try to pause and wait for God to help me get up when I've taken a spill. I need to cry out and wait just like we encouraged my mother-in-law to do. He's just an outstretched hand away. Do you pause and wait for God when life gives you a spill?

"For I am the Lord, your God, who takes hold of your right hand
and says to you, Do not fear; I will help you."
Isaiah 41:13

Is it difficult for you to ask for and receive help?

I come from a family of worriers so it comes naturally to me. I can worry about everything from the lights being shut off, to a door being closed. In fact it seems I worry more about the little stuff than I do about the big things. I have kept journals for years. I keep them so I can go back and read what I was feeling at different times in my life. They are filled with "what if's" and concerns, which have all been resolved one way or another. Worrying is one of the least productive activities we can do. It's also a sin. God has told us not to worry because worry changes nothing. It stems from fear, and fear stems from a lack of trust, which stems from a lack of faith. So if I have a worry problem—I have a faith problem. Once I started to view it from this light, it became easier to let it go. I didn't one day just quit worrying, but now I make a conscious effort to replace worry with praise. Whenever I catch myself worrying, I lift a prayer of praise that God will take care of my concern. Replacing worry with praise works for me. I also remind myself how futile worry is—like being concerned that the sun won't rise. It's a waste of time. I have never given the rising or setting of the sun a second thought, but I have worried about things equally beyond my control. The next time you find yourself worrying, thank God for being in charge and, remember, the sun will rise in the morning. It's all in His hands. Are you a worrier?

"Who of you by worrying can add a single hour to his life?"
Matthew 6:27

"Blessed be the Name, blessed be the Name,
Blessed be the Name of the Lord!
Blessed be the Name, blessed be the Name,
Blessed be the Name of the Lord!"

Make a list of your worries, throw them away,
and thank God for being in charge.

> *"Glorious freedom, wonderful freedom,*
> *No more in chains of sin I repine!*
> *Jesus the glorious Emancipator,*
> *Now and forever He shall be mine."*

A study was conducted with children playing in an open playground versus one with fencing. Without defined boundaries they tended to play in the center, bunched together and did not venture out. But in a playground with fencing they would spread out feeling confident that if they stayed within the fenced area they were safe. We need defined boundaries and limits and yet it is a natural instinct to test them. Children and teenagers push the rules to see what they can get away with. I remember my teenagers confiding in me that even though they pushed the limits they were glad the boundaries held firm and they could use me as an excuse not to do something. God has set clear boundaries in the Bible and they never change. As long as we play within the defined boundary we need have no fear, knowing we are safe in His care. But if we walk out the gate and leave the protection of the Good Shepherd behind we might find ourselves alone and in grave danger. God's commandments are not meant to take away our joy, but to give us freedom to live life to the fullest. Are you always pushing against God's boundaries?

"I am the gate; whoever enters through me will be saved. He will come in and go out, and find pasture. The thief comes only to steal and kill and destroy; I have come that they may have life and have it to the full."
John 10:9 & 10

Compare the difference of raising a child now than when you were a child.

When I was expecting my second child it was sugar beet harvest season and my husband was working from sun up to sun down fifteen miles away. My remote home did not have telephone service and I was left with my 18-month old toddler, over fifty miles from the hospital. My husband set out an old tractor tire and a can of diesel in the field beside the house and told me to light it if I went into labor. Everyone was instructed if they saw the black, billowing smoke to tell my husband or get me to the hospital. Even though I didn't have to use this communication tactic it was in place if I had needed it. There are many times in life when we need to call to others for help, but we often do the opposite. When we find ourselves slipping into depression, fighting a sin temptation, struggling in our marriage or sliding in our spiritual walk we often feel ashamed or embarrassed and try to hide it from those who care most about us. If I had gone into labor, it would have been foolish and possibly life-threatening to keep it to myself, ashamed to send up smoke signals for help. It's just as dangerous to hide struggles in life instead of calling out to those who can help us. The next time you feel alone and afraid send up a smoke signal and see if those who love you don't come to your rescue. Have you ever hid a difficult time in your life because you were ashamed?

*"The Lord is close
to the brokenhearted
and saves those who are
crushed in spirit."
Psalm 34:18*

*"From sinking sand He lifted me,
With tender hand He lifted me;
From shades of night to plains of light,
Oh, praise His Name, He lifted me!"*

If you are struggling with something don't hide it, but confide it to a friend.

> *"Hallelujah! What a Savior, who can take a poor, lost sinner,*
> *Lift him from the miry clay and set me free!*
> *I will ever tell the story, shouting glory, glory, glory,*
> *Hallelujah! Jesus lifted me."*

Do you struggle with forgiving yourself for past mistakes and sins? I think most of us disappoint ourselves at times and then find it difficult to move on and not let it get us down. There are things in my past that I'm ashamed of. Even though it's been many years since I've confessed them I still remember as if it were yesterday. Psalm 103 says "as far as the east is from the west, so far has He removed our transgressions from us." But I have days when it doesn't feel like they're gone. I know the problem lays inside me not with God's forgiveness. In Isaiah 44 God compares our offenses to the morning mist. Frequently, when I rise in the morning there is a mist above the river, winding like a silky ribbon along the valley floor. As the sun comes up the mist evaporates leaving a fresh sprinkling of dew to start the day. God says that once our sins are confessed and forgiven they too evaporate and we are only left with the lessons learned to guide us through the day. When I dwell on these forgiven sins it's like wearing a dark cloak over my head that leaves me burdened and confused. Instead I should see them like the morning mist, here for a moment but soon gone under the loving "Son"shine of Jesus. Every day is a new day; a day that He has made. Let us throw off everything that burdens us, let us lift our eyes to Heaven and give a shout of praise to the God who loves us enough to forgive us forever. Do you need to free yourself from past sins you've given to God?

> *"I have swept away your offenses like a cloud, your sins like the morning mist.*
> *Return to me for I have redeemed you."*
> *Isaiah 44:22*

Write what is bothering you on a slip of paper,
confess and ask forgiveness, then throw it away.

> *"It is well, with my soul,*
> *It is well, it is well, with my soul."*

Have you ever tried to catch a piece of paper in a wind storm? The paper and the wind seem to play a game of tag, laughing, as I scramble after the elusive paper. I get close, but just as I reach over to grab it the wind whisks it away. This game of chase goes on until either I give up, or the paper becomes caught long enough for me to grab it. Finding satisfaction in this world can be similar to chasing paper in the wind. Worldly satisfaction is elusive and impossible to grasp. I have tried to find it by purchasing something I really wanted or by traveling somewhere special. But with each experience I felt unfulfilled and the pursuit began again. I believe the things of this world will never bring satisfaction. God has placed a longing inside us that only He can fill through a relationship with Him. It is only when we quit chasing wind-blown papers, and ask Him to come inside our heart, that we start to feel the peace and satisfaction we've been running after all along. Have you been looking for peace in all the wrong places?

> *"Yet when I surveyed all that my hands had done*
> *And what I had toiled to achieve,*
> *Everything was meaningless, a chasing after the wind;*
> *Nothing was gained under the sun."*
> *Ecclesiastes 2:11*

Think of a time you purchased something
and evaluate if it increased your sense of peace and satisfaction.

November 11

Read 2 Timothy chapter 2

"Endure hardship with us like a good soldier of Christ Jesus. No one serving as a soldier gets involved in civilian affairs—he wants to please his commanding officer."
2 Timothy 2:3 & 4

> *"Onward, Christian soldiers, marching as to war,*
> *With the cross of Jesus going on before.*
> *Christ, the royal Master, leads against the foe;*
> *Forward into battle see His banners go!"*

Whenever someone enlists in the military they go to boot camp in preparation for military duty. All status is stripped away as those enlisted become equal in their commander's eyes. For the next several weeks their personal agendas and spirits will be broken as they are formed into a unified division responsive to authority and direction. They are pushed mentally, emotionally and physically in preparation for active duty. When we become a Christian we sign up for the Lord's army and for the rest of our lives we will be in boot-camp training. Our personal agendas, status, rank and honor are set aside for serving our Lord. We undergo rigorous and difficult periods of training as we are molded for His service. We learn to hear and be responsive to Christ, our Commander and Chief, and not question His leading. We become physically fit, mentally competent and spiritually strong for the battles we will face. Some of us live as if we are on a long furlough and resist boot-camp training. Others become deserters of the faith finding the requirements more than they are willing to endure. Still others understand the commitment they have made, the oath of honor they are called to and are obedient and faithful even unto death. Where are you in your Christian military training?

Reflect on how a recent challenge prepared you for Christian service.

Lions are majestic animals and fun to observe in a zoo. But I don't think many of us would want to be inside their cage or have one approach us in the wild. We wouldn't think of packing a picnic lunch, crawling into their cage and sitting down to eat. We wouldn't play a game of Frisbee or baseball around them, running here and there oblivious to them. We wouldn't work, play, or worship in their space. It would be foolish to court such obvious danger. The Bible tells us that the enemy, Satan, roams around like a lion looking for whom he might devour. Yet are we always on the look-out for him? Do we eat, play, work, and worship with him right beside us and pretend he won't harm us? God has given us a very vivid picture of how Satan behaves and how dangerous he is, but we're often casual about sin. It's time we start behaving as if we're in a battle, because we are. We're in a fight for our life and Satan will do anything he can to distract, scare, confuse, discourage, or destroy us. Do you live your life on the look-out for Satan or are you playing in the lion's den?

"Be self-controlled and alert. Your enemy the devil prowls around like a roaring lion looking for someone to devour. Resist him, standing firm in the faith, because you know that your brothers throughout the world are undergoing the same kind of sufferings."
1 Peter 5:8 & 9

"All hail the pow'r of Jesus' Name! Let angels prostrate fall;
Bring forth the royal diadem, and crown Him Lord of all;
Bring forth the royal diadem, and crown Him Lord of all."

Memorize God's Word to protect you from Satan's attacks.

> *"O love divine, 'tis wonderful that mortals here below*
> *May share thy grace most excellent, thy wondrous power know!*
> *Around our hearts fore'er entwine, and let thy beauties in us shine,*
> *That we may be, O love divine, completely lost in thee."*

When my grandchildren leave after visiting me I often find tell-tale signs that they were there—a toy stuffed under the couch cushion, fingerprints on the glass door, a raisin dropped on the floor, a bent playing card on the chair or a half-full glass of water left on the counter. These reminders bring a smile to my face. I know when my grandchildren grow up I will miss the little fingerprints they leave behind everywhere they go. Do we live our lives in such a way that we leave God's fingerprints on those we touch? Do our actions and words leave tell-tale signs that bring a smile to the faces of those we've just been around? A warm encouraging word, a gentle pat on the shoulder, an inviting smile, attentive ears—all are fingerprints of God expressing His love. It doesn't take much to make a lasting impression. I want to touch those I'm around in such a way they feel they've just been touched by the hand of God. Do you leave God's fingerprints on those you meet?

> *"Be imitators of God, therefore, as dearly loved children and live a life of love, just as Christ loved us and gave himself up for us as a fragrant offering and sacrifice to God."*
> *Ephesians 5:1 & 2*

Leave a fingerprint of God on someone's life today.

My daughter-in-law raises chickens. Some are for laying eggs and others are for meat. Chickens peck what they eat. They peck grain, vegetables, weeds, insects and anything else around them. They will also peck each other and if mad or threatened can peck each other to death. We have had to rescue a young chicken that was attacked by the older chickens in the coop. People can peck at each other too. Criticizing, complaining, correcting or just plain nagging are all ways we peck each other. I'm afraid I often resemble a chicken in my behavior towards my husband—pecking at this and that until he flies the coop into the pasture with his cows who enjoy his presence without complaint. God has told us we need to encourage one another and not be judgmental. Constant criticism is hard to endure and something dies inside us when we are around someone who is relentless in their pecking. It's an area I have to continually surrender to God. I don't want to be like a mother hen who pecks at everything. Are you prone to pecking or are you the one who feels pecked?

> *"Do not judge, and you will not be judged.*
> *Do not condemn, and you will not be condemned.*
> *Forgive, and you will be forgiven."*
> *Luke 6:37*

"More about Jesus I would know,
More of His grace to others show;
More of His saving fulness see,
More of His love who died for me."

Compliment, not criticize those close to you.

November 15
Read Galatians chapter 6

I recently received a card from a friend containing words of encouragement that uplifted me. Little did I, or my friend, know that God had put it upon his heart as part of a much bigger plan. The next day during my devotional time the same words my friend had used were in a passage from one of my favorite devotional books. I had read the page so many times before, but this time it was as if God Himself was speaking to me in a new and powerful way, affirming something He wanted me to know. I don't believe the timing was coincidental. No, I believe it was planned by God all along and I am so thankful my friend was attentive and responsive to the Lord's nudging when he sat down and penned his thoughts. God desires to include us in His work and we need to pay attention to His prodding, no matter how small it seems. Is there something God has been nudging you about lately? Who knows, it just might be part of something much bigger than you think.

*"Let us not become weary
in doing good,
for at the proper time
we will reap a harvest
if we do not give up.
Therefore, as we have
opportunity, let us do good
to all people, especially to
those who belong
to the family of believers."*
Galatians 6:9 & 10

*"Make me a channel of blessing today,
Make me a channel of blessing, I pray;
My life possessing, my service blessing,
Make me a channel of blessing today."*

Write a letter to someone God has put on your heart
and let them know you're thinking of them.

I read an article about the scientific search for the Higgs particle that some believe will settle the debate about how the Big Bang made the universe we live in today. Some believe that this particle, nicknamed "the God particle," allows all other particles in the universe to have mass and form. Scientists, realizing something has to tie all the particles together, have spent millions of dollars and years of research to find it. I wonder why they cannot accept that God is the answer? Why do they reject Christianity and search for a more tangible explanation? Believing in God requires faith, which is "being sure of what we hope for and certain of what we do not see," Hebrews 11:1. It means we accept something that is humanly impossible to prove or explain. Maybe that is why they continue to search—they need to find something they can prove. But I know God is the "Higgs particle" they are searching for. Except He's not a particle—He's the Creator of heaven and earth. The evidence needed to prove He exists begins in the heart, not the head. Do you believe God created you?

"Lord, you have been our dwelling place throughout all generations.
Before the mountains were born or you brought forth the earth and the world,
from everlasting to everlasting you are God."
Psalm 90:1 & 2

"Church of the Living God, we wait no future time,
But now on earth with joy we dwell within thy courts sublime;
Oh, thou dost triumph now, and shalt at any cost;
And if thy glory be unseen, 'tis hid but to the lost."

Take a drive and enjoy God's amazing creation.

I have struggled with receiving love and at times have behaved in unloving ways to reinforce my belief that I'm difficult to love. My perfectionist nature has compounded the problem as I've tried to earn love rather than embrace it. But as my love relationship with Jesus has deepened, my struggles with accepting love from others has greatly diminished. At a recent convention I attended, the speaker shared the importance of understanding the depth of God's love for us. She challenged us to pay attention to how He loves us so we can model that same love to others. Our ability to love others is directly linked to our ability to understand God's love for us. He loves each one of us as deeply as He loves His own son, Jesus Christ. He calls us His child and heirs to His Kingdom. He speaks of being our great Shepherd and tenderly cradling us in His arms when we are lost or afraid. The Bible is filled with analogies of a great and gentle Father who loves us completely and unconditionally. I want to fully embrace His love so I can extend that same love to those around me. Have you experienced the deep and rich love of God in your own life?

*"A new commandment
I give you:
Love one another.
As I have loved you,
so you must love one another."
John 13:34*

*"O love divine! no soul has e'er. Thy wondrous depths explored;
O priceless gift! We fain would have Thy riches on us poured.
Let mortals join with all their might, let earth and heaven both unite
To sing thy praise both day and night—The half can ne'er be told."*

List all the ways God has loved on you this week.

"Arise, shine, for your light has come, and the glory of the Lord rises upon you.
See, darkness covers the earth and thick darkness is over the peoples,
but the Lord rises upon you and His glory appears over you."
Isaiah 60:1 & 2

> *"Down in the human heart, crushed by the tempter,*
> *Feelings lie buried that grace can restore;*
> *Touched by a loving heart, wakened by kindness,*
> *Chords that were broken will vibrate once more.*
> *Rescue the perishing, care for the dying, Jesus is merciful, Jesus will save."*

In order for water to become ice it has to be exposed to cold temperatures for a period of time. The colder the temperature and the longer it is exposed, the more solid the ice becomes. But if the ice, no matter how solid it is, is exposed to warmth it starts to thaw and if left long enough in the warmth will become water again. When I meet someone who is cold as ice I believe they have been exposed to something really cold in their life that has given them their icy composure. How long they have been exposed to this cold environment determines how hard they are frozen If we expose them to Christ's love, no matter how frozen they are, something inside them will start

to thaw. If we continue to shine love and warmth on them we will eventually see their icy exterior start to break down. If we have the chance to keep them in the light long enough, eventually all their coldness will disappear and they'll become filled with the living water of Christ. The worst thing we can do is allow them to stay in the freezer just because it's uncomfortable to be around them. Something has caused them to freeze up and we can help warm them by bringing God's love into their life. Do you know someone who is icy cold and have you thought of it as an opportunity to warm them with God's love?

Bring some warmth into someone's life by a deed of kindness today.

November 19

Read 2 Chronicles chapter 7

*"Sweet hour of prayer! sweet hour of prayer! Thy wings shall my petition bear
To Him whose truth and faithfulness engage the waiting soul to bless.
And since He bids me seek His face, believe His Word and trust His grace,
I'll cast on Him my every care, and wait for thee, sweet hour of prayer!"*

A volunteer for Love INC called one day requesting time to visit with me about a new task we had given him. He was to call clients enrolled in our long-term programs and offer prayer and encouragement. It didn't seem like a difficult assignment and I had a lot of other things I needed to get done. It was with some reluctance I agreed to set aside some time but felt torn between other pressing issues and honoring his request. As we talked I could see he had put a lot of thought into this new role. He had a list of questions about what he should do if this or that was said or happened. As we worked our way through his thoughts I realized my priorities had been all messed up. I have always said and believe that prayer is the real work of any ministry and everything that follows is a result of the prayers. His desire to offer the best prayers he could for each client helped me focus on what was most important. Prayer is the key to power. It opens the door for God to do amazing work. I almost didn't take time to talk about how his prayers could impact the future of our ministry. It's so easy to get busy doing things that taking time for prayer can be pushed to the side. I'm so grateful that this faithful servant of God followed the Lord's nudging and reminded me what's really important. Have you been so busy lately that you've forgotten to make prayer your highest priority?

*"If my people, who are
called by my name,
will humble themselves
and pray and seek my face
and turn from
their wicked ways,
then will I hear from heaven
and will forgive their sin
and will heal their land."*
2 Chronicles 7:14

Move prayer to the top of your priority list.

Watching little children learn to walk holds many lessons for us. They may fall and get up many times in one day. For weeks they hang onto Mom's fingers trying to learn this thing called balance. Parents set them on their feet, help them find their center and then let go and beckon them to come. Even though they fall down repeatedly, they don't give up and they don't get mad because we encourage them to learn something new. No, they keep trying until they master it and before we know it they're running everywhere and into everything, delighted in their new-found freedom. So why is it that when we become adults we try something once, twice at best, and then give up saying we can't do it? Why are we so easily defeated in learning a new skill or talent? And why do we often get mad at others if they encourage us to keep trying? Who knows, if we stayed with it maybe we would find a new freedom in life too. We should be encouraged by the tenacity of little children. Is there something you've given up on that you need to try again?

"As you know, we consider blessed those who have persevered. You have heard of Job's perseverance and have seen what the Lord finally brought about. The Lord is full of compassion and mercy."
James 5:11

"O God, our help in ages past,
Our hope for years to come,
Our shelter from the stormy blast,
And our eternal home."

Think of something that has discouraged you
and resolve to give it another try.

November 21
Read Psalm 90

> *"Give of your best to the Master;*
> *Give of the strength of your youth;*
> *Clad in salvation's full armor,*
> *Join in the battle for truth."*

I hired a new employee who was excited to join the Love INC team. He received a call one day about picking up items that hadn't sold at a community yard sale. Wanting to do a good job he said he could make it happen even though it was going to require extra hours on a Saturday. By the time I heard about it the commitment and arrangements had been made. I explained that had he asked me I would have turned it down. We usually don't get many useable donations from what has not sold at a yard sale. I would not have asked him to work extra hours on a Saturday for something so minimally profitable. He then realized I did not expect him to try to do everything that came his way. It took a lot of his Saturday and another day to unload. Almost everything had to be passed through because we couldn't use it. I think many times we make this mistake when doing ministry. We want to do everything that comes to us thinking that's what God wants. In reality, much of what consumes our time is not what God would deem worthy. We get so busy doing other things that we're too preoccupied to do the work God has for us. Before we engage in any ministry activity we need to ask God what we should do. Let Him weed out those distracting opportunities so we're ready and available for the real work He has for us. Do you pray before saying yes to an opportunity to do ministry?

> *"May the favor*
> *of the Lord our God*
> *rest upon us;*
> *establish the work*
> *of our hands for us—*
> *yes, establish the work*
> *of our hands."*
> *Psalm 90:17*

Decide never to say yes or no without praying first.

"Oh, send Thy Spirit, Lord, now unto me,
That He may touch my eyes, and make me see:
Show me the truth concealed within Thy Word,
And in Thy Book revealed I see the Lord."

When a professional analyst is trained to detect counterfeit money they only study real money. They spend hours becoming familiar with every detail no matter how small. They never study counterfeit bills, only the real thing. They become intimately familiar with real money so they can easily spot anything that is counterfeit. The Bible warns us repeatedly that there will be false prophets who will try to get us to believe in a counterfeit religion. They will not have the things of God in mind but their own agendas. People will quit seeking the truth and "gather around them a great number of teachers to say what their itching ears want to hear. They will turn their ears away from the truth and turn aside to myths." 2 Timothy 4:3 &4. In order to discern truth we need to study the Bible, the true source of God's Word. We need to become intimately familiar with God and His ways so we know when others are trying to lead us astray. While it is good to read books by different authors and study under trained teachers, hold everything they say up to the light of God's Word and discern for yourself if it is accurate. Don't take anyone's word for it— look it up yourself. Become an expert on God's Word and then you'll be able to spot counterfeits no matter how good they are. Do you know God's Word well enough to discern when someone says something that isn't accurate?

"I urge you, brothers, to watch out
for those who cause divisions
and put obstacles in
your way that are contrary
to the teaching you have learned.
Keep away from them.
For such people are not serving
our Lord Christ,
but their own appetites.
By smooth talk and flattery they
deceive the minds of naïve people."
Romans 16:17 & 18

Always go to the Bible when seeking advice on what is right.

When the fog rolls in it obscures everything around us. I dislike driving in the fog. I lose my bearings as the usual landmarks are hidden and everything seems strange and distorted. I find myself creeping along, wondering if I'm even on the right road. And then, just as quickly as I've driven into it, I drive out from the thick oppression into the sunlight. Almost instantly I feel grounded again, recognizing the world around me. Life at times can feel like a dense fog has descended over it. Everything becomes obscure and unfamiliar, and making decisions or moving forward is difficult and frightening. I've learned from experience that when I feel this way I need to stop moving and gather myself. I need to wait upon the Lord to reveal the next step and not feel pressured into making a decision. God is the one who lifts the fog, in His time, and my way becomes clear once again. Until then, it's best to slow down, stay the course and wait for the fog to lift. Have you ever felt foggy about something and had to wait for things to clear before you knew which way to go?

"Once more Jesus put His hands on the man's eyes.
Then his eyes were opened, his sight was restored,
and he saw everything clearly."
Mark 8:25

"Following Jesus from day to day,
Gently He leads me along the way;
E'er will I trust Him all foes despite,
By faith and not by sight."

Write a note to someone who is seeking direction encouraging them that God will guide them.

*"They devoted themselves to the apostles' teaching and to the fellowship,
to the breaking of bread and to prayer."*
Acts 2:42

*"Then in fellowship sweet we will sit at His feet,
Or we'll walk by His side in the way;
What He says we will do, where He sends we will go;
Never fear, only trust and obey."*

I love to bake from scratch. But if I want it to turn out right, I have to be sure and put in all the ingredients. One time I was making a batch of molasses cookies and left out half the sugar. I put my first tray in the oven and couldn't figure out why they weren't melting like they should. As I took them out, I tasted one—boy was it bitter. I realized that when I doubled the recipe I hadn't doubled the sugar. Even though I had some in the dough it wasn't enough to make the cookies turn out right. Being a well-rounded Christian is multi-faceted. We are told to study the Bible and spend time alone with God. Prayer needs to be an integral part of what we do. We also need to worship God, both privately and in fellowship with other believers. Many

times Christians do part of these things but they don't do them all. They leave some out and hope they'll still turn out alright. But just like my cookies left a bad taste in my mouth, Christians who are lopsided may not be so sweet either. We can't skip our personal study and prayer time with God but we are also told to gather with other believers and worship God corporately. Have you got all the ingredients for being a Christian in your life or is one of them missing?

Invite other believers to your house for fellowship.

November 25
Read 1 Thessalonians chapter 5

"Be joyful always; pray continually; give thanks in all circumstances,
for this is God's will for you in Christ Jesus."
1 Thessalonians 5:16

> *"Jesus, Jesus, how I trust Him!*
> *How I've proved Him o'er and o'er;*
> *Jesus, Jesus, precious Jesus!*
> *Oh, for grace to trust Him more!"*

We teach our children to say thank you when they're given something, or someone does something for them. And we say thank you when people extend a helping hand to us. Saying thanks when we get our way is easy, but the Bible tells us to be thankful in all circumstances. That's not quite so easy. Are we supposed to be thankful when someone hurts us? Are we supposed to be thankful when we're sick or lose our job? It's not being

thankful for the circumstance that counts, it's being thankful that God is in the circumstance. It doesn't matter what happens or how difficult things may be, we can be certain that we aren't alone. God promised that He will never leave us. He instructed us to "draw near to Him and He will draw near to us" (James 4:8). During this Thanksgiving season I'm going to focus more on my relationship with God and less on the circumstances around me. After all, with God on my side, I can be thankful in all circumstances. Does your thankfulness ebb and flow with your circumstances?

Count your blessings. Name them one by one.

> "I once was an outcast stranger on earth,
> A sinner by choice, an alien by birth,
> But I've been adopted, my name's written down,
> An heir to a mansion, a robe and a crown."

A friend of mine adopted a special needs girl. For her first twelve years she had been greatly abused and mistreated. My friend is committed to helping her heal and live a full life, but it's not been easy. Her adopted daughter finds human touch difficult, responds inappropriately and has a multitude of trigger points. Progress is slow and measured but my friend has lots of love to give her and sees great potential hidden deep inside. God has adopted us into His family, we are His children. As I listened to my friend share about her adopted daughter I wondered if we don't often behave inappropriately as children of the King. Do we reject His love and pull back when He tries to help us? Are we easily upset by things He allows to come our way? Do we distrust Him? Do we lash out in anger when the hurt we feel inside has been done by others, not Him? I'm sure when God looks at me He finds my progress slow and measured. I've got a lot of baggage to be worked through. I'm guarded, unappreciative at times and don't behave like His child. But God's not giving up on me, just like my friend is committed to her daughter. He'll continue to love and teach me how I should behave. Little by little I'll learn He's not going to abuse or mistreat me. I need to remember He chose me because He loves me, not because He had to. I have a home with Him forever—He said so. Do you feel you're a child of the king?

> "In love He predestined
> us to be adopted as His sons
> through Jesus Christ,
> in accordance with His pleasure
> and will—to the praise
> of His glorious grace,
> which He has freely given us
> in the One He loves."
> *Ephesians 1:5 & 6*

Spend time reflecting on how much God loves you.

*"When you ask, you do not receive, because you ask with wrong motives,
that you may spend what you get on your pleasures."*
James 4:3

*"More love to Thee, O Christ, more love to Thee!
Hear Thou the prayer I make on bended knee;
This is my earnest plea: More love, O Christ, to Thee;
More love to Thee, more love to Thee!"*

Marriage needs to be founded on love and commitment or it is nearly impossible to sustain. A young couple I knew struggled in their marriage from the day it started. She was a young mother with two children when she married. Many felt she lacked love for her new husband. She had struggled providing for her family and it seemed she was marrying as a means of support. The new husband failed to meet her expectations and tragically the weak foundation failed in a short period of time. Many Christians try to build their relationship with God on the wrong foundation also. They expect that He will meet all their needs and they enter into the relationship for what they can get out of it, not what they must put into it. God loves us completely and unconditionally. He will do anything to help us be transformed into what He has created us to be. But He's not sitting at an order desk waiting

for us to send our next request so He can fill it. Often He knows that what we want will not help but hurt us so He sets our order aside. Instead He sends us a trial, challenge or opportunity that will grow our faith and dependence on Him. God wants us to love Him and not be in relationship with Him for what He can give us. When a relationship is healthy both parties work hard at pleasing the other. It becomes less about what they get out of it and more about what they put into it. Is your relationship with God based on what He can do for you or what you can do for Him?

Think back on your recent prayers and evaluate your relationship with God.

"Abide with me; fast falls the eventide;
The darkness deepens; Lord, with me abide;
When other helpers fail and comforts flee,
Help of the helpless, oh, abide with me."

I have a dark cloud over me today. I have felt the oppression of the storm moving in, day by day my thoughts slowly retreating into feelings of confusion, fear, and discouragement. I have tried to rise above it, but awoke this morning deeply discouraged and enveloped in darkness. I find myself lethargic and weak—I sit before the Lord, crying out for Him to lift the depression and shine His light down on me once again. Over the last few days, words spoken by others have convicted me, causing me to question what I am doing. My feelings arise out of my inability to know if God is speaking to me through them or if the enemy wants me to stumble. My desire is to faithfully serve God and do whatever He wants. If I need to adjust my way or turn back from the direction I am going, I am willing. But if the enemy wants me to retreat, than I want to stand my ground, knowing God has called me to do this work. I want to please God and so I will wait for clarity from Him. I will stay close to Him, in spite of the extreme darkness I feel until the storm passes. He will shine His light back into my life in His time and I will know if He is turning me around or if I need to denounce the enemy and push forward. What do you do when you feel confused and lost?

"I will stand at my watch and station myself on the ramparts;
I will look to see what He will say to me."
Habakkuk 2:1

Spend time in prayer, seeking God's direction in your life.

"Your beauty should not come from outward adornment, such as braided hair and the wearing of gold jewelry and fine clothes. Instead, it should be that of your inner self, the unfading beauty of a gentle and quiet spirit, which is of great worth in God's sight."
1 Peter 3:3 & 4

"More like the Master I would ever be,
More of His meekness, more humility;
More zeal to labor, more courage to be true,
More consecration for work He bids me do."

When I was a teen and young adult looking fashionable was important to me. I liked to wear the current style and loved to shop for new clothes. I spent a lot of time focusing on my outward appearance and never left the house without looking as good as I could. I always had my makeup in place, hair fixed and wore the newest fashion in clothes. I worked out, kept in shape and tried not to carry extra weight. My physical appearance was important to me and I spent a good deal of time focused on it. I'm not the only one who has concentrated on their outward appearance. Many of us strive to look good and take care of ourselves. As I've matured in my relationship with Christ my outward appearance is no longer my primary focus. I still want to look attractive but I no longer hope to be noticed for my physical appearance. I want people to see Christ in me. I desire that the beauty of my inner spirit transcends my outward look. If I am noticed by others I hope it is because they see something beneath the surface that attracts them. Physical beauty is fleeting but an inward beauty continues to develop and blossom, getting better with time. Do you spend more time on your outward appearance than your inner development?

List characteristics you find attractive in others.

When I read or study self-help books I like to highlight and underline things that stand out to me. I find highlighting serves two purposes— it ingrains the thought in my mind because I read it at least twice and it is easier to find if I want to look it up later. Have you ever approached reading the Bible with anticipation that God will highlight something He wants to tell you? Often when reading familiar passages a Scripture will jump off the page and speak to me in a new and powerful way. When this happens I believe God has His highlighter out and is pointing out something specific for me. I even date certain passages when I feel they were emphasized by God for that day. As I look back I can see how God was speaking and moving through my life. It has become a diary of my personal journey with God. We don't have to write in our Bible, but we all need to approach the Word of God as a time of personal communication between God and us and expect Him to highlight special passages as we read. Have you ever had a familiar passage catch your eye in a new way?

"As for God, His way is perfect; the word of the Lord is flawless.
He is a shield for all who take refuge in Him."
2 Samuel 22:31

"I am so glad that our Father in Heav'n
Tells of His love in the Book He has giv'n;
Wonderful things in the Bible I see,
This is the dearest, that Jesus loves me."

Journal or highlight a Scripture that speaks specifically to you this week.

> *"Following Jesus day by day,*
> *Following Him—His will obey,*
> *Following Him, I cannot stray,*
> *I'll follow Him all the way."*

One of the things I have noticed while working in ministry is the importance parents play as role models in their children's lives. Kids learn as much from watching as from being taught things. It is not uncommon to have several generations of one family go through our long-term accountability program, all seeking to learn the same skills which were absent in the home while growing up. As a parent, I see my adult children have adopted lifestyles and habits they saw modeled in our home. I find them following in my footsteps like tracks in the snow, and I pray I've blazed a good trail for them. It's important to model a direction we want our children to follow; we could be shaping future generations. Who do you think is following in your footsteps and does that thought make you want to change direction?

"Train a child in the way he should go, and when he is old he will not turn from it."
Proverbs 22:6

Pray a special prayer for someone over whom you have influence,
asking God for wisdom and guidance.

> *"Blest be the tie that binds*
> *Our hearts in Christian love;*
> *The fellowship of kindred minds*
> *Is like to that above."*

Being part of a family is special. My two brothers and I were close growing up and have maintained a close bond in our adult years. Even though we haven't always lived near each other, it's just like old times, filled with laughter and love when we do get together. I think one of my favorite things about being part of the Body of Christ is the sense of belonging that exists between Christian brothers and sisters. I have the privilege of working with Christians from around the nation and find there is a feeling of family and acceptance from the first minute we meet. A mutual bond seems to exist even between strangers once it is known that God is their Lord and Savior. Believing that we are part of the extended family of God unites us and breaks down the barriers of loneliness and fear. When the love of Christ is our common denominator there always seems to be something to talk about. The family of God should know no strangers and always be ready to welcome a new brother or sister into the fold. Have you ever met someone new, and instantly felt a kinship with them because of your shared faith?

"Consequently, you are no longer foreigners and aliens, but fellow citizens with God's people and members of God's household, built on the foundation of the apostles and prophets, with Christ Jesus himself as the chief cornerstone. In Him the whole building is joined together and rises to become a holy temple in the Lord. And in Him you too are being built together, to become a dwelling in which God lives by His Spirit."
Ephesians 2:19–22

Thank God for being a part of His extended family.

December 3

Read John chapter 15

> "I'm pressing on the upward way,
> New heights I'm gaining every day;
> Still praying as I'm onward bound,
> Lord, plant my feet on higher ground."

In Matthew 22:14 we are told many are called but few are chosen. We have all been created to do good works for the Lord which He prepared for us in advance (Ephesians 2:10) yet many are not engaged in those works. Why? It might be similar to applying for a job. Often one open position will receive hundreds of applicants hoping to get an interview. Out of the mass of applications, a few will be chosen for the first interview. There will be additional interviews and skill testing with only a few chosen to go on until one person is hired. The manager is looking for the best person for the job and all aspects of the applicant's work history, abilities and personality are considered. Desiring to work for the Lord follows a similar process. Many think they want to do Christian work but they have been slack in preparing. Their work history and character are not adequate for the call. Others cannot endure the testing of their faith that is required for ministry work. God is looking for those who can endure incredible persecution and trials. The work will be tough so the application process is difficult and many are weeded out. There were multitudes of people following Jesus yet only a handful became His disciples. "The harvest is plentiful, but the workers are few and it is the Lord who sends out His workers into His harvest field," Matthew 9:37 & 38. Those chosen have proven themselves worthy and ready for such a high calling. What are you doing to prepare yourself to be one of His chosen ones?

"You did not choose me,
but I chose you
to go and bear fruit—
fruit that will last.
Then the Father
will give you whatever you ask
in my name."
John 15:16

Identify areas in your life you want to improve to help prepare you for His call.

There was a time in my life when I faced one of my greatest trials. I had taken a stand and refused to be a part of something that I felt was not honoring God. It was a tumultuous time and people with strong opinions on both sides of the issue got involved. Unfair accusations were made and I found myself labeled the villain and the problem, not part of the solution. Everything within me wanted to stand up and fight in my defense, yet God wanted me to learn a difficult lesson. This battle was His, not mine, and He wanted me to keep still and let Him fight it for me. The days and nights dragged on as the battle raged all around me. I didn't know what to do but felt doing something would have to feel better than just standing on the sideline watching the debate take place. It didn't resolve quickly and those weeks of trusting God seemed like an eternity. In time resolution was found and I was given the opportunity to again be part of something that was very dear to me. There continued to be many challenges but God needed me to be about the task at hand not defending a war already won. God wants us to learn that the battle or victory isn't ours and we must be obedient to where He places us. We may be on the frontline or we may be asked to stay at camp while others fight the cause. It's not easy to be still when everything inside us screams differently, but I learned lessons through that time that prepared me for the days ahead. Have you ever had to stand back and let others go to battle for you because that was what God called you to do?

"The Lord will
fight for you;
you need only
to be still."
Exodus 14:14

"Simply trusting every day, trusting through a stormy way;
Even when my faith is small, trusting Jesus, that is all.
Trusting as the moments fly, trusting as the days go by;
Trusting Him whate'er befall, trusting Jesus, that is all."

Reflect on a time of conflict and how it was resolved.

December 5
Read Psalm 37

"He abides, He abides;
Hallelujah, He abides with me!
I'm rejoicing night and day
As I walk the narrow way,
For the Comforter abides with me."

My husband and I both felt led to build a home we could share with others who wanted to rest and refresh. For six years we searched through four states looking for that perfect place. I had grown discouraged with searching so did not accompany my husband on the first trip to what would become our new home. After he returned he shared that it had a beautiful view but would take a lot of work. Then he added how intrigued he had been by two doves in a mulberry tree on the land. They cooed the whole time he was there as if they were speaking to him. He found this odd as doves normally fly away when humans are around. Tears sprang to my eyes as I confided that I had put a fleece out to God asking Him to put two doves on the land where we should build. God had given us our answer but little did we know what a journey of faith it was going to be. We put an offer on the land and was informed it had sold. This was the first of many "no's" that turned to "yes's" along the way including getting a second chance to buy the land at a cheaper price. God proved faithful as we faced multiple obstacles only to have Him turn them into blessings. "Selah," the name of our home, has been a blessing to us and many others through the years. When God births a passion He also shows the way even if it takes years and a pair of doves to do it. Has God put a passion in your heart that you've yet to realize?

"Trust in the Lord and do good;
dwell in the land
and enjoy safe pasture.
Delight yourself in the Lord
and He will give you
the desires of your heart."
Psalm 37:3 & 4

Think of a time when a 'no' turned to an even better 'yes' down the road.

*A*s the morning sun mounts up over the valley, it can create an amazing winter wonderland scene. From the inside of my house, the sunbeams sparkling off the freshly fallen snow can look warm and inviting. Their magnetic pull speaks of beautiful and wonderful things, enticing me to enter into it. But as I open the door and step out into the winter scene, the bitter cold hits me in the face. While it's invigorating to feel the brisk morning air, it's not long before the reality of the coldness starts to seep into my body and I return to the warmth of my house to carry on my day. Sometimes we can look from within the warmth and security of God's presence and feel the world enticing us to step into it. It looks inviting and mysterious, seeking to pull us from under His loving care and into its attractions. But if we step into these worldly enticements, we will feel the cold, uncaring atmosphere attack us—driving us back into our Heavenly

Father's loving arms, to be embraced by His love and presence. The things of the world often look appealing from a distance, but the cold harshness of life without God is not where I want to spend my days. Have you ever been enticed by worldliness, only to have it sting you when you got close to it?

"The Lord is my rock, my fortress and my deliverer;
my God is my rock, in whom I take refuge, my shield and the horn of my salvation.
He is my stronghold, my refuge and my Savior—from violent men you save me."
2 Samuel 22:2 & 3

"Safe in the arms of Jesus, Safe from corroding care,
Safe from the world's temptations; Sin cannot harm me there.
Free from the blight of sorrow, Free from my doubts and fears;
Only a few more trials, Only a few more tears!"

Take a walk in the brisk air and thank God for His love and warmth.

ithing is Scriptural and usually private and personal to each individual. There is much written about how one cannot out-give God and how He will rain down blessings upon those who give. But you don't usually hear someone bragging about how they gave to God and what He gave in return. It's just not spoken publicly. In our long-term relational program we teach Biblical principles of finances, including tithing. Often as the clients begin to understand that God owns everything, they begin to practice tithing for the first time in their lives. Because we are monitoring their financial decisions we are aware when tithing becomes a part of their budgets. We have seen the Lord's blessings in the lives of those who begin to tithe. Debts are forgiven, interest rates dropped, pay-offs negotiated, people will receive raises, bonuses, or a better paying job offer—we have witnessed the principle of tithing come full circle in life after life. When we submit everything in our life, even our finances, God is pleased and honors our obedience. While we should not tithe to receive, if we tithe with a pure heart we will receive the Lord's blessings in one way or another. Do you believe and practice tithing in your life?

" 'Bring the whole tithe into the storehouse, that there may be food in my house.
Test me in this,' says the Lord Almighty, 'and see if I will not throw open the floodgates
of heaven and pour out so much blessing that you will not have room enough for it.' "
Malachi 3:10

"Give of your best to the Master; give Him first place in your heart;
Give Him first place in your service; consecrate every part.
Give, and to you will be given; God His beloved Son gave;
Gratefully seeking to serve Him, give Him the best that you have."

Give your best to the Lord.

My grandchildren and I love to put puzzles together. They learn on easy puzzles with the borders defined and only a few pieces to fit together. As they advance they move to puzzles that are more difficult. I have taught them to put the border together first giving them the structure and boundaries they need to complete the inside. I often work with them helping them see how the pieces and colors combine, especially when it's a harder puzzle. Picture your life as a puzzle with all the pieces jumbled together and some even face down. Imagine yourself as God's child holding out your hands with the scrambled pieces of your life and asking Him to help you figure it out. If we ask, He will help us put the boundaries around our life so we can focus on piecing together who we've been created to be. I like to think that He takes great delight in working with me, just as I do with my grandchildren. It's a process that will take time and contemplation, and I will try many pieces that do not fit where I thought they might. But if I ask Him to join me, together we will complete the puzzle and not one piece will be missing. Have you thought of your life like a puzzle and asked God to help you fit it together?

"For we are God's workmanship, created in Christ Jesus to do good works,
which God prepared in advance for us to do."
Ephesians 2:10

"Take time to be holy, the world rushes on;
Spend much time in secret, with Jesus alone.
By looking to Jesus, like Him thou shalt be;
Thy friends in thy conduct His likeness shall see."

Put a puzzle together with a child.

December 9
Read Mark chapter 2

*H*ave you ever thought about what our world would be like if we could read each other's minds? I would be embarrassed if everything I thought was known by others. Some of it should not even be thought much less known. I like to watch people but catch myself critiquing them: how they look, how they act, comparing myself to them. Sometimes when someone asks if they can talk to me, outwardly I smile and say sure, but inside I wish I could continue with what I'm doing and not be bothered. I don't say most of what I think because often it would discourage rather than lift up others. If people

knew what was on my mind I would have to control my thoughts more than I do. But Jesus knows everything that's on our minds. He knows when our thoughts are prideful, judgmental or selfish. We may fool the rest of the world, but we never fool Him. He judges us by what's inside our heart not what we let the world see. In Proverbs 21:2 we read, "All a man's ways seem right to him, but the Lord weighs the heart." This truth needs to become more of a reality so we control our thoughts better, knowing the One who really counts is reading our minds—all the time. Does your thought life line up with your "talk" life?

"Now some teachers of the law were sitting there, thinking to themselves. 'Why does this fellow talk like that? He's blaspheming! Who can forgive sins but God alone?' Immediately Jesus knew in His spirit that this was what they were thinking in their hearts, and He said to them, 'Why are you thinking these things?'"
Mark 2:6–8

"Search me, O God, and know my heart today,
Try me, O Savior, know my thoughts, I pray;
See if there be some wicked way in me;
Cleanse me from every sin, and set me free."

Make a conscious effort to rebuke impure or critical thoughts.

> *"Praise God, from Whom all blessings flow;*
> *Praise Him, all creatures here below;*
> *Praise Him above, ye heav'nly host;*
> *Praise Father, Son, and Holy Ghost."*

I'm a morning person and enjoy watching the morning sun introduce a new day. As it first peeks over the horizon another day with new opportunities begins to dawn. Little by little beams of sunshine start spilling across the land, chasing away the stars and breaking through the darkness. Each new day is a gift from God and should bring hope and anticipation of what it will hold. It's another day to see God's blessings and to be used as a blessing to someone else. Sometimes the night has been hard and we don't feel like walking into another day. It's at those times we need to open ourselves to God and let His love spill out on us one ray at a time until it spreads through our entire being, filling us with joy and peace. He can chase away the dark corners in our mind and give us a sense of His love and presence. Each morning before we jump, or crawl, out of bed let's take a minute and thank God for a new day. Imagine His love filling your being from the tip of your toes to the top of your head, and He'll create a wonderful sunrise in you that will warm others who cross your way.

"This is the day the Lord has made; Let us rejoice and be glad in it."
Psalm 118:24

Try to catch the sunrise one day this week.

Have you ever had a relationship go bad and been unable to reconcile it? I have a few scattered through my life and I still remember each one of them. When I reflect back on them, I'm saddened that I have been unable to bring resolution or reconciliation to them. I like to fix things and I'm uncomfortable with unresolved conflict. But sometimes, despite my desire and efforts for a peaceful settlement, the conflict remains. It takes two people to have conflict and two people must desire resolution or it won't happen. I have a responsibility to do everything I can according to God's teaching. It is important to discern any wrongs I have committed and seek forgiveness. I must extend grace to others for any wrong they have done to me and hold no grudges so no bitter root of anger can grow in my heart. But after I have done what I can I have to leave it with God. This is the hardest part for me but I cannot control the outcome when others are involved. I have found that if I continue to pray for them, truly caring about them and the situation, God helps me deal with it. Do you have any broken relationships that are unresolved and have you done your part in reconciliation?

"Make every effort to live in peace with all men and to be holy; without holiness no one will see the Lord. See to it that no one misses the grace of God and that no bitter root grows up to cause trouble and defile many."
Hebrews 12:14 & 15

"Take the Name of Jesus with you,
Child of sorrow and of woe,
It will joy and comfort give you;
Take it then, where'er you go."

Pray for God to give you wisdom in a relationship that is strained.

> *"All creation, join in praising
> God, the Father, Spirit, Son,
> Evermore your voices raising
> To th'eternal Three in One."*

As the Executive Director of a ministry that unifies Christian churches, I have the opportunity to worship with many different denominations and experience their worship styles. I recently was invited to a Pentecostal church and experienced church in a way I never had before. When they pray—they pray loudly and with great energy. When they sing, it resembles a workout session with lots of clapping, jumping, shouting, and joy. At first I felt out of my comfort zone, having never seen this degree of enthusiasm during a service. Then I tried to imagine how it must look and sound to God, and I thought what joy He must feel as He looks down and sees all their praises rising to the heavens. I have also worshiped in very quiet services, where meditative thought and prayer are whispered from the depths of the soul and I believe God is pleased with that also. It is not so much how we worship that matters to God, because every church I have attended is worshiping Him in their own style. I think it is the condition of the heart that God is looking at. Whether we are noisy or quiet, reserved or expressive, reflective or ambitious is not important. What matters is the attitude of our heart and why we are worshiping. Style is not important, but if we don't enter into it with a pure heart, no style of worship will please God. Have you ever experienced a different style of worship than you are accustomed to and how did it make you feel?

*"God is Spirit,
and His worshipers
must worship in spirit
and in truth."*
John 4:24

Attend a church different from your own and worship with them.

December 13
Read Amos chapter 8

"Back to the one foundation, from sects and creeds made free,
Come saints of every nation to blessed unity.
Once more the ancient glory shines as in days of old,
And tells the wondrous story—One God, one faith, one fold."

Many of us live very blessed lives and take for granted the things we have. We only have to lose something to realize how much it meant to us. Ask someone who is struggling with a chronic illness and they will tell you how blessed you are to have your health. Someone who has lost a child or spouse will tell you how blessed you are to have your loved ones around you. Someone who is struggling to find a job will tell you how blessed you are to have employment. The list could go on and on—we all have things to be thankful for. One blessing many take for granted in America is the freedom to worship as we like. We are not persecuted or killed for attending a church of our choice and we don't have to hide our gatherings in a dimly-lit room. Most of us own Bibles. We do not have to hide them and they've not been confiscated. Do we take the freedom to gather, read God's Word and worship together for granted? What if one day we are persecuted for worshiping God and our Bibles are taken from us? Will we then realize how blessed and privileged we were? Let's not wait until we've lost this privilege before we cherish it. Nothing except God is forever—the freedom of religion may end one day. What do you take for granted that would devastate you if lost?

" 'The days are coming,' declares the Sovereign Lord, 'when I will send a famine through the land—not a famine of food or a thirst for water, but a famine of hearing the words of the Lord. Men will stagger from sea to sea and wander from north to east, searching for the word of the Lord, but they will not find it.' "
Amos 8:11 & 12

Imagine how different your life would be
if you couldn't worship God or read the Bible openly.

When we first begin our journey with Christ most of what we know is head knowledge—what we have read and been taught. As our relationship deepens we move from just having head knowledge to heart knowledge. We feel Him living in our heart and experience the Holy Spirit moving within us. We connect emotionally with God. As we continue to mature our relationship with God deepens until we move beyond what we have learned or felt, into the assurance of a living God in spite of any circumstance that surrounds us. We believe God is still on the throne when all emotion is gone, our prayers seem unanswered and we feel dried up and left to die. He is the rock we stand on no matter what is happening around us. We believe when everything says we shouldn't. We praise even when our emotions are torn and erratic. Our hope stands unshakeable in a fragile and broken world. He is our Alpha and Omega, the Beginning and the End. He reigns above heaven and earth, and all things are in His hands and under His control. Can anything shake your faith?

"I am the Alpha and the Omega, the First and the Last, the Beginning and the End."
Revelation 22:13

"Crown Him with many crowns, the Lamb upon His throne;
Hark! How the heav'nly anthem drowns all music but its own!
Awake, my soul and sing of Him Who died for thee,
And hail Him as thy matchless King through all eternity."

Compile a list of the attributes of God and praise Him for being sovereign.

December 15
Read John chapter 1

"The Word became flesh and lived for a while among us. We have seen His glory,
the glory of the one and only Son, who came from the Father, full of grace and truth."
John 1:14

"It came upon the midnight clear, that glorious song of old,
From angels bending near the earth, to touch their harps of gold;
'Peace on the earth, good will to men, from Heav'n's all-gracious King.'
The world in solemn stillness lay, to hear the angels sing."

The Christmas season is supposed to be a time of celebrating Christ's birth, a time of reflection on the gift God gave us in the form of His Son Jesus Christ. But I struggle, fighting hard to keep the reason I celebrate in the center of all my activity. Some of my past Christmas's have not been enjoyable as I frantically tried to decorate, buy gifts, bake all the goodies we didn't need, and get ready for family and friends to come. God's gift wasn't a thing, it was His Son, sent to give each of us the opportunity to enter into a

relationship with Him. It was personal and given at great cost. I wonder how much the Christmas season could change if I would focus on giving the gift of myself instead of things? Maybe, in place of the frenzy of buying gifts, decorating the house, and endless baking, I should visit a shut-in, write a note of encouragement, and increase my prayer time with Christ. I think giving the gift of friendship and celebrating God's gift of life could simplify the season and magnify the reason. Does the Christmas season wear you out? What things might you do differently?

Do a secret good deed for someone who is alone
or lonely during the holidays.

*I*roning is not nearly as common today as when my mother was growing up. They ironed everything—clothes, sheets, napkins, whatever was made of fabric. Nowadays we prefer to buy wrinkle-free or permanent-press materials. I still iron my husband's shirts because he prefers the crisp, clean look. They do look much nicer but it takes time and effort. To get a really good crease I have to do all the steps: applying starch, steam and heat. I think many Christians want a wrinkle-free, permanent-press kind of faith. They don't want to go through all the effort of having their faith starched, steamed or pressed. They would rather stay away from the heat and look a little frazzled than let God apply pressure. But the kind of faith God wants us to have requires heat and pressure. You can't cut corners and end up with the real deal. The next time you want to circumvent the faith-growing process, remember—it takes heat and pressure to look and be your best for Christ. Are you trying to have a wrinkle-free faith without the effort?

> *"See, I have refined you, though not as silver;*
> *I have tested you in the furnace of affliction."*
> *Isaiah 48:10*

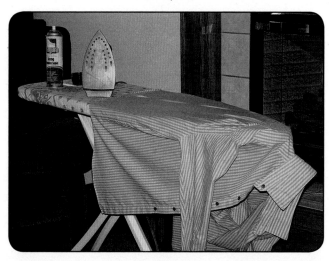

"Lord, I would be wholly Thine, I would do Thy will divine,
From the world and sin and self I would be free;
On the altar now I lie, and with all my heart I cry,
Let the holy fire from heaven fall on me."

Iron out some of those areas you've been neglecting.

December 17
Read Isaiah chapter 55

ave you ever wondered why bad things happen to good people? Sometimes life seems so unfair and it's hard not to question what God is doing or why He allows such things. I have met people whose faith was shattered due to some extreme situation in their life. The reality of life is that we live in a fallen world and some things are not fair, but God can work everything to His glory if we allow Him. My husband's mother lingers, her quality of life poor. She can't get around, feed or care for herself and seldom communicates due to several strokes. I've wondered why God hasn't called this faithful and dear Christian woman home. But my husband reminds me that God will keep her here as long as she is being used in His work. Often the circumstances or challenges we face may be more about what God is teaching someone else through us, than about us. When life is hard, we should not question why something happened but ask instead how we can honor God through it. God's perspective is all-inclusive not narrow like ours. He knows how everything fits together in His perfect plan. We need to keep our eyes on Him and let Him use us as He sees fit, trusting that His purpose will be accomplished and that we are part of a much greater plan. Have you ever wondered why God has allowed something to happen in your life?

"'For my thoughts are not your thoughts, neither are your ways my ways,' declares the Lord.
'As the heavens are higher than the earth, so my ways higher than your ways
and my thoughts than your thoughts.'"
Isaiah 55:8 & 9

"Be Thou my Vision, O Lord of my heart;
Naught be all else to me, save that Thou art;
Thou my best thought, by day or by night,
Waking or sleeping, Thy presence my light."

Tell God your feelings about a difficult time in your life.
He desires you to be honest with Him.

December 18

The story of Hannah in the Old Testament touches my heart. Hannah was barren for years and had to endure ridicule and taunting from her husband's other wife, Peninnah. Each year the family went to the temple to worship and sacrifice to the Lord. One year as she prayed fervently at the temple, pouring out her heart to God, Hannah promised Him she would give her son back to Him if He would grant her wish. God heard her prayer and within the year she had her first son whom she named Samuel. True to her word, once he was weaned, she took him back to the temple and left him in the care of the priest, Eli, for the rest of his life. What love and faith Hannah displayed. I remember wanting a piano so badly and how excited I was when I finally got it. The thought of then giving it to a church or someone else never entered my mind. Give up that which I had prayed and waited so long for? That is what Hannah did. She remembered her promise to God and He blessed her with many more children. When we pray for God to give us something, is our focus on using it to further Kingdom work on earth? Or do we covet it, hanging onto it for dear life? God gives us the desires of our heart, but we should hold everything lightly in our hands. The things that God gives us should never become more important than serving Him. Do you have prized possessions you couldn't imagine losing?

"And she made a vow, saying, 'O Lord Almighty, if You will only look upon your servant's misery and remember me, and not forget your servant but give her a son, then I will give him to the Lord for all the days of his life, and no razor will ever be used on his head.'"
1 Samuel 1:11

"There's a song in the air! There's a star in the sky! There's a mother's deep prayer and a baby's low cry! And the star rains its fire while the beautiful sing, For the manger of Bethlehem cradles a King!"

Ask God if you should simplify your life and give away some of your things.

"Oh, come, all ye faithful, joyful and triumphant,
Oh, come ye, oh, come ye, to Bethlehem.
Come and behold Him, born the King of angels;
Oh, come, let us adore Him, oh, come, let us adore Him,
Oh come, let us adore Him, Christ the Lord."

Our ministry, Love INC, recently started a resale shop. I was amazed at how many new volunteers came forward to help work with the product we would sell. They were eager to sort, clean, fix, price, display and help sell donated items. Their gift of service blessed us and allowed us to open the store. Finding volunteers to mentor clients in our long-term relational programs has been more challenging. These volunteers have to form a relationship with their client, not just give of their time and skills; it requires a personal, emotional investment on their part. Those who work with things see progress and feel a sense of satisfaction in their work, while volunteer mentors often cannot see measureable change for a long time. They have to believe that their efforts are making a difference even when progress is slow and difficult. I think this concept is also true in our relationship with God. Many of us are drawn to work for Christ more than we are drawn into relationship with Him. We can do all sorts of things in His name and still neglect Him. When we actively serve Him we usually feel satisfaction for a job well done. When we enter into a personal relationship with Him it requires an investment of ourselves and progress is often slow and discouraging. God wants us more than He wants our works. What we do for Him can impact ourselves and others, but what God can do in us through relationship will be life-transforming. We should not neglect serving God and others, but our first priority must be growing our relationship with Him, so our work flows from Him. Are you more prone to work for Him than spend time with Him?

"You see that his faith and his actions were working together, and his faith was made complete by what he did."
James 2:22

List how much time you spend alone with Him
and how much you spend serving Him—do they balance out?

> *"Good King Wenceslas looked out on the Feast of Stephen,*
> *When the snow lay round about, deep and crisp and even.*
> *Brightly shone the moon that night, though the frost was cruel,*
> *When a poor man came in sight, gath'ring winter fuel."*

My father grew up in North Dakota and has shared many stories of the difficult winters they had there. He said they used to tie a rope between the house and the barn so they could find their way from one to the other in a blizzard. Without that rope to guide them it was easy to become blinded in the snow and get lost. Life can become like a blizzard around us and we can't see our way through the storm. But if we have anchored ourselves to Jesus Christ, we'll always be able to find our way home. We'll have something to grab onto when nothing makes sense around us— He will guide us out of danger and into the warmth of His love. Have you ever felt blinded by a storm in life and had to grab onto Jesus to pull you home?

> *"I will lead the blind by ways they have not known, along unfamiliar paths*
> *I will guide them; I will turn the darkness into light before them*
> *and make the rough places smooth."*
> *Isaiah 42:16*

Think of something or someone you're anchored to and thank God for them.

December 21

Read 1 Thessalonians chapter 3

Have you ever felt overwhelmed wondering what Christmas gifts to buy your siblings? I have often been clueless what to get mine as Christmas approached. They either buy what they want when they want it, or don't live close enough for me to know what they need or like. We've tried not buying anything for each other, but there's always one who breaks the agreement, and pretty soon we're all back to buying gifts. I think my husband found the solution when he suggested we plan a vacation together. The reason we exchange gifts is that it's a token of our deep love for each other. We enjoy getting together and sharing life. So he suggested we plan a vacation together. Our gift to each other will be the time we share doing something we enjoy with those we love. It sounds like a winning combination and something we can look forward to. I think the best gift we can give someone is the gift of friendship and fellowship. Sometimes we get caught up in worldly things, but what's really important is family and relationships. Do you know someone who needs your gift of friendship?

"May the Lord make your love increase and overflow for each other and for everyone else, just as ours does for you."
1 Thessalonians 3:12

"God be with you till we meet again,
By His counsels guide, uphold you,
With His sheep securely fold you,
God be with you till we meet again."

Plan a family outing and give the gift of your time.

*"Hallelujah! Thine the glory.
Hallelujah! Amen.
Hallelujah! Thine the glory.
Revive us again."*

When trials come we often ask God to remove the difficulty. Trials are sent by God to teach us and help us grow, but they also serve another purpose—to glorify Him. To be relieved or saved from some great trial diminishes our ability to praise Him and show His miraculous faithfulness as He takes us through it. We are His witnesses to others and as we experience victory we can encourage our brothers and sisters during their difficult times. Often we are so focused on having our own pain relieved that we tarnish the opportunity to shine for God. When storm clouds gather they often hide the sun and everything becomes dark and gloomy, but inside those clouds is life-giving water. The same thing happens in our dark times. During the storm everything rages around us and we get drenched in the downpour, but afterwards new growth springs to life. Storm clouds often reflect the sun hidden behind them like a halo. Let us seek to bear His glory during our trial, reflecting light in the midst of our dark times so others will see and praise Him. When life gets dark is God's light shining through you?

*"When you pass through the water, I will be with you;
and when you pass through the rivers,
they will not sweep over you. When you walk through the fire,
you will not be burned; the flames will not set you ablaze."*
Isaiah 43:2

What life experience has enabled you to be a comfort
to someone going through a similar experience?

December 23

Read 2 Corinthians chapter 5

My husband believes people buy gifts for others that they would like to get themselves. We don't give gifts we hate, but select things we like. I started paying more attention to the gifts I received and found this observation to be true. I also found I gave things I wouldn't mind receiving myself. This same principle applies to the gift God gave us. He gave us His Son, Jesus Christ, as a sacrifice for our sins. He knew that Jesus would have to give up His life that we might share eternal life with Him. We are also asked to give up our life—to die to self and be born again. Jesus told Nicodemus, "I tell you the truth, unless a man is born of water and the Spirit, he cannot enter the kingdom of God." I need to give up my own desires and pick up my cross to follow Him. I know the gift of Christ is the best gift I've ever been given and giving God my life is the best gift I can give Him. Have you and God exchanged gifts yet?

"For Christ's love compels us, because we are convinced that one died for all, and therefore all died. And He died for all, that those who live should no longer live for themselves but for Him who died for them and was raised again."
2 Corinthians 5:14 & 15

"I surrender all,
I surrender all;
All to Thee, my blessed Savior,
I surrender all."

Give someone the gift of your friendship this year.

"However, as it is written;
'No eye has seen, No ear has heard, No mind has conceived
What God has prepared for those who love Him,'
But God has revealed it to us by His Spirit."
1 Corinthians 2:9 & 10

"Away in a manger, no crib for a bed,
The little Lord Jesus laid down His sweet head;
The stars in the sky looked down where He lay,
The little Lord Jesus, asleep on the hay."

There isn't much written in the Bible about how Mary felt as she carried the Christ Child and prepared for His birth. When the angel told her she would conceive through the Holy Spirit and give birth to the Son of God, she responded, "I am the Lord's servant. May it be to me as you have said." We are left to contemplate the emotions she must have felt as the birth approached. I would have expected God to provide a safe, clean, and protected place for the child to be born. After all it was His Son, and He could do anything He wanted. Instead, Mary found herself traveling a long journey with Joseph to Bethlehem, and giving birth in a stable because the inn was full. I wonder if she was perplexed and surprised at the Lord's provision. I may never know, but I think God often works His will in ways that puzzle us. There have been times in my life when I was sure I was following Him, and yet found the way confusing and difficult. It seemed His plan often took a turn or curve I did not expect. God has told us we cannot conceive what He has planned for those who love Him. What is important is that we are obedient to whatever He calls us to do. Have you ever been puzzled by how things worked out as you sought to serve Him faithfully?

Read the Christmas story in the book of Luke, Chapter 2.

December 25
Read John chapter 3

Can you remember the excitement you felt as a child waiting for Christmas to arrive so you could open your gifts? When I was young it seemed the last few days just crept by as I waited for the big day. Now that I'm an adult I get more excited watching others open the gifts I have bought for them. I'm notorious for giving gifts early because I can't wait until Christmas day to see their faces as they open something I have purchased especially for them. I can't imagine how disappointed I would be if they refused to accept my gift and didn't care that it was an expression of my love for them. God must feel this way when His most precious gift of all, His Son, Jesus Christ, is not accepted. He sent His Son to earth and we celebrate Jesus' birth on Christmas Day. God knew all along that Jesus was going to die an ugly death for our sins so He could offer us the ultimate gift—eternal life. God doesn't force anyone to accept this gift and waits for us to come to Him. The gift of salvation is free for all who will receive it, yet there are many people who have rejected it. This Christmas share the good news with those who may not have heard it so they too will know God has a gift just for them. Is there someone close to you who needs to hear the real reason we celebrate Christmas?

"For God so loved the world that He gave His one and only Son, that whoever believes in Him shall not perish but have eternal life."
John 3:16

"Hark! The herald angels sing, Glory to the newborn King;
Peace on earth, and mercy mild, God and sinners reconciled!
Joyful, all ye nations rise, Join the triumph of the skies;
With th'angelic host proclaim, Christ is born in Bethlehem!"

Reflect on when you accepted Christ as your Savior
and thank God for the gift of eternal life.

I usually feel a sense of relief the day after Christmas. There is always so much to do before the special day and afterward I find myself ready to return to normal. It doesn't take long before I start to put away the gifts and box the decorations until next year. But when we're putting Christmas away are we also packing Jesus away in some corner of our heart until the Easter season rolls around? Is Jesus just a part of the holiday festivities and the reason we have Christmas but nothing more? Jesus wants to be a part of our life every day of the year. He doesn't just want to be remembered during the holiday seasons of Christmas and Easter. This year make sure you leave Him out as you pack the holiday decorations. Perhaps we should leave one decoration out as a reminder that Jesus wants to be remembered in our house 365 days of the year. What can you do to remember the real reason for the season after the holiday is over?

"This is love: not that we loved God, but that He loved us and sent His Son as an atoning sacrifice for our sins."
1 John 4:10

"What Child is this who, laid to rest on Mary's lap is sleeping?
Whom angels greet with anthems sweet, while shepherds watch are keeping?
This, this is Christ the King, whom shepherds guard and angels sing;
Haste, haste, to bring Him laud, the Babe, the Son of Mary."

Pick one ornament and keep it out to remind you of Jesus.

> *"Then pealed the bells more loud and deep:*
> *God is not dead, nor does He sleep;*
> *The wrong shall fail, the right prevail*
> *With peace on earth, good will to men."*

A barometer is an instrument used to measure atmospheric pressure and can forecast short-term changes in the weather. My parents always had a barometer in their house. I remember my mother tapping it and saying the weather was going to change. Often when the barometric pressure drops people feel it in their joints and bones, almost as a warning of the coming storm. Our conscience can serve as a spiritual barometer helping us determine if we're engaging in something we shouldn't. If we feel a need to hide our actions from others it's a good indication they are wrong. If we would be embarrassed or feel ashamed if others found out about what we were doing, we should probably stop doing it. If we have to sneak around to do something, deceiving others so we don't get caught, we probably are up to no good. When we behave in any of these ways, it's probably because we know what we're doing is wrong. Our spiritual barometer is warning us a storm is coming. While we may be able to deceive others God knows exactly what we're up to—nothing is hidden from Him. If your spiritual barometer is warning you that what you're doing is bound to bring a storm into your life—quit it. Make the necessary changes before the storm hits. Do you need to quit doing something you know is wrong?

"For we must all appear before the judgment seat of Christ, that each one may receive what is due him for the things done while in the body, whether good or bad."
2 Corinthians 5:10

Confess any known sin and ask for forgiveness.

> "Whiter than the snow, the beautiful snow,
> Whiter than the snow He has made me;
> Whiter than the snow, the beautiful snow,
> Whiter than the snow He has made me."

Newly fallen snow is virgin white, pristine, and unblemished. Muddy tracks across it leave dirty prints that stand out and mar the clean surface. Anyone looking will notice the stark contrast between the pure white and the dirty, ugly brown. However, if you walk on dirt with muddy shoes, you might leave a few traces of mud here and there, but it could easily go unnoticed. Our lives can bear the same contrasts. We are told no one is without sin. In a life that is committed to following Christ and seeking to serve Him faithfully, sin will show like muddy footprints in the snow. Those who earnestly seek to walk with the Lord will find every sin they commit stands out in their life and is obvious to those around them. But to those who live in the world and don't care if they walk in Christ's steps, sin is not as noticeable. The difference between their everyday walk and sin bears little contrast. When you sin, is it in stark contrast to your daily life, or does it blend right in?

> "Cleanse me with hyssop, and I will be clean;
> Wash me, and I will be whiter than snow."
> Psalm 51:7

Go for a walk and thank God that He can cleanse you from your sins.

Most of my life I have participated in some sort of exercise program. Sometimes I'm more committed than at other times and starting over after a long break is anything but fun. At first I struggle to do the program and have to fight against quitting. But after several weeks my body begins to respond positively and I push to do more. I don't start a program hoping to stay at the beginner level forever. My goal is to become stronger. The mindset for our Christian journey should be similar. When we first come to Christ the trials will be difficult and we may feel discouraged and weak. As our personal relationship with God grows our faith grows and we endure more difficulties without discouragement, knowing God is our strength. But don't expect things to level out and your life to plateau. You will always be challenged and stretched beyond what you think you can do. As long as you're submitting to His leadership He's going to push you further than you presently are with new and more difficult challenges. You're in His class for life—be committed to become all He has planned for you and don't give up. Are you allowing God to stretch your faith?

"For physical training is of some value, but godliness has value for all things,
holding promise for both the present life and the life to come."
1 Timothy 4:8

"I want to scale the utmost height
And catch a gleam of glory bright;
But still I'll pray till heav'n I've found,
Lord, plant my feet on higher ground."

Commit to a regular exercise program.

When I started writing this book, I listed the days of the year and randomly wrote each day's devotional. I feared my changing thoughts might be reflected if I wrote chronologically. Today is my last devotional. As I pen these words I am reminded of going on mountain hikes as a young girl. Our family would set out to conquer some large hill sure that once the summit was reached we would be on top of the world. But each time we reached the top there were other hills or mountains before us. We could have hiked forever and never have arrived at the final peak. That's how I feel about this part of my journey. I have climbed the first hill but from my vantage point I see new hills before me. It's been a long and sometimes hard climb but I've not arrived and realize I never will. There will always be new, unexplored territory before me to be conquered. Life really isn't a destination; it is a journey. Wherever you are in your journey, keep looking up and moving forward. There's something new and exciting at the top of your hill. You're not there yet but the walk is invigorating and exciting. You don't need to go alone—Jesus is with you each step of the way. Are you moving forward?

"Grace, mercy and peace from God the Father and Christ Jesus our Lord."
2 Timothy 1:2

"Jesus, Jesus, Jesus,
Sweetest Name I know,
Fills my every longing,
Keeps me singing as I go."

Think back over your year and list the hills you have climbed.

December 31
Read Romans chapter 12

> *"I am Thine dear, blessed Jesus, all Thine,*
> *All of self now to the death I consign;*
> *Gladly, gladly all I have I resign,*
> *That salvation in its fullness be mine."*

As the end of a year draws to a close, television stations, radio shows, and magazines are all recounting what has happened throughout the year. So much of what is reported is subjective and not anything I found newsworthy when it happened, much less historic in the year. But it is a good time to reflect on my own year and remember what took place. A few questions worth asking could include the following. What took most of my time and attention throughout the last twelve months? Did I spend time with the Lord daily or was it hit and miss? Did I receive direction from the Lord and was I obedient? How would I rate my Christian growth over the past year—was it substantial or minimal? Did I thank God for all the blessings He bestowed upon me and all the challenges He brought me through? Can I see transformation in my life as a result of a growing personal relationship with Christ? And finally, what are my goals for next year? Just what am I going to do with the rest of my life, for Heaven's sake? Take a minute and ask yourself these same questions reflecting on your Christian walk through the last year.

> *"Therefore, I urge you, brothers, in view of God's mercy, to offer your bodies*
> *as living sacrifices, holy and pleasing to God—which is your spiritual worship.*
> *Do not conform any longer to the pattern of this world, but be transformed*
> *by the renewing of your mind. Then you will be able to test*
> *and approve what God's will is—His good, pleasing and perfect will."*
> *Romans 12:1 & 2*

Rate your Christian growth over the last year.

Index to the Scriptures

Index to the Scriptures

Index to the Scriptures

Index to the Scriptures

Index to the Hymns

Index to the Hymns

Index to the Hymns

Index to the Hymns

Index to the Hymns

Index to the Hymns

Index to the Hymns

Index to the Hymns